SOCIAL WELFARE AND SOCIAL DEVELOPMENT

PUBLICATIONS OF THE
INSTITUTE OF SOCIAL STUDIES

PAPERBACK SERIES

V

PROCUL CERNENS

CLARIUS OBSERVAT

INTERNATIONAAL INSTITUUT
VOOR SOCIALE STUDIËN - 'S GRAVENHAGE
1972

SOCIAL WELFARE
AND
SOCIAL DEVELOPMENT

by

EUGEN PUSIĆ

Professor of Administration
University of Zagreb

1972
MOUTON
THE HAGUE - PARIS

LIBRARY OF CONGRESS CATALOGUE CARD NUMBER: 79-189707

Printed by Geuze, Dordrecht

ACKNOWLEDGEMENTS

Acknowledgements are due to the publishers and editors of the books and journals in which the material reproduced in this volume was originally published.

The Introduction and the chapter on "Human Rights and Social Welfare in a Responsible Society" are based on "Social Policy as a Factor of Social Change", a contribution to *Sozialpolitik und persönliche Existenz*, Festgabe für Hans Achinger (Duncker & Humblot, Berlin 1969). "Welfare and Development" was partly published under the title "The Political Community and the Future of Welfare" in John S. Morgan (ed.), *Welfare and Wisdom* (University of Toronto Press, 1966).

"A Theoretical Model of the Role of Professionals in Complex Development Situations" appeared in *Agents of Change: Professionals in Developing Countries*, edited by G. Benveniste and W.F. Ilchman (Frederick A. Praeger Inc., New York 1969). "Power, Planning, Development" was first printed in *Development and Change*, Vol. I, No. 1, 1969.

"Social Planning — Interests and Techniques" was presented to the Planning Conference held in Puerto Rico, July 1966, and subsequently published in *Social Planning: Puerto Rican Papers* edited by E. Reimer (Editorial University of Puerto Rico, 1968).

"Patterns of Administration" appeared as "Territorial and Functional Administration in Yugoslavia" in *Administrative Science Quarterly*, Vol. 14, No. 1, March 1969, and "Area and Administration in Yugoslav Development" in UNESCO's *International Social Science Journal*, Vol. XXI, No. 1, 1969.

In the Appendix to this reader an abbreviated version of a report to the United Nations is reproduced. "A Reappraisal of the United Nations Social Service Programme" (UN Document E/CN.5/AC.12/L.3/Add.1) was submitted to the Ad Hoc Working Group on Social Welfare on 17th February 1965. Permission has kindly been given by the Social Development Division of United Nations to publish the report in the present volume.

EUGEN PUSIĆ

CONTENTS

1

INTRODUCTION

Welfare today is at the crossroads. The controversy about what welfare really is begins with the term itself,[1] but does not end there. Is welfare, or social welfare, an activity or a cluster of activities aimed at helping people under certain types of social stress to regain their balance, their self-reliance, by removing the causes — material, psychological and other — of their predicament? Is it a system of general measures — legislative, planning, economic — intended to promote a more equitable or more desirable redistribution of the national income? Is it something in between these models? Or is it all things at the same time? If so, where is the common denominator that makes it meaningful to classify all these relationships, functions and orientations under the heading of welfare?

A more pedestrian approach understands social welfare simply as the collective name for a number of organized and institutionalized activities performed by a network of agencies, whether or not attached to various levels of government. But even this restrictive interpretation of social welfare as social service does not settle the question. What services can legitimately be considered social? The term sometimes covers health services and education in addition to social security, physical rehabilitation and crime prevention. Is social welfare just a department of government as distinct from public health or education? What about the quite respectable number of activities which are controversial and marginal even in a

---

[1] Three altogether different concepts of welfare are found in the American Constitution, for example, or in "welfare economics", or in a welfare department. In other languages, the situation becomes even more complicated. *Le bien-être social* in French is a rather clumsy expression, too broad for the technical sense of "welfare" and ill-adapted to its other uses. The French sometimes speak of *prévoyance sociale* or *action sociale* but are not altogether happy about either. The German *Wohlfahrt* is nearest to the narrow meaning of "social welfare" as a service to help people in social difficulties. In the Slav languages, again, *dobrobit, blagostanje* and their equivalents are very broad expressions denoting many things from good health to economic affluence.

purely administrative and jurisdictional sense, such as community development, housing, population policy, education of the physically and mentally handicapped, parole supervision, kindergartens, geriatric care, handicapped war veterans, etc., etc.?

Assuming even that after much effort, thorough discussion and with the participation of all concerned, agreement is reached as to the meaning to be attached to the elusive term of welfare, chances are that this success would prove ephemeral. Whatever social welfare may signify at any given moment in a given country it almost certainly does not have the same significance in another country or even in the same country at a different point in time along the endless line of social change. If all functions in society were arranged on a scale according to their susceptibility to transformation, to take on new meanings in the course of social development, welfare would be necessarily near the top of the list.

Turning finally to welfare as a field of knowledge, the same phenomenological dilemmas are reflected in the level of study. Is the study of social welfare a discipline in its own right? Or is it the focus for practitioners of various disciplines, for the political scientist, the public administrator, the economist, the psychologist, the lawyer, who find in problems of welfare a basis for practical interdisciplinary collaboration?

If there are easy answers to these questions, they are unknown to me. I proceed on the assumption that the study of welfare must include many things, must leave many avenues and approaches open. It should lead to a way of seeing the world and understanding people and their problems rather than impart a closed body of knowledge for whatever it is worth. And understanding the world and our place in it means, first of all, perceiving it as a process in which all things, values, institutions, even those which seem most stable and permanent, are constantly and endlessly changing. Only against this background can we attempt to discern better what people have done and are trying to do about human suffering, about those of their fellows who are unable to function in a normal way within a given social framework; or what they were trying to do or are doing about social frameworks which preclude large numbers of human beings from optimal functioning.

The essential dimensions of development and the various trends in welfare considered together should provide an introduction to this method.

I

Ideas about social development are part of the general picture which people have of society, of their position in it, and of the change or permanence of social relationships. For all people, whatever the social and economic system in which they live, social development has two aspects: it is a question of goals and a question of possibilities, of what they want and of what they are able to achieve, or in the most general sense of these terms, a problem of values and a problem of techniques.

In the last resort, values and techniques determine people's ideas of their place in the world. The development of every human community is the result of the interaction of forces shaping and limiting the possibilities of purposeful activity, with interests motivating people to make use of these possibilities or to decide not to use them. What interests can be expressed in a socially meaningful way and by what methods depends on the technological capacity of a society. And the dominant interests summed up in the abstract scale of socially accepted values in turn define the goals towards which the existing technological potential will be used and developed, and the degree of intensity with which this is done.

In the early phases of development man is relatively helpless. In the face of scarcity and imminent disaster, he must make use of the available technology in defending his physical existence against hostile environmental forces. This gives rise to sharp differences of values and interests.

Unconditional solidarity within the group and ceaseless, unbridgeable hostility between groups. On the one hand, the reality of power in society, the domination of minority interests over the majority through direct physical force, political sovereignty and subjection, property and economic exploitation. On the other hand, the ideal of liberation from all entanglements with this-worldly things. A motive common to all great religions tends towards development of the individual on the moral plane. By his efforts and conscious renunciation, man should strive towards the ideals of asceticism and sainthood. He should leave all mundane interests behind him, thus closing one of the main sources of social conflict.

With greater possibilities of action, attention shifts to ways and means by which to improve man's lot in this world. The basic ideas on how this should be done stem directly from the two traditional orientations discussed above.

One group of concepts starts from the reality of power and the corresponding values. In people's consciousness, the historical experience of naked force is gradually displaced by the model of benevolent power. Property and power are not only rights but social duties. The ruler becomes the "father" of his subjects, caring for them and promoting their welfare by a system of wise measures.

The other basic orientation takes the individualistic values of the religious relationship as its starting point. Man is personally responsible for his own salvation. In the same way that he had to work at his moral perfection, so he should work at his economic advancement, should create riches as a symbol of divine grace.

Both these orientations disregard the opposing interests in society. Both operate under the concept of a common social interest representing the simple sum of all individual interests of the people who make up a society. Paternalism does not even see a problem. Individualism assumes some kind of automatic social mechanism for the adjustment of interests.

These views were effectively criticized during the 19th century, since when the existence of different and possibly incompatible interests within the same society has become an accepted social fact. The historical dialogue between paternalistic and individualistic models of social welfare development had to be conducted on a more sophisticated level. The naïve view of society has been replaced by a more critical attitude. Interventions by political power on the social scene have to be checked and balanced by mechanisms for the expression and defence of interests and by processes of economic as well as political democracy leading to a consensus of interests, binding power and its exercise to this expressly formulated consensus. On the other hand, the individualism of social and economic action has to be fitted in one way or another into the framework of a common goal, development or plan.

In the present day, people who consider central power institutions to be the main source of initiative and the principal agency for regulating the development toward social welfare, and who would rely chiefly on government planning and legislation in this development process, give modern expression to the paternalistic tendencies of the 18th century and might be called "the social etatists".

On the other hand, those who believe that the individual should take care of himself under all circumstances and who admit the intervention of "public authority" only as an exception, must necessarily look upon the conscious regulation of social development as an exceptional activity. The heredity of individualistic ideas from the beginning of the industrial revolution is evident. "Social marginalism" would seem an appropriate term with which to describe such ideas.

The present phase is characterized by the converging movement of "etatists" and "marginalists" towards a consciously-regulated pluralism within the framework of a more complex view of social development.

II

Ideas of social etatism find their common denominator in the dominant position accorded to the state in social development, arising from the following considerations:

— The State extends its control over the means of production, gradually or with revolutionary abruptness, and thus becomes the main factor of economic development.

— The political power of the State is seen as the most useful instrument for implementing social change and adapting traditional social institutions to new circumstances.

— Social development is primarily the result of conscious action by the State within the framework of a coordinated and all-inclusive State plan.

These basic ideas take many forms, the most significant being the doctrine of social development accepted officially in socialist countries during their centralistic phase. In this case, however, it should be remembered that practice does not necessarily and completely correspond to theoretical tenets.

In socialist theory, belief in the importance of the State as an instrument of social development is based on the analyses of society made by Marx and Engels. However, the relative economic underdevelopment which prevailed at the moment when socialist countries, particularly the U.S.S.R., underwent their re-structuration, was decisive for the further development of this approach.

The starting point of classical socialist theory in this respect is that society is a system of phenomena classified into different layers. The basic layer includes economic phenomena, primarily the forces and relationships of production obtaining in a society. On this foundation stands the social superstructure, consisting of political and cultural institutions and all other societal elements which are not directly economic. The basis and the superstructure influence each other.

It is thus possible to use political power to bring about change in productive relationships, but in the long run conditions in the superstructure are determined by the base.

The principal goal of a socialist society is therefore to change its economic base as quickly as possible, thus enabling a socialist transformation of the whole society. This means giving priority to the increase of production and productivity, to reaching a level of affluence at which material goods lose their character of wares to be bought and sold, and become freely accessible to all members of society according to their needs.

In order to increase production, facilities for production must be expanded; this can be achieved, first of all, by channeling a larger part of the national income into productive investment. The less developed the country, the larger the necessary investment, and the smaller the national income. It is then incumbent upon government and governmental planning to maximize saving and optimize productive investment towards accelerated economic growth. During this period of greater strain, all other social interests should be satisfied only to the extent necessary to prevent dysfunctional consequences dangerous to the existence of the community or which inhibit the push towards its principal economic and social goal.

The lower the starting level of development, the sharper the dilemmas over priorities. Everything which does not directly contribute to production and to the expansion of production should temporarily remain constant or even be reduced. All non-productive consumption should be subjected to exacting economic criteria. The population generally is considered from the point of view of production: how much can it contribute as working force? Or from the point of view of consumption: what are its absolute needs in the distribution of the newly created value? Central control and centrally guided direct action are the preferred methods of development.

Within this framework, social development is part of general social and economic progress. Faster economic growth ultimately entails a more favourable social development. It is therefore inapposite to consider problems of social development by themselves, while the belief that it is possible to find their solution independent of the total transformation of society is illusory. Only social structures which are radically changed can protect the numerous interests and needs of a community from being ruthlessly dominated by egoistical aspirations and capacities of individuals and groups, typical of a class society.

In the course of time, however, this simple picture becomes more complex as a result of living through development and of confrontation with the experiences which development teaches. The process of creating and building the socialist states is a political process subject to the specific rules of political action. The economic and political struggles of the working class, the main social group representing socialist political tendencies, cause it to develop certain demands related to welfare, such as a larger share of the national income, greater social security, reduction of the working day, better working conditions, the right to work, etc. After coming into power, the leadership of the working-class political movement must make allowances for these demands even if they frequently conflict with the absolute priority of saving and economic growth over all other requirements. In this way, social benefits and social services in socialist countries are sometimes from the very beginning more developed than is consonant with the strictly economic calculus of levels of productivity reached and further productive investment needed.

The expansion of productive capacity and the changed social conditions result in greater and more varied interests as well as in improved possibilities for their satisfaction. These interests cannot always manifest themselves as demand on the market because of the policy which restricts consumption and favours the production of capital goods.[1] This leads to difficulties in optimizing the utilization of produced goods, to reduced motivation on the part of the workers, and thus to a slump in productivity. Heavy reliance on government as the main instrument of development also has its dangers. Hardening of bureaucratic structures necessarily reduces the value of government as an instrument in stimulating economic progress, innovation and adaptability. The bureaucracy tends also to appropriate an increasing share of resources and to expend them unproductively on enlarging the machinery of government and

---

[1] The introduction of the concept of "economic efficiency of investments" in the economic theory and practice of the USSR bears witness to the emergence of more sophisticated points of view. Cf. Alexander Baykov, "Some Observations on Planning Economic Development in the USSR", L. J. Zimmerman (ed.) *Economic Planning* (The Hague: Mouton & Co., 1963), p. 43.

proliferating its agencies. Finally, these epiphenomena of development tend to compromise certain fundamental human values which are the starting point of the socialist movement and the deepest motive for all its efforts in the struggle for social progress.

All this leads to a more sophisticated version of the originally simple ideas of "social etatism". Social development continues to be seen as part of the total movement of society, but there is a much clearer awareness of the specific problems to be encountered on this road and much less voluntaristic faith in government and planning as a panacea for all ills.[1] It becomes clear that an over-strained effort to save is self-defeating. At the same time, more resources are available for social needs. It is now better understood that exaggerated centralization makes the whole system inelastic and critically reduces the level of initiative. Ideas about the necessity for local action in development,[2] about participation and the sharing of responsibilities by a larger number of people in all social activities, gain wider acceptance.

From a distant general goal, social aspects of development are becoming concrete and relatively urgent tasks of society. General working and living conditions are improving as a result of the fact that a larger part of the growing national income is being employed for social services in their widest sense. A social security and social services system tending towards general coverage for all is no longer felt to contradict the differentiated and individualized approach to the actual needs of the individual.[3] Social development is seen as a dynamic process requiring stricter centralization of resources and the temporary setting-back of non-economic factors only in the early phases of relative underdevelopment. Later on, social needs

---

[1] Oscar Lange thinks that cybernetics represent a further development "in concrete and mathematicized form of the basic ideas of materialistic dialectics of Marx and Engels". Oscar Lange, "The Role of Science in the Development of Socialist Society with Special Regard to the Science of Economics", J. C. Fischer (ed.) *City and Regional Planning in Poland* (Ithaca N.Y.: Cornell University Press), p. 468.

[2] It is significant that the advantages of local action are pointed out by representatives of developing countries where the benefits of energetic centralized direction could be more easily assumed than anywhere else. "If there is no participation of local communities and no planning, no programme of social action can be effective..." M. Senkatuka, "Planification sociale dans l'Ouganda", in *Le Progres social par les plans de developpement social* — Compte Rendu de la XIIe Conference international de service social (Athenes 1964), p. 48.

[3] Among the principal characteristics of social planning in Poland, Strzelecki includes "the generalization and the adaptation to the individual of the social services", which are beginning to be applied. Edward Strzelecki, "Planification sociale en Pologne", *Ibid.*, p. 63.

should be considered and satisfied on an equal footing with demands of the economy, through a system of expanding social services and benefits.

The rational kernel of the socialist conception of social development and the contribution this represents in the evolution of thinking about development, is contained in the idea of development as a many-sided process combining economic, political and other elements into one whole which can be only understood as a whole. An essential factor in this process is the existence of social groups with different and divergent interests. Conscious planning of the broad outlines of the development process is a necessary condition for making it more rational and for reducing the social costs of development.

III

Similarly, the otherwise widely different ideas about social development which we have tried to include under the term "social marginalism", start from several common basic assumptions:

— In early marginalist models, society is seen as the more or less fortuitous result of the autonomous activity of all its members interacting with each other.

— Under normal circumstances, individual activity oriented towards the satisfaction of individual interests results in the maximal satisfaction of the general interest.

— The intervention of social forces and institutions in the general life of society is an exception from normal conditions.

From these basic premises follow several practical consequences for social development. The assumption that individual personal interests are the motives of every action leads to a classification of interests into egoistic and altruistic, and to the further assumption of a motive of social justice for all forms of behaviour occurring in a society which cannot be explained by the personal utilitarian motives of the actors.

The principal source of need satisfaction and interest realization in an individualistic society and a money economy is a personal money income. Consequently, measures of social welfare are oriented primarily toward supplementing, insuring, increasing the individual's money income and only exceptionally towards services or benefits in kind. A corresponding value-idea develops about the greater "dignity" and autonomy of the personal money income, of its moral superiority over other forms of social distribution.

Social marginalism classifies people in a society into two unequal parts. The "normal" majority which is self-reliant and self-supporting, and the "socially threatened" minority requiring some form of intervention and help by its fellow citizens.[1] A problem of priorities does not arise in this context, and even less the question of methods of social development. Marginal welfare activities are initially left to private initiative and individual expediency.

The drawbacks of the initial conceptions of marginalism soon became apparent. In the wake of industrialization and particularly of urbanization, what was an exception in the marginalist view is transformed into the rule. The entire industrial urban population is now exposed to the risk of a situation which was formerly considered abnormal, that a person is not able to provide for the needs of self and family without systematic outside help. Problems of free education, public health protection, insurance against general working and other risks, arise through a series of crises and social calamities. Technological progress causes work to become more and more collective and interdependent. This interdependence is constantly being translated into new collective, social services. Increasingly, activities develop for which the assumption no longer applies that personal material interest is the main incentive and the best regulating device.[2]

In the same way, ideas about the natural harmony, or at least automatic adjustment, between individual and general interests clash more and more openly with the reality of social relationships. Social structures embodying domination by minority interests become increasingly visible. These interests not only delay the process of economic and social development, they are in flagrant opposition to the common weal.

---

[1] Even today, representatives of the marginal conception evaluate negatively this presumed minority of "socially threatened" individuals, describing them as "asocial", "undeveloped" etc. Cf. Charles Pean, "Peuple sous-développé en pays sur-développé", in *Schweizerische Zeitschrift für Gemeinnützigkeit*, 106 Jahrgang, Heft 4/5 (April/May 1967), pp. 89-92.

[2] On the level of economic theory Tinbergen points out that Pareto is wrong in asserting that rising marginal costs and the absence of external effects constitute the common characteristic of all productive activities. It is relatively easy to show — on the examples of transportation, air pollution, or education — that many activities have, on the contrary, diminishing marginal costs and that they produce very significant external effects. Jan Tinbergen, "Aspects sociaux de la planification économique", in *Le Progres social*, *op.cit.*, p. 31.

The principal factor in the evolution of these initial ideas of social marginalism is again a growing production and productivity, expanding possibilities and parallel rising needs and aspirations. Here, also, social services and social benefits gradually assume increasing importance and become factors to reckon with at the national economic planning level.

In the first vague approaches to social planning, the term means simply the activity of coordinating existing social services and institutions usually at the local level, forming combined boards and other mechanisms intended to bring together various actors in the social field, thus increasing the effectiveness and efficiency of the whole activity. This is the first beginning of planning within the framework of an individualist view of society, and in this sense there is truth in the saying that socialist countries start with capital planning and capitalist countries with social planning. Gradually, social planning develops towards greater comprehensiveness and better methods. At the same time, static models of society are replaced by changing social structures viewed as a normal phenomenon of social dynamics.

The development of marginalist ideas under the influence of practical measures of social policy points in the same direction. Beginning with a few laws about factory inspection and measures of the law-and-order type, social policy is growing into a system of benefits and services aimed, in principle, at the total population. These benefits and services include social security, national health, free and compulsory education, and essentially influence the distribution of the national income. Social policy theoreticians consider the redistribution effect of social measures to be their main goal.[1]

However, old patterns of thought have not yet disappeared. Redistribution of the national income needs a moral legitimation which is found in the ideas of social justice, of the expanding responsibility of society for an increasing number of individuals, of social solidarity.[2] Personal money income continues to be consider-

---

[1] See Elizabeth Liefmann-Keil, *Oekonomische Theorie der Sozialpolitik* (Springer Verlag, Berlin, 1961) and Pekka Kuusi, *Social Policy for the Sixties, A Plan for Finland* (Kuopia: Finnish Social Policy Association, 1964).
[2] The moral justification of redistribution policies is found firstly in the social policy views of religious communities. See e.g. the Encyclical of Pope Paul VI "Populorum progressio", ed. *Hrv. književno društvo Sv.Cirila i Metoda* (Zagreb, 1967), particularly pp. 8 and 40.

ed the main form of participation in the distribution of national income, the greatest achievement of social security. In societies with highly developed economies, the idea of an annual guaranteed minimum income for all is no longer beyond practical discussion. There is at least some new wine in the old bottles. The purely quantitative increase in benefiits and in the number of clients implies change in the quality of the whole system. The State operates an increasing number of public services; in dispensing benefits, it is no longer merely the depository of organized violence and monopolized coercion. To adjust its ramifying activities to the complexities of economic and social development, at least a modicum of planning and foresight is necessary.[1] Greater involvement of the citizen as user and as client of services stimulates demands for wider participation. There is better understanding of the immediate and possibly beneficial economic effects of measures which were formerly treated as expenditure pure and simple.[2] Finally, social policy as a system by itself exercises a function of social criticism, levelled at the reality of interest relationships, and dispelling the illusion that all members of a society are treated alike.

Through these changes, marginalist ideas converge toward the line which is approached from the other side by social etatism. Marginalism also has a rational kernel, a contribution to make to the thinking about human welfare, i.e. its orientation towards the individual and his personal development as being the supreme value and ultimate aim of any form of social development.

IV

In the wake of the anti-colonial revolution, problems of the accelerated development of formerly colonial populations eager to make up for lost historical time, to create the preconditions of progress, and to enter the community of free nations on an equal footing,

---

[1] "To speak about development means to speak about something which includes social progress in the same way as it does economic growth. *Ibid.*, p. 21.
[2] The position is taken that work as a factor of production is not a natural factor as is, for instance, untilled land, but a produced factor in which human work is already invested. The most important and most profitable of all the elements invested in the creation of working capability is education. The profitability of resources invested in education exceeds the return on funds sunk into capital assets. Ingo Hochbaum, "Bildungsförderung und wirtschaftliche Entwicklung", in *Politische Vierteljahresschrift*, 8 Jahrgang, Heft 2, 1967, p. 234.

gave special impetus to the idea that social development is an interconnected and complex process.

On all sides, the most evolved thinking, stemming from marginalist or from etatist sources irrespective of the practical political moves of one or other great power, agrees that accelerated development of former colonies and semi-colonies is the common task of mankind. These formerly dependent areas usually suffer from low production and productivity, a low level of organizational capacity and capability of action, and from most other indicators of a defective social situation. In comparison with countries which preceded them in the earlier stages of the development process, they have the advantage of being able to profit from the experience of others. In the area of social welfare, they will be confronted with both etatist and marginalist traditions. One group of experts will be likely to advise developing countries to rely chiefly on government and political power for the achievement of welfare aims, considering political revolutionary action by the former colonial peoples as prerequisite to any development whatsoever. Others will tend to emphasize practical measures of everyday care for people, not stopping to consider the general social meaning which such measures can assume within a given social and economic framework.

However, both traditions will have to relate themselves to the whole complex of development; in doing so, they will be exposed to stronger pressures toward convergence than ever before. This effect is already visible in the field of academic theory as well as in the realm of practical action, particularly within the framework of the United Nations. A cursory glance at the former will facilitate understanding of the other.

The classical economic model of development as a balanced process in which saving, investment, production, national income, etc., gradually increased toward higher levels achieved by the manipulation of material factors, was early exposed to criticism. Even economic theoreticians have pointed out the importance of the human factor, of the existence of social structures which enable and give meaning to certain economic decisions and moves, of initiative, of the will to work, of entrepreneurial capability and motivation.[1] More and more it seems that in the total sum of conditions for development, human qualities are decisive for the potential of a

---

[1] Cf. W. Arthur Lewis, *The Theory of Economic Growth* (London: Allen & Unwin Ltd., 1956).

community to initiate, sustain and accelerate the process of economic growth.

The basic assumption of an inverse relationship between consumption and saving or investment is exposed to doubt. A change of people's attitude can result in increasing effectiveness of work and, consequently, in a simultaneous expansion of consumption and saving. A change of attitude, however, is a social change which is not brought about automatically by a mechanical increase or reduction of economic parameters. Balance can and often does mean stagnation, and so the doctrine of balanced development is sometimes replaced by the slogan of unbalanced growth.[1]

The next step induced by the experience of some countries in Western and Northern Europe, is to see the positive economic effects of a policy of redistribution through social benefits. The equalization of incomes stimulates the market and the whole economy, reinforcing the "multiplier" effect, while stagnating and poor social groups and geographic regions act as a retarding factor on the development process as a whole. At the same time, experience has at least partially disproved dogmatic expectations about larger social benefits being the main factor which inhibits saving and investment and produces inflationary movements.

Other disciplines also increasingly orient their efforts toward the reason why human communities experience historical periods of intensive and successful creativity in economics and politics, in culture and in the development of social institutions, more active and more ambitious than ever before or since. At present, the main accent is on the collection of materials which document similar development cycles and illustrate certain collective attitudes preceding such "golden ages". As yet, we lack systematic and analytical explanation of these observed and obviously very complex manifestations of development.[2] Scientists who have hazarded some preliminary interpretation of the facts can be classified from extreme economic determinism to a psycho-analytical understanding of economic élites.[3]

While theory pertaining to social development has hardly progressed beyond its 19th century foundations, practical life re-

---

[1] Albert O. Hirschman, *The Strategy of Economic Growth* (Yale University Press, 1958).
[2] David McClelland, *The Achieving Society* (London: Van Nostrand, 1961).
[3] Everett E. Hagen, *On the Theory of Social Change — How Economic Growth Begins* (Homewood Ill.: The Dorsey Press, 1962).

quires practical answers to pressing everyday questions. The most interesting forum in which to follow practical thinking and action on development problems confronting the experience and divergent doctrinal orientations of the whole world, is the United Nations.

UN doctrine on development has changed and evolved during past years with surprising speed. No longer ago than the end of the 1950s, conceptions of development current in UN circles were based on the classical model of economic growth through intensified investment activity. Caught in the dilemma between economic systems of private ownership and state ownership, the UN tends towards the compromise that the State should take upon itself "basic" investments, primarily heavy industry and transport, and that private economic activity should be simultaneously stimulated. In addition, there should be a general development programme, with which citizens are acquainted by means of a systematic campaign of information. The human factor is also present in the "general conditions of development", including government activity in guaranteeing law and order, personal security, governmental anti-cycle measures in economic policy, a minimum of social security and a gradually rising level of education.[1]

The best known official UN document on development is *General Assembly Resolution No. 1710 (XVI)* concerning the UN Development Decade, adopted at the 1084th plenary session on December 19th, 1961. The decade 1961-1970 was declared the "UN Development Decade", the main aim of which was to reach during this span of time a minimal rate of growth of national income of 5% per annum in all countries of the world. Although this goal is characteristically economic, the resolution treats on the same plane the aim of "advancing towards self-sustaining economic growth" and the objective of "social betterment". The concrete measures advocated for achieving the objectives of the programme include "the mobilization of manpower". Four aspects related to the human factor are discussed in detail: the role of youth as a dynamic factor in social change; training and education as a prerequisite for successful economic and social growth; vocational training and formation as a specific activity in introducing new professions, new branches of economic activity, new institutions; and finally, community development as a specific approach, developed within the UN, to the task

---

[1] Jan Tinbergen, *The Design of Development* (Baltimore: The John Hopkins Press, 1962).

of mobilizing the masses in the course of development by making them participate in democratically chosen, programmed and led local action.

This political act by the United Nations provided new impetus to theoretical thinking which is immediately related to action on an international level. Development is now understood as a proces through which people aim at satisfying their aspirations and realizing their interests. These interests and aspirations are by no means only economic. It is rather the reverse. The goals of development are primarily human in the broadest sense of the word, i.e. improvement in the quality of human life. An increase in economic resources appears as a means towards this end. Economic factors receive a broader interpretation, they acquire "human colour". Problems of distribution are thus no longer considered less important than production. Development has often been inhibited by the fact that resources do not reach the people who would be willing to employ them productively. Planning is now definitely accepted as a technical instrument for the orientation of development. Certain social problems of development — the population explosion, the revolution of rising expectations, the human difficulties of industrialization — are treated for the first time as central questions and not as secondary dysfunctional consequences of the economic process. The fact is beginning to be understood that the distance between developed and non-developed countries might increase instead of being reduced.

This orientation towards the human factor in development has been strengthened by the influence of the experiences gained during the first half of the Development Decade. These were analyzed at the end of 1965 and the results showed the difficulties to be greater than expected. The average annual increase in national income in developing countries, which had reached 4.5% during the lustrum 1955-1960, fell to 4% between 1960 and 1963. Agricultural production in these countries has increased at an approximate 1% per year, less than half the average rate of population increase. It seems impossible to maintain even the present standards of nutrition, which are considered inadequate for about two-thirds of the world's population. In most developing countries the annual increase in population exceeds 2%, in many it is over 3%. The population explosion is becoming the major long-term problem. The UN *Report on the World Social Situation* (1965) lists the main social factors which inhibit the participation of people in the development effort and thus compromise the whole plan. These are the existing patterns of land-ownership and land-utilization, castes and classes, extreme poverty and apathy, absence of technical know-how, lack of appropriate institutions, mistrust of government and over-dependence on it, isolation and illiteracy, the conflict between suggested changes and existing cultural and religious values, the insufficiency of the existing administrative machinery.[1]

Perspectives are not favourable. All signs indicate that the situation in the 1970s is going to become more difficult. This applies to food and employment, and to social problems generally in a world which is urbanizing at an increasing speed and is becoming too small for its billions of inhabitants. At the same time, a certain disillusionment with classical economic methods becomes noticeable, and efforts to apply them in the development process are slackening. Under the impact of these problems, it is not surprising that the social-policy aspects of development are receiving increased attention. A new UN doctrine on development is in the making which emphasizes the human factor over and above the purely material instruments of social progress.

The basic demand is for better, more realistic and more democratic social planning. The people must accept the plan as their own programme. The accent is therefore on a system of communication which makes it possible to present the aims and advantages of the plan to all — not through proclamation and oration but by convincing demonstration and instruction in new working methods.

The central problem on which hinges the realization of development plans is manpower, causing education and training to become the basic investment, the prerequisite of development. Youth is the main potential instrument with which to achieve the indispensable changes in social structure, traditional relationships, patterns of behaviour and ways of work. Incentives must be discovered with which people may be induced to work better, to acquire necessary knowledge and skills, to move to areas where conditions of work are difficult. Among the many forces which could be made to work in this direction, motives of idealism and ideological commitment have been particularly effective. The administrative machinery also plays a significant role in development, the quality of local government being of particular importance. Moreover, a modicum of stability

---

[1] United Nations, *1965 Report on the World Social Situation* (New York, 1966), pp. 1, 3, 5.

must be achieved among the labour force in the new industrial enterprises, giving a significant task to the trade unions. However, the aspect which is given particular emphasis by the new development doctrine is the participation of the people in industry and agriculture, in urban as well as rural settings, i.e., the full commitment of the masses to the goals of social development.

V

All that has been said so far provides a composite picture of a modern orientation in social development policy, towards which the various, widely different historical lines of thinking converge. Convergence, however, does not mean fusion. Sufficient differences exist among the approaches adopted in various parts of the world to supply the dialectics of debate and mutual criticism so indispensable to theoretical and practical progress.

What are the principal points of such an orientation?

— Firstly, social policy is seen increasingly as an integral part of the general development of a community. The question is: how much does social policy contribute to development, including economic growth. Increasing acceptance is given to the concept that social development implies social change, i.e. change of social structures in industrialization and urbanization, in the position of the family, in the relationship among classes, and in relation to political power.

— The second main characteristic of the modern view is realization of the significance of interests and of the role they play in social development. It is perhaps a weakness of UN doctrine that the interest-aspect of development is not sufficiently emphasized in official UN documents. The process of changing a whole society is obviously more than an exercize in planning. Refusal or failure to realize the focal point which the interests of principal social groups occupy in this process implies that development plans are built upon unrealistic foundations, leading inevitably to "surprises" and failures. Development is an interest-process and this means a political process.

— In its political aspect, development is being accepted more and more as a democratic process. Social policy undoubtedly presents a number of technical problems which demand skilled analysis and professional solution. However, key decisions should not be taken away from those with whom the development plan is chiefly concerned, the people living in the community, and usurped by an élite, technocratic or otherwise. The limitations which the democratic principle imposes on development planning must be accepted. It is not possible to undertake everything a planner may find technically desirable and feasible, but those projects should be concentrated upon for which interest consensus and adequate support of the majority of the population can be obtained. In addition to the democratic principle, there are other and more practical reasons for proceeding in this way. Any development plan is doomed to remain on paper if the active participation of the citizens is not obtained.

— This implies that any kind of monopoly in development activity must be rejected and a polycentric approach adopted. The objective is not to realize one central plan, but a series of plans and actions which are integrated with each other according to the logic of their technical interdependence, and based on consensus achieved by interaction among social interest groups.

— At the same time, however, development continues to be the responsibility of society as a whole. Basic measures for the framework of development must be decided upon at levels at which the whole of society is represented. Such measures include the broad lines along which the national income is distributed, the construction and quality of the large social services networks, social security systems, the fundamental regulation of the economic process.

— People represent the ultimate goal and value of development. In addition to its main task of protecting the living standards of the non-active population, social policy must adopt more versatile methods which should be adjustable to the manifold and varied needs of individuals.

— Modern development policy is becoming increasingly complex. It does not only consist of general directives, plans and broad moves; success or failure depends on their adequate implementation in a growing number of special fields which then have to be integrated into large functionally-meaningful wholes. A multitude of general ideas cannot take the place of detailed analysis and thorough knowledge of the many problems of the labour force, of housing, of children and the family, of education, public utilities, administration and all the other sectors which, in their total sum, make up the everyday life of society.

— Finally, modern development policy is international. The 19th century demonstrated the unity of individual countries and saw this unity expressed in the nation State. In the second half of the 20th century we begin to see the reality of the unity and the interdependence of the whole world. During the 19th century individual countries were divided within themselves along lines of class and other social and economic contrasts into a rich and civilized minority and a poor and underdeveloped majority. Today, the same picture is presented by the world. The action of conscious and progressive social forces changed the relationships of appalling inequality and unrestricted exploitation in individual countries. The same task awaits the same forces today on the level of the planet.

To this task we are all committed. On the manner of its solution depends not only the quality of the world's future development, but to a certain extent also the answer to the question: will anything be left to develop?

VI

Social welfare and social development belong to the class of very complex problems. Their understanding, adequate analysis and particularly their solution require the largest calibre of capabilities, the highest quality of thinking.

Can people be taught at the required level? Can they be trained to be original and creative in matters in which their basic interests, prejudices, traditions and fundamental personality structures are involved? Can they be prepared for tasks whose successful fulfilment demands not only the finest types of skill but also detachment, which has been always considered a privilege of morally outstanding personalities?

It has to be done, and it will be done. If it is not yet done it is because we have not developed the methods necessary for introducing capable people to novel and unprecedented problems in a way which is both stimulating and enlightening. These methods must now be evolved, starting from our present position. Already it is widely understood that teaching does not mean transferring so much as associating, stimulating people to participate in the groping process of thought.

On the problem of welfare and development this process takes place along three lines.

— In efforts toward attaining better theories of social development. Without the successful theoretical solution of some key problems, practical activity can be little more than a particularly hopeless kind of trial-and-error process in which experience cannot be accumulated because of the complexity of interconnections and the quickly changing character of initial conditions; therefore, every new trial is exposed to the same chances of error as any of the previous cases. In this context, the motto: nothing is as practical as a good theory, sounds very convincing.

In the sciences which pertain to welfare and development, we are actually at a stage at which a theory's best service consists of the opportunity it offers for refutation, making it valuable as an instrument for the development of advanced thinking. To follow the construction of a hypothetical system from its beginning, to discuss it, find flaws in it, replace some of its parts by better ideas, to rescind and pull down the whole structure altogether, is at present the most promising kind of training for original and critical thinking.

— Practice, at our present stage of awareness, is most meaningful if related to specific circumstances of place and time. This increases the value of the case study, the more profound description shedding light on the background, probing towards roots and dwelling on the ideographic uniqueness of the concrete event. This approach is dangerous only if used in isolation, because then it cannot but lead to unwarranted generalization. Discussions of what has happened at some place at some time should certainly be compared with each other. But this should not be done too quickly or superficially, trying to fit experiences into the Procrustean bed of a theory by misinterpreting individual facts or by discarding any that may be inconvenient.

— The international scene is where it is most possible and really indispensable to draw generalizations from practice. In assessing the efforts made in welfare and development on the international level, however uncoordinated, initially clumsy and generally deficient these efforts may be, we cannot help but draw conclusions from the application of a particular doctrine or theory to similar problems under widely different circumstances. Again, there would be the temptation to make facts fit the theory were it not that case studies have sharpened our awareness of the differences, and that theoretical training has taught us that incontrovertible stubbornness is not a virtue.

2

WELFARE AND DEVELOPMENT

If we do not find a way, and soon, to adapt politically to the decisive increase in both productivity and destructiveness, any discussion of human welfare is irrelevant. The choice we have to make is, unhappily, as simple as that. I say unhappily, because we all find it extremely difficult to face the implications of circumstances that are really and radically new.[1] Always, however, at crucial turns in history, some momentous change in the external or internal situation has had to be compensated by a decisive breakthrough in the pattern of our thinking and functioning. It looks as if the next great inventions might have to come in the political field in order to neutralize the dangerous combination of new technological development and old ways of thinking and feeling about man in society.

I

Life in society, as far as we can see through history, seems to have been determined by two basic and complementary facts: the necessity of cooperation and the inevitability of conflict.[2]

---

[1] One of the typical defence mechanisms against an unfathomable reality is "to face the situation squarely", to try to calculate the number of the dead and to imagine the next technical tasks of those still alive. It seems redundant to point out to those who write "On Thermonuclear War" and similar "hard headed" studies the many unwarranted assumptions they make in the technical field. Their main omission seems to be not to take sufficiently into account the unstabilizing social and psychological effects of a traumatic experience of that order of magnitude.

Another reaction is to project the present into a still uncertain future. So Raymond Aron: "L'économie s'efface avec la rareté. L'abondance laisserait subsister des problèmes d'organization, non des calculs économiques. De même, la guerre cesserait d'être un instrument de la politique le jour où elle entraînerait le suicide commun des belligérants. La capacité de production industrielle rend quelque actualité a l'utopie de l'abondance, la capacité destructrice des armes ranime les rêves de paix éternelle" (*Paix et Guerre entre les nations* [Paris: Calman-Levy, 1962], p. 30).

[2] The complementarity of cooperation and conflict as basic principles of social life seems to be presently accepted even by the most pronounced theoreticians of a har-

In the history of ideas the emotionally intensive experience of conflict attracted earlier and wider attention than did the equally obvious concept of cooperation. In the early religious systems conflict is already projected into the realm of the transcendental, into the never-ending struggle of good and evil. On a higher level of religious development the metaphysical representations are retroprojected[1] into society: what are the implications of this all-embracing war between light and darkness for practical human action? Sometimes conflict is given a positive value as an expression of solidarity of the faithful and a method of spreading the faith. In other instances, conflict is transferred to the intra-personal field. Man has to combat evil in himself in order to be counted on the winning side of the metaphysical battle, or for more disinterested reasons of personal spiritual improvement.

Cooperation was given more systematic thought only when the development of economic productivity made coordination of human effort one of its most obvious prerequisites. The growth of commerce and industry and the concomitant need for public peace and security, which alone could satisfy the requirement of "laissez faire, laissez passer", found expression in corresponding ideologies of cooperation, in theories of natural law and of social contract. The assumed primaeval, chaotic state of "bellum omnium erga omnes" gave place to a state of "prestabilized" harmony within the framework of supposedly aprioristic rules.

In the history of institutions, however, in the reality of their social life and whatever the current ideologies of the time, people have always had to cope with the simultaneous tasks of finding the most appropriate method of cooperating with each other and the most effective means of fighting against each other. These two aims were sometimes fused into one overriding objective: to work together in order to survive in conflict.

For a long time the possibilities of cooperation were defined by the scope of the human eye and the power of the human voice, and were limited essentially to the face-to-face group. As with

---

monious view of society. Cf., Talcott Parsons, "Die jüngsten Entwicklungen in der strukturell-funktionalen Theorie", *Kölner Zeitschrift für Soziologie und Sozialpsychologie*, No. 1, 1964, pp. 30-49. It would seem easy to make the additional step of understanding "homeostatic" processes in society as complementary to social change.
[1] The mechanisms of projection and retroprojection have been studied in detail by Ernst Topitsch, *Vom Ursprung und Ende der Metaphysik* (Wien: Springer Verlag, 1958).

organic forms, however, the range of adaptability of institutional structures is not unlimited. The increased division of labour and the accelerated rate of change have put increasing strain on the face-to-face group. The ever-more detailed specialization of tasks has called for additional precision in the determination of behaviour. On the other hand, a more rapid succession of shifts in the social situation has intensified the requirements of elasticity, of a speedier response to change. These two tendencies have exerted a heavier and heavier pressure on the existing institutional structure. Reaching the end of its capacity for adaptation the primary group has developed pseudo-solutions of considerable interest. Behaviour patterns prescribed in the most minute detail, as in marriage ceremonies or in commercial transactions, are evidence of the attempt to find an answer to the problems imposed by the advance of the division of labour. What was won in precision, however, was lost in elasticity. The initially rational definition of individual tasks lost its meaning with the changing situation, but the behaviour, learned through repetition of the same situation in the group and reinforced by a battery of social and magic sanctions, persisted as formalized ceremonial conduct. It still yielded the social benefit of generating feelings of solidarity and security, but these advantages had to be measured against the growing handicaps to practical and efficient action.

A second contradiction in the crisis of the face-to-face structure was the opposition between the requirement for greater differentiation in social relationships and at the same time greater stability in human relations. It was evident that with trade, with migration, with colonization, it was practically useless to think of all people in black and white patterns. There were in-between relationships which could be quite profitable. One would trade with people not of one's own group, and at the same time establish quite friendly relationships. It would obviously be beneficial if this kind of relationship could be made more stable—if it did not have to be conducted under the always existing risk that any such relationship could immediately turn into open hostility.

This double challenge—detailed allocation of tasks and speedy adjustment to the changing environment, and greater differentiation in human relationships and greater stability in them—was beyond the structural possibilities of the face-to-face group. In order to find an answer a new institution was necessary, and in time a new institution was evolved: organization, one of the most remarkable social inventions of man. Organization is an instrument for achieving consciously chosen goals. It relates ends to the means necessary for achieving them by setting up a stable structure of relationships among people at work. It makes possible the planning of ongoing activities, the devising of detailed programmes and blueprints for action. This is achieved by dividing the overall task into smaller and simpler parts and by subdividing these parts until individual operations are defined to the last movement, where necessary. The lines traced in the course of this process constitute the network for the co-ordination of the total planned activity and its orientation towards the established goal. At the same time the whole system can be changed with an ease and speed difficult to imagine under earlier conditions. From the most general goal to the most specific element of action, everything can be subjected to scrutiny, analysed, compared and changed in the same way in which it was introduced in the first place, by explicit arrangement. Organization is a powerful new instrument for cooperation towards the satisfaction of human needs.

Human needs, however, have to be satisfied under conditions of scarcity of resources and within human society—conditions which define conflict as a situation where the needs of an individual or a group can be satisfied only at the expense of the needs of another individual or group.[1] There are several possible answers to a situation of conflict: one party dominates the others and satisfies its needs without regard to anyone else's needs; one or several parties abandon their original aims and reorient their wants towards other objectives; the conflicting parties reach a compromise where everyone gets some satisfaction but nobody fully realizes his original goals.

Each of these methods, in the course of social development, evolves its corresponding set of institutions. Domination is socially stabilized through power; reorientation is expressed through the great systems of religious thought and aesthetic creation; and compromise is regulated through the institution of contract, through systems of rules and through the judicial process.

The original methods employed within this institutional framework are determined by the type of structure available for social

---

[1]   Needs, and therefore conflicts, are not limited, of course, to material necessities. They range all the way to Coser's "non-realistic" conflicts generated by the need to release tensions (L. Coser, *The Functions of Social Conflict* [Glencoe, Ill.: The Free Press, 1956], p. 156).

action generally. Power is based on actual physical violence or on the immediate threat of it; religious communion is achieved through direct charismatic experience; the institutions of compromise function in face-to-face contact only.

In conflict, as well as in cooperation, the coming of organization marks an epoch. The field of action of the different institutions is decisively widened, the methods are transformed, their mutual relationships are altered. Power develops the continuity, the territorial links and the relative permanence we associate with the more modern notion of political power;[1] religious movements consolidate into organizations of churches with a considerably widened span of influence; contracts and rule systems become independent of the physical presence of the affected parties. At the same time power becomes less dependent on the immediate use of violence: religious experience loses some of its emotional pitch as charisma becomes gradually bureaucratized; and the area of compromise is widened in an increasingly rational atmosphere. In the mutual relations among the different institutional systems political power comes to occupy a central place. As power-systems become larger and more stable, the traditional systems of reorientation, such as religion, lose some of their former conflict-solving capacity and are relegated to the inner councils of the individual—if the corresponding church-organizations do not in turn develop some form of political power— while institutions of compromise are integrated into the political power system and become, at least in principle, dependent on it.

II

Organizations are groups of people who in one of their social roles are bound by specific sets of rules to apply given resources in order to achieve prescribed ends by performing one of the activities into which the overall task is divided and by submitting to coordination for the most efficient achievement of the general goal. The simultaneous presence of the opposite tendencies in organization— division and fusion—is the principal source of its achievements and also the ultimate cause of its demise. There can be no doubt that

---

[1] The characteristic of legitimacy of power, made popular through Max Weber, pertains to a different point of view: the motivation why people obey. That some of his subjects are prepared to obey a monarch in exile does not yet invest him with political power.

today organization as an institution is facing a crisis. It seems that organization has completed its circle and in its turn has reached the limits of its capacity to adapt to changed circumstances. The crisis of organization is brought about by its role in human cooperation as well as by its place in human conflict.

As indicated earlier, the tension between the need for precision and the requirement of elasticity was too great for the face-to-face group. In the same way a new antithesis between the drive towards specialization and the necessity to co-ordinate is developing into a force likely to destroy the traditional structure of organization.

The process of differentiation of labour tends, within organizations, to take two different forms. One, implied in the organizational process itself, consists in the division of complex tasks into progressively more detailed and less complex action-elements. The result of this "crumbling"[1] of work is the production line, the conveyer belt, the standardized simple action prescribed to the last detail of time and motion, and fitted into larger schemes independently of the will or even the knowledge of the individual worker. The advantages of precision and of simplicity have to be paid for by a loss of meaningfulness, by the deadening effect on the relation between man and his work.

The other form which the differentiation of labour takes is that of professional specialization. There are activities which cannot be usefully broken up into simpler elements. They are based on a systematic knowledge of more complex relationships among natural or social phenomena and on the learning of more intricate skills. Here the differentiation of labour proceeds through a progressive narrowing of the range of concern, a reduction of the field of interest, while the action-processes themselves within the smaller field remain intact. A cardiologist, for instance, does not perform simpler functions than a general practitioner, nor is a specialist of international law less qualified than a general lawyer.

In organizations the differentiation of labour develops both ways, up to a point. Comparatively early in the development of the division of labour the standardization of individual operations implicit in the first method—that is of breaking up an activity into simpler components—suggested the transfer of these well defined movements to machines. But in very recent times developments based

---

[1] According to the expression by Georges Friedmann "l'émiettement du travail" made popular through his book *Le travail en miettes: spécialisation et loisirs* (Paris: Gallimard, 1956).

on cybernetics and information theory have made possible the construction of large-scale chains of action where the standardized elements are performed without human intervention. The development of automation spells an end to the first method of differentiation of human labour in organizations by dividing the work-process. Whatever can be standardized can, in principle, be transferred to machines. This increases considerably the importance of the other method, the differentiation of labour by professional specialization.[1]

Professional specialization leaves the specialist in possession of the necessary knowledge and skill to perform complex and meaningful activities. He is much less in danger of being separated from the meaning of his work and, therefore, much more independent. He knows his work and does not need to wait for others to assign tasks to him. Still the work of the individual specialist has to be coordinated and integrated into larger contexts. An individual physician in a hospital, a social worker in an agency, a scientist in a laboratory, a teacher in a school, an administrator in an office can make their full contribution only as their work is brought into rational relationships with the work of others. The very independence of their individual activities, however, makes coordination both more necessary and more difficult. The classical school of administrative science early became aware that the span of control —the number of people to be coordinated by one superior—was in inverse proportion to the professional level of the work coordinated.

The methods of coordination practiced within the traditional structure of organization seem to be ill adapted to the task of tying together the work of professional specialists. The work of individuals is coordinated within an organization by a hierarchy of superiors who are responsible for the allocation of work tasks to those below them as well as for the control and necessary correction of their work performances. With the increasing complexity of organizations and of the work done by their individual members the hierarchical method of coordination requires more and more of everybody's time. The flow of directives down the line and of reports up the line becomes more abundant. More time is spent in

---

[1] At least in one of the aspects of their role Gouldner's ideal-types of "cosmopolitans" and "locals" are related to the difference between professional specialization and the fragmentation of the work-process. Gouldner does not seem, at least in his original formulations, to have taken into account the probable influence of automation on the relationship between his two types (cf., A. W. Gouldner, "Cosmopolitans and Locals: Toward an Analysis of Latent Social Roles", *Administrative Science Quarterly*, No. 3, 1957; No. 4, 1958).

meetings and other forms of face-to-face contact. More writing and reading for purposes of coordination have to be done at all levels. Administrative procedures become more involved, formalities more numerous as the organizational system tries to counteract the centrifugal tendencies of specialization. This increase of coordinating activities, however, has to find its place within the fixed time-budget at the disposal of the organization. Coordination can ultimately expand only at the expense of the main activity, which is the initial social reason for the existence of the system. More coordination means less health work, less social welfare services, less education, less research by the respective organizations. The point of diminishing returns can be clearly seen: it is the moment when the balance between coordination and basic activity becomes so unfavourable that organization will no longer be the socially most economical method of human cooperation.

Also, the method of coordination prevailing in organizations is based on the assumption that the existing inequalities among individuals as to their respective possibilities of contributing to the common goal are, on the whole, correctly expressed through the existing hierarchy. Individuals at lower levels perform simpler tasks and have, therefore, to know less than those at higher levels who instruct and control them and who should possess greater insight into the more complex interrelationships between the more elementary contributions of their inferiors. With the possibility of eliminating these simpler tasks altogether by transferring them to machines and with increasing professional specialization, this assumption no longer holds. Those members of the organization who are directly performing its basic activity, and who are therefore at the bottom of the traditional hierarchical pyramid, have really to be the most knowledgeable and skilful. What wonder that they adjust less and less easily to the traditional method of coordination which is based on the assumption that the higher echelons of the hierarchy are manned by people who are necessarily wiser and whose contribution is more valuable than that of their inferiors. This new situation is finally irreconcilable with the organizational relationship of subordination and super-ordination.

In its other aspect as well, its place in human conflict, organization is approaching the point of crisis. Organization implies a substantial increase in the efficiency of power. Through organization, power becomes impersonal and can exert a greater pressure on the individual who most fears what he cannot grasp and know: he tends to respond by aggressive and hostile attitudes to power-in-organization which present the blank facade of anonymity to his hostility. Through organization, also, power gains a stability and continuity, an independence from the turnover of its personnel never before imagined. To human ambition organization offers the prize of power without necessarily requiring the Alcibiadic[1] talents of moving people, which imply at least a minimum of empathetic identification of the leader with the led. Power based on huge organizational systems develops a gravitational pull strong enough to draw into its orbit existing interests over a wide field. The rulers rule; the growing bureaucracy derives its living and its sense of personal value from its position; more and more people feel somehow protected by power, dependent on it, or simply fear change more than the status quo, having carved, by thousands of small adjustments, a nook for themselves. Organization makes power at the same time more all-pervading and more remote, more intermingled with everyone's interests and more independent of them. Techniques developed in order to control power of a different magnitude become manifestly inadequate.

The crucial new element in power based on organizational systems is not only its increase in quantity and stability, but the phenomenon of displacement of goals. Every organization develops a kind of staying power expressed in the loyalty of its members, in their readiness to find new tasks for it when the original purpose has been exhausted, in their commitment to values implicit in what the organization has set them to do. This loyalty, however, is to the organization more than to any other value. The existence and growth of the organization become a goal in their own right—a goal which commands, more and more, the emotions and the motivations of people working for the organization, and dominates, by its importance and appeal, the original aims for the pursuit of which the organization was created. As long as these aims justify the development of the organization and contribute to its prosperity they are maintained and used in order to legitimate the organization's activities. When they no longer perform this function they are discarded and other aims are put in their place. The organization is important, not the aims. The existence and growth of the organization are becoming its institutional goal, in contrast to the

---

[1] The reference is to the imagined conversation between Socrates and Alcibiades in B. de Jouvenel, *The Pure Theory of Politics* (Cambridge: at the Clarendon Press, 1963).

functional goals which its creators had in mind. This institutional goal tends, in the long run, to dominate and to displace also the individual objectives that the organization's members might have at any time and to subordinate their strivings, sociologically as well as psychologically, to the "reason of State" of the organization.

This displacement of individual goals and interests by the institutional goal of the organization increases with the size of the organization, in order to reach a practically inescapable level of intensity in the large organizational systems which are the basis of political power. The reason of State, the cause of the preservation and the aggrandizement of the power system as such—whatever the form in which this cause is rationalized—becomes the supreme law not only for members of the organization, but also for the political rulers and even for their opponents, the "loyal oppositions". A situation may then arise when mere "bystanders", the ruled, people who apparently have everything to lose by the complete subordination of their interests to the State, are drawn into the magnetic field of the system and its institutional goals. The climate created by the endless echoing process of reinforcement of emotions similar to physical induction, makes it possible to impose the existential goals of the organizational system not only against the interests that the system was supposed to serve in the first place, but sometimes also against the manifest, basic interests of all the people concerned. And, most dangerous of all, the intrinsic purposes of different large power systems are by definition opposed to each other. While it is conceivably possible, with an increase of resources, to satisfy a multiplicity of material interests formerly conflicting in a situation of scarcity, rival power goals admit, logically, of no simultaneous satisfaction.[1]

To summarize the argument: no sooner did organizations come to dominate the institutional scene than they entered an epoch of crisis resulting from the conflict in their internal structure between specialized service and the growing need for coordination in large organizational systems. This tension became intensified by the parallel tensions between the independence of the professionals and the presumptions of the hierarchy. Moreover there was in the social

---

[1] "If the purpose of States were the wealth, health, intelligence or happiness of their citizens, there would be no incompatibility; but since these, singly and collectively, are thought less important than national power, the purposes of different States conflict, and cannot be furthered by amalgamation" (B. Russell, *Power — A New Social Analysis* [London: George Allen and Unwin, 1938], pp. 179-80).

role of the organization the increasing difficulty of controlling political power based on organizations, as well as the danger inherent in the opposition between the institutional goals of different power systems.

III

Before we move on to the present let us take a look at the field of values. If our analysis claims a measure of generality it should be applicable not only to the more technical subject of cooperation and the obvious phenomenon of politics, but also to the more elusive representations which influence human striving sometimes just as decisively as the most palpable conditions of material life.

Let us take, by way of example, human dignity as the expression of the values of freedom and equality.

1. Dignity is a value, and as such depends on the total value framework which obtains in a given society at a certain point of its development. Understood as criteria of choice or as measurable entities, values change with time and place. They change in content and in rank-order, they change also in inclusiveness. However, while there is no predictable direction of change in the first two dimensions, the circle of persons who are regarded as rightfully sharing an existing value in a community, generally expands with time.

Dignity, as a value, begins as the prerogative of the elite. The elders, the aristocracy, the free as distinguished from the slaves or the serfs, are considered to be invested with a special quality which makes them more valuable than other members of the community. Dignity is a concomitant of social status. As a rule, it implies power over others, and is protected as a social institution by special sanctions. Attempts on the life or property of the dignitaries are considered more grievous offences than similar crimes toward others and are subject to severe punishment.

As dissatisfaction with this state of scarce dignity—the expression of general scarcity—spreads and the material productive capacity of a society grows, dignity for all becomes a practical ideal, a goal of social and political action, in its later stages a normative concept by which to judge and to measure people and movements. The doctrine of general brotherhood, common to the great religions, finds an echo, on the institutional plane, in the postulate of equal membership in a universal church or equal citizenship of a universal empire.

But it is quite a distance from an ideal, even a practical ideal, to its realization. For a long time yet, some will be more equal than others; even among the privileged minority dignity will be a possession which has to be reconquered whenever it is tested. The quality of personal honour becomes the institutional expression of dignity in the upper status of the social pyramid. Each individual is responsible for his personal honour and has to defend it, if need be, at the point of the sword.

The third and present stage in the development of the concept of dignity is characterized on the institutional level by the expanding legal and social guarantees of a minimum of human dignity for all. Feudal serfs and slaves—where slavery still exists—become emancipated and similar relationships of dependence crumble and disappear everywhere. The principle of personal freedom is reinforced by more equality. Equality of citizens before the law, universal suffrage, religious tolerance and abandonment of the institution of the official church, equality in conditions of the work-contract and, at least in principle, equality of economic opportunity for everyone. Even if some of these principles are today honoured mainly in the breach in many parts of the world, an institutional beginning has been made. Few indeed would be the voices that would dare to attack the pronouncement of dignity as a necessary condition for all. And legal guarantees, developed and improved in use, begin to tell even against inveterate prejudice and actual inequality of economic conditions. They begin to function as proclamation and as indictment. An indictment of the injustice of those who still try to withhold the institutional conditions of human dignity from their fellows. And a proclamation calling into action all people of good will to realize these conditions in their countries.

On the personal level, also, the concept of dignity is evolving toward a more complex and more sophisticated understanding. It is the experiencing, by the individual, of his own internal balance and of a harmonious relationship with his environment. Master of no man and servant to none, the individual lives the experience of dignity as consciousness of his own worth, based not on status but on moral action, not on what he is but on what he does.

Dignity is seen as a social relationship, with a greater or lesser institutional supporting structure; at the same time it is lived as a moral experience. On both levels it is defined as freedom on the one hand, and as equality or equilibrium on the other.

2. The meaning of dignity is changing because the content of freedom and quality does not remain the same through the life history of the individual or through the course of civilizations.

The conditioning framework of freedom and equality, and therefore of dignity, is man's material and social environment. There is no dignity without elementary freedom from the forces of nature and from subjugation by man, without elementary equality with one's fellows.

In the elementary stages of social development freedom can be achieved either by isolation or by domination. Roving hunters, farmers on scattered farmsteads, nomads following their herds across the open steppes, these and similar examples exist of people who have succeeded in establishing and maintaining their freedom, however precariously, by reducing ties with their fellowmen to a minimum or by cutting them altogether. Within society, the only lasting chance of freedom for an individual or a group was in wielding superior force, in the possibility of employing, and the actual use of, the means of overwhelming physical violence. Freedom was for the strong only, in the most literal and inhuman sense. And it was a very poor freedom at that, established within the narrow limits permitted by stern nature, depending often on unstable alliances, coalitions and compromises.

Equality, consequently, was usually equality within an alliance held together by sheer necessity, not infrequently characterized by mutual fear and distrust, as in the war-band and similar associations in which people decided overtly that they could only stand or fall in common, but were afraid of internal treachery no less than of external defeat. The clan and the tribe represented efforts to put this defensive equality on a more permanent basis. The blood-relationship, actual or assumed, among the members helped in creating and reinforcing rules of morality and of political behaviour which today appear sometimes surprisingly democratic and egalitarian. This equality again, however, was not only narrowly circumscribed by the size of the group and the extent of its activities, but was bought at the price of a nearly absolute rejection of all out-groups: material and permanent hostility toward all who did not belong to the in's.

One of the outstanding examples of institutional equality in early times is undoubtedly the peasant family. Born out of the meeting of nomadic cattle-breeders with sedentary fruit-gatherers, the peasant household, as a unit of production and consumption, was based on a complementary division of labour, giving to every member a useful role and therefore a certain degree of independence. It is the first institutionally regulated instance of equality between the sexes built upon the prevailing agricultural technology. The peasant household is relatively self-sufficient materially and, to some extent, even culturally. It is therefore economically independent of contacts with other people and, to that extent, free by isolation. Here again, the freedom and equality of the peasant are at the mercy of favourable natural conditions—the alternative is hunger—and a propitious social situation. Militarily, the peasant household is insignificant and military attack on peaceful peasants has always been a tempting undertaking.

However precarious, what dignity there was for man grew from the freedom of his force or isolation, from his equality within a community, however small and vulnerable.

For a long time, however, the odds were against freedom and equality. Insecurity and fearsome risks were characteristic of the situation of most people most of the time. The small groups—from peasant family to city-state—were enclaves in a hostile world. What security there could be within the narrow limits left by undomesticated nature and human aggression had to be paid for by large portions of freedom and equality. Initially, slavery was the alternative to immediate violent death for a population defeated in war. Feudal serfdom developed, at least in part, through the voluntary subordination of free peasants to the lords of fortified castles where they sought protection in times of danger. People consented to indenture and to sell their labour to the owners of land, factories and other instruments of production lest they and their families should suffer hunger. They were prepared sometimes to give up their political franchise to dictators and strong men who promised to allay their many fears and apprehensions.

It seems that we may venture a general conclusion: without greater security from the common risks of human existence there can be no progress in freedom and equality for all and, therefore, no increase in human dignity.

IV

The present situation, where we have to look for a solution to the institutional crisis of our society, is affected in two important ways by technological development.

The one, and most pressing, new factor is the present level of destructiveness of weapons. Conflicts which would involve their use (i.e., conflicts between large political power systems) have to be avoided. The obvious solution is the establishment of a world community. Before this can be attempted, however, it will probably be necessary to relax gradually the structural base of the big concentrations of power as well as to modify their emotional and ideological superstructures. A process of deconcentration will have to be devised which does not aim at the utopian goal of preorganizational simplicity but is able to reconcile the increasing interrelatedness of people and their activities with an expanding multiplicity of goals, orientations, and interests.

The other important technological factor is the accelerating increase in productivity. Estimates may differ as to the moment when we have reached, or shall reach, the level of productivity where it becomes possible to satisfy the basic material needs of all inhabitants of this planet. The reality of want and poverty in which the majority of the earth's population are still living today may label as impractical all discussions of this possibility. Still the fact remains that, technologically, the possibility is within our reach. The traditionally fundamental source of conflicts among people, competing claims for scarce resources, would then play a considerably reduced role.[1] The consequence would probably be a phenomenon which we are already witnessing today in its beginnings, the dispersion of interests.[2] What I mean by the dispersion of interests is that people participate in a greater number of various interest groups than before while the hierarchical ordering among their different interests becomes less clear and less well determined. Their various interests associate them with various, and only sometimes partially overlapping, interest groups, so that it is more unlikely that large numbers of people will become polarized into large classes based upon opposing interests.

Both technological factors point in the same direction and two general conclusions can be drawn immediately about the forms of

---

[1]   Barring development which can be prevented by rational action, such as "the population explosion".

[2]   The term "interest" is used in the meaning "situation permitting the maximization of a socially accepted value in relation to an individual or to a group of individuals". The purely subjective aspect of interest — the motivational orientation independent from the real-world situation—is called subjective interest. An interest group is a group of people who are in the same objective interest-situation. "Conflict of interests" denotes a situation where the maximization of a value for an individual or group of individuals is possible only at the expense of another individual or group.

institutional transformation that must necessarily take place. The new structures will have to be, in a way, looser and more unified at the same time. They will have to give greater scope to the individual, to his creativity, to the independence of his specialized professional contribution, to the multitude of existing interests. They will have to isolate conflicts instead of reinforcing them to the highest emotional pitch. They will have to diffuse power into a network of mutual influence instead of concentrating it. Instead of facilitating goal-displacement they will have to counteract it. At the same time, these new institutional structures will have to simplify large-scale planning, to reflect the growing interrelatedness of human activity, in order to prevent an uncontrolled increase in social entropy.[1]

In the institutional system that must now be evolved, the process of the realization of interests will have to be integrated with the handling of interest conflicts. What we identify today as the service aspect and the political aspect of organizational systems will have to be understood as two sides of the same coin.[2] Assuming a growing dispersion of interests it would, perhaps, be more appropriate to speak of diverging rather than of conflicting interests.

This new social process which might tentatively be called the process of social self-management, will have to be carried by a new institutional structure. The process of social self-management will have to provide the means to integrate the activities of individuals aimed at the realization of socially accepted interests under conditions of diverging individual interest positions, with the maximum social efficiency compatible with respect for the autonomy of the

---

1 Students of the problem at present seem to be primarily preoccupied with the loosening of organizational structures. The tenets about the span of control are turned upside down by the suggestion to increase the span in order to prevent the managers from managing too much. Cf., W. F. Whyte, "Human Relations— A Progress Report" in A. Etzioni, ed., *Complex Organizations* (New York: Holt, Rinehart & Winston, 1961), p. 111. D. Katz feels that "we must be able to tolerate the ambiguity of a loose organization with wide margins of tolerance with respect to meeting role requirements" ("Human Relationships and Organizational Behavior" in S. Malick and E. H. Van Ness, *Concepts and Issues in Administrative Behavior* [New Jersey: Prentice Hall, 1962], p. 173). Even direct contradictions and unrealistic requirements in role definition are justified as "creative disorder" and its stimulating effects pointed out (A. G. Frank, "Goal Ambiguity and Conflicting Standards: An Approach to the Study of Organizations", *Human Organization*, vol, 17, no. 4).

2 Here as well, usually that side of the picture is pointed out which is new. Conflict is seen as the essence of the functioning of complex organizations (cf. M. Dalton, *Men Who Manage—Fusions of Feeling and Theory in Administration* [New York-London: J. Wiley-Chapman & Hall, 1959]) and a constructive role in organizational change ascribed to it (cf., L. Coser, *op. cit*, p. 154).

individual contribution. Whether we shall call the institutional structure designed for this process an "organization" or invent another name for it is a matter of personal preference. But what points can be indicated to sketch, at least in outline, the emerging structure?

If the nature of the process is to be reflected in the structure, then the institutions of social self-management will have to be constructed around opposite focal points. The first pair of these points might be the individual and the work team. The important difference from organization as we know it today is a shift in accent. The starting point in organizational structuring is the overall objective. This is divided and subdivided until each individual can be assigned his function, as it were from above; and in the course of action everything is again oriented to and measured by the general goal. Organization by its very structure pushes its members into purely instrumental roles.

The new structure starts from the individual specialist who is supposed to know his function by diagnosing given situations in the light of his knowledge and applying his skill to them without any assignment from outside. This basic element of the individual contribution is then integrated into progressively wider patterns, the basic unit of integration being the work team. The work team does not detract in any way from the professional autonomy of each of its members, but it gives to each individual activity its social meaning. In tackling the situation of a family in trouble, for instance, or planning the rehabilitation of a decaying neighbourhood, the work team will be composed of social workers, sociologists, psychologists, psychiatrists, public health specialists, lawyers, town planners, architects, and possibly others. The contribution of each is independent because his very profession is independent, and it cannot be overruled except by technical argument on its own professional ground.[1] At the same time, the socially indicated objective—to help the family, to rehabilitate the neighbourhood—can be reached only by integrated action. There are situations where there can be no action at all without a team. Surgical operations or the acting of a play are obvious illustrations. The integration of the individual professional specialist into the team has to be based on his own free acceptance and has to respect the conditions imposed by his exper-

---

[1] On the other hand, the dispersion of interests counteracts the possible tendency towards narrow-mindedness and one-sidedness inherent in an increasingly detailed professional specialization.

tise. The coordination by hierarchical decree or by the order of a superior is unacceptable on sound logical grounds as well as for psychological reasons. It is meaningless to give anybody the responsibility of giving orders to specialists outside his own field. Within the same field, things have to be decided by technical argument on the basis of the actual accountability for the result.

We can already point to examples of this process taken from fields where professional specialization prevails. In order to make this situation general the process of transferring standardized, routine operations in factory and office from people to machines will have to progress far beyond the point reached at present. Only when the professional specialist becomes the prevailing type of worker, and the menial worker performing simple repetitive operations the exception, can the rigid normative structure of most of our organizational systems be replaced by the freer atmosphere of the work team. But even when the dominance of the norm is succeeded by the "hypothetical imperative" of the technical rule, there will be considerable areas left for normative regulation.

In the field of human relations especially, the internalization of the norms of professional ethics and the development of other appropriate attitudes will be another prerequisite for the functioning of the individual in the work group. The successful integration then promises to be, among other things, a better solution of the problem of the opposite drives towards new experience and towards security than anything that is possible under present circumstances. In the freedom of their professional work, people ought to find a better outlet for their tendencies towards achievement than in the discipline of the organization, while the equality of the working group might be more favourable to security than the competition for hierarchical advancement.

Human dignity might thus also be provided with a more stable basis. In a world of insecurity, dignity, as a personal moral experience, independent of social status and power over others, is the privilege of the saint and the hermit. It is only on the solid foundation of increasing technological and organizing capabilities in a society, that a greater number of individuals can share that experience. But it should be well understood that the relationship is not automatic. Higher economic and organizational levels are a necessary but not sufficient condition of greater personal dignity. People generally can progress on the road to personal perfection only when they are freed from debilitating conditions of subjection through fear and material insecurity. But they have to do the walking themselves. It is only by individual action that the individual can mature as a personality. It is only by personal experience that a person can abandon the crutches of social status and hierarchy, disengage from too strong attachment to his socially-defined self, escape from consuming egotism and self-importance. Only after this cathartic process has progressed far enough, can dignity be experienced internally — as internal freedom from obsession with the self and internal equality between the opposing drives toward achievement and toward security, dynamic internal equilibrium among various individual interests, among different points of view and perspectives within one personality. Only when it is psychologically possible to satisfy the desire for new experience without aggression towards others, to feel secure without buttressing by social approval and social institutions, can true dignity be divorced from relationships of power.

The work group is only the basic unit of a much wider process of integration. With ascending levels two complexes of problems are likely to grow more intricate: the heterogeneous character of the work and the divergence of interests. With the multiplication of the number of work teams in a system an increase in the variety of functions is to be expected. New auxiliary and secondary functions become necessary simply because of the expansion of the network. Traditionally, these secondary and auxiliary functions are the background of the coordinating activity of the hierarchy in organizations. In the new structures they will have to become the task of specific work teams who will service, on a basis of equality, a number of other professional teams. For example, no consequences as to the subordination or superordination of the different individuals or groups would necessarily follow from the fact that a team is engaged in testing or examining personnel for other teams, or that it is constructing and implementing a system of salaries, or keeping a number of accounts. Even today there is no reason why an executive officer of a university or an administrator of a hospital should be hierarchically superior or inferior to the different functional specialists working in the institution. By their very function the work teams performing secondary auxiliary functions for other teams will come to represent for them a sort of contact point, a platform for wider integration on a basis of service and not of hierarchical command.

Still, decisions will have to be taken, decisions on higher levels of integration affecting a substantial number of individuals and work teams and involving, to a greater or lesser degree, their diverging interests. The logic of the system requires that the interested individuals be associated, in one way or another, with decisions affecting their interests. The functional contact points between the work teams will have to be supplemented by a system of collective bodies with changing membership and very elastic rules of procedures which will have to be convened at various levels whenever a decision about indeterminate alternatives involving interests—i.e., not a purely technical decision—has to be taken. The membership in each instance will depend on the content of the decision, giving voice or fair representation to the individuals or the work teams whose interests are touched. The functioning of a hospital board or of a faculty meeting are rudimentary examples of what these interest-decision-making bodies might be. The general application of this method will require, besides much greater elasticity in composition and procedure, the invention of a process of selection by which the handling of most divergencies of interests will be kept as near their source as possible and only those will be filtered to higher levels of integration where this more costly alternative might be worthwhile from a social point of view.

The relationship between the work groups serving as contact points for other teams and the collective bodies responsible for interest decisions should be purely functional, i.e., exist when necessary, as long as necessary, and to the extent required in a specific case, instead of the actual permanent ties of organization. This also applies to the relations between each of the two structural elements and the individuals and teams involved in their activities. All these relations have to be seen as much more fluid than the present organizational rigidities.

This leads to the third pair of problems posed by the new institutional structure: what about the interests of people affected by the activities of the professional teams, as users or consumers, and not as members of other work teams? And how is the looseness of the relationships among work teams, contact points, and decision-making bodies to be reconciled with the requirement of a more dependable prediction of human behaviour in social situations?

The obvious answer to the first question is to include the representatives of the consumers in the decision-making bodies. As consumers they are vitally interested in the "product" of the work teams concerned, in the quality of their work, but not primarily interested in the personal or institutional goals of the teams and

their members. The consumers, then, are theoretically in an ideal position to voice constructive criticism of the professionals in the teams. They are clearly well-intentioned with regard to the function and able to see and to point out quickly dysfunctions. At the same time their presence could function as a diluting and sedative agent on the intensity of conflict brought before the collective bodies by the interested members of the work teams. Finally they would act as an additional factor of integration counteracting possible technocratic tendencies and clannishness on the part of the professionals.

On the other hand, the participation of the consumers in the decision-making bodies, besides involving a number of puzzling issues of recruitment and representation, might run counter to the tendency towards the differentiation of work and the dispersion of interests. If brought to its logical conclusion, the principle of representation of consumers would involve every individual in all the activities from which he derives a benefit, directly or indirectly. That is manifestly impossible and irreconcilable with present levels of technological development. The basic interest of each individual is that the multitude of services and activities necessary for the satisfaction of his needs should function normally and satisfactorily without his intervention. That means that consumer representation can be only an auxiliary or temporary device, and that the basic mechanism of integration has to be found elsewhere.

My first question was how to ensure the participation of consumers in the decision-making process. In the light of my analysis, this question now converges upon my second question: how to combine a minimum of intervention with a maximum of predictability of behaviour? The conditions for the creation of some kind of automatic regulation of behaviour in society have been considered before by utopian and by more practical thinkers. The efforts to set up "steering situations", to discover "laws of the situation"[1] are not without precedent. The imposition of negative sanctions, requiring a power relationship, can be dispensed with where the infraction of rules is followed by the loss of benefits independently from any sanctioning activity. The rules of exogamy (marrying outside one's own group), for instance, were probably most effectively "enforced" by the prospect of the offender's going

[1] The expression "steering situation" is derived from the terminology of cybernetics; the term "law of the situation" belongs to Mary Parker Follett (cf., H. C. Metcalf and L. Urwick, *Dynamic Administration, The Collected Papers of Mary Parker Follett* [New York: Harper, 1942]).

without dowry and missing the opportunity to establish friendly relations with another clan. The market economy, as compared with a slave-holder or a feudal economy, has a "built-in" system of sanctions, and demands the intervention of power, in principle, only in order to guarantee the rules of the game. The public service systems, such as social security, health, education, and others, can impose a rather elaborate and sometimes vexing system of rules on their consumers simply by the threat of withholding their services or benefits. There are, therefore, no essential difficulties in establishing such services organizationally outside the system of governmental administration, which is actually done, particularly for social security, in a number of countries. Here again the intervention of power becomes necessary the moment when consumers do not want to "consume"—e.g., in order to enforce school attendance—or when the service, instead of giving, is asking for something—e.g., collecting fees or premiums. The relative number of public services of that type seems to be on the increase. Manifest danger from disobeying regulations, danger for the transgressor stemming from the situation created by disobedience, obviates enforcement in a majority of cases. It is well known, for instance, how difficult it is to enforce traffic regulation below a given level of density of traffic, while beyond that level people will tend to conform to the commands given by automatic traffic lights.[1]

Even the idea of "creative conflict" was institutionally anticipated in practical attempts at large-scale regulation, as in the mechanism of the separation of powers. In order to avoid the overriding social influence that a large system of political power necessarily has, the attempt was made to partition power. Its various attributes were vested in different carriers—legislative assemblies, courts, executives—at least in part independent of each other. Conflicts among them were not only anticipated but regarded as the main method by which they might check each other and achieve a balance of power diminishing, to an extent, their cumulative influence in the social universe.

The relationship between interest decisions and technical decisions is basically affected by the introduction of planning. The logic of

---

[1] On situations of this kind B. de Jouvenel bases his "law of conservative exclusion" and his argument for the social usefulness of power. It seems, however, that these are precisely the examples where people will have the least difficulty of finding ways to "eliminate conflicting signals" without the intervention of power (cf., B. de Jouvenel, *op. cit.*, p. 111).

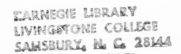

planning calls for such long chains of interconnected decisions that interests can be expressed only on the most general levels and at crucial points. All other decisions are determined by previous choices to such an extent that their technical determining factors can be comparatively little affected by interests. Besides, the network of possible consequences grows so complex that it becomes increasingly difficult for the persons involved to foresee the consequences of alternative modes of behaviour. Planning, in a way, transfers the solving of interest conflicts to an earlier point in time before they have had the opportunity to reach dangerous levels of intensity.

With the dispersion of interests the old calculus of lost opportunities, used at one time to discredit the psychological credibility of the *homo œconomicus*, could reappear in a possibly more realistic form. More and more interest conflicts may become intra-personal instead of inter-personal. The individual deciding to pursue one of his many interests through the collective bodies for the regulation of interest-conflicts will have to balance very carefully the maximum benefit obtainable from this course of action against the loss of opportunity to follow at the same time a multitude of other interests. This appraisal might contribute significantly to the limitation of conflicts introduced into the solving-mechanisms and burdening the collective decision-making bodies.[1] On the other hand, this internalization of conflict does not mean necessarily an intensification of internal conflict in the individual. Different interests which are in conflict simply by having different subjects might well find, in one individual, an ordered scale of individual preference assigning to each of them rank and precedence.

Around the three levels of constructive points already identified, the new structures will have to be built according to general principles somewhat like the following. The starting point would have to be, not the common task, which is then subdivided into more elementary action elements, but the other way around—the expertise of the individual specialist. For example, if we plan to

---

[1] It is interesting that in a socialist economic system as well deliberate planning seems to be supplemented by processes independent from active intervention. Nemčinov defines planning as the "harmonious coordination of the economic principle of conscious control of social production—in accordance with the known objective laws of economic development—with the cybernetic principle of the automatic, autoregulatory and autoorganizing flow of the economic process" (V. S. Nemčinov, *Ekonomiko-matematičeskije metodi i modeli* [Moskva: Izdatelstvo socialno-ekonomičeskoj literaturi, 1962], p. 52).

dig a ditch with a number of people employed, we will normally keep in mind the totality of the task—where we want the ditch to go, how deep it is to be, etc.—and assign to each of the men a task according to this common plan. It is unnecessary that each of the men should know what we are trying to do, why we are digging a ditch, how long and how deep it finally is going to be; everybody knows exactly what he has to do, and that is enough. But if we take a surgical team at a surgical operation, this method does not hold. We do not have an idea of a total operation which is then to be divided into action tasks. On the contrary, each of the specialists in the surgical operation has to have his own judgment and to behave according to his own judgment, and the whole undertaking can function only if nobody has to tell each specialist what to do, only on condition that each member of the team, through his expertise and through analysing the situation before him on the operating table, knows exactly what to do.

The second characteristic change in the new situation would be the unity between administrative and political processes, in the widest sense of the term. This is a rather far-reaching change if one thinks of the implications. For example, if a faculty of a school in the university today has a meeting to decide on the curriculum, here it is very difficult to separate administration from policy-making. The people who are to decide on the curriculum will also implement it, which is usually considered administration. Their experience from their past implementation will influence their own policy decisions. Institutions like faculties, hospitals, research institutions, etc. are already foreshadowing the future general types of cooperative action.

So far, I have identified a number of changing patterns of human behaviour in the institutional situation. I have suggested that we must recognize and put to constructive use a number of pairs of contrasting and potentially conflicting roles. First, the autonomy of the individual in his work as contrasted with the equality of members in the work team. Second, the parallel functioning of professionals and administrators without hierarchical relationships as contrasted with collective bodies for the regulation of conflicts. Third, the representation in the decision-making process of all the interests at risk as contrasted with attempts at the development of self-regulation and self-regulating situations. All of these phenomena are embodied in a number of institutional examples that exist today. The critical task for the future seems to me, however, to be to investigate their mutual interconnections, to trace these inter-relationships as they merge into a balanced system of social relations and, in particular, to examine their implications for human well-being.

V

Let us now take up this development at the level of concepts and try to analyze more systematically what it implies for the professions in the field of welfare.

The concept of welfare emerged relatively early in human com-munities as a kind of minimum level in the standard of living and behaviour of its members. Situations below that level were valued negatively from the social point of view. The reaction of the community to such situations varied all the way from repression and punishment to the mobilization of feelings of social solidarity and the creation of institutions of social support. As a rule, to fall below social minimum standards and to cause appropriate social inter-vention on one's own behalf was considered the opposite of dignity. Dignity being an institutionalized positive privilege, welfare as an institution was a sort of negative privilege. It was considered to apply to marginal cases and, if one can speak of social policy at these early stages, it consisted of keeping these exceptions to as small numbers as possible.

Further development in welfare as a concept and welfare as an institution was induced, in the ultimate analysis, by the increase in man's power to provide for his needs. Greater capabilities resulted in greater expectations. Socially accepted minimum levels of sustenance rose, the mechanisms triggering social intervention became more sensitive, their threshold was lowered, needs them-selves became more numerous and more diversified. With increasing levels of aspiration the dissatisfaction of the under-privileged majority became a political factor. The political struggle of the disenfranchised "third estate" in feudal Europe, of the restive settlers in colonial America, and then of the working class in the 19th and 20th centuries, contributed decisively to shaping the notion of general welfare as we know it today. Also, the spread of industry and the growth of cities created essentially new situations in which the traditional institutional framework proved inadequate. For millenia, what social security there was was based on the family and its various extensions, the household, the clan, the agricultural family cooperative, etc. The family was not only a unit of production and consumption. It provided education, health care, recreation and welfare or security for those who could not provide for themselves with the work of their hands. In an industrial and urban environment most of these functions of the family were socialized. The place where people worked became divorced from the place where they lived. The required level of education began to transcend the educational possibilities of the urban family. With the development of medicine, health services had to be put on a professional basis. Recreation became an industry in its own right. In an industrial and urban society the common risks of existence were expanding at the same time as the capability of the nuclear family to cope with them grew smaller.

The consequences of this development were, first of all, ever-wider circles of recognized social responsibility. From the family, clan, tribe, household, estate, city, it extended gradually to the country and the nation and is moving towards encompassing the whole world. Also, there is better understanding of the relationship between existing social conditions and individual success or failure. The morally dangerous assumption of the complete responsibility of every human being for what is happening to him or to his dependents, economically and socially, was gradually replaced by a more complex view. Finally, the idea of general welfare, as a positive state of wellbeing of all members of a community, has become an ideal, an ideology, a force able to mould human action, far beyond the original marginal and subsidiary concept of welfare from which it started. In today's explosive growth of human productive and destructive capabilities, in the growing interdependence of people everywhere, in the continuing struggle for the emancipation of man from any form of "freedom" or inequality, welfare is not only a force in the realm of ideas. Work has already started on its transformation into a planned system of satisfying basic human needs of all people in all countries.

(a) The type of need

Welfare (or well-being) in the most general sense is a state where certain needs are satisfied. The needs whose satisfaction is considered, however, are not always the same. Material needs expand with the possibility of their fulfilment from the minimum necessary to physical survival[1] to more and more elaborate levels of material comfort thought indispensable for welfare. With other types of needs it is less easy to establish a clear-cut line of development. But variety there certainly is. Emotional needs, for instance, seem to be more constant in time, less subject to expansion, than material needs, but their expression as well as the means of their satisfaction changes with the prevailing culture and the concrete institutional structures. Aesthetic values and standards change even while the aesthetic feeling itself remains relatively constant. Political needs of active participation in community affairs, of freedom, of equality, of condition, change in inclusiveness, in interpretation, in institutional expression. Spiritual and religious needs as well as the impulse towards philosophical speculation or ideological commitment seem to go through periods of greater and lesser intensity and generality. The basically opposite tendencies toward new experience, creative achievement, towards activity on the one hand and towards security, the preservation of acquired positions and relationships on the other, have demonstrated practically unlimited variability. The content of welfare consists of an ever-changing level of satisfaction of psychological and material needs.

(b)   The subjects of welfare

The number of persons for whose welfare other people feel concern and responsibility is, on the whole, expanding: from the family, the clan, the village, the tribe, towards the community, the nation, the world. Working through the mutual interaction of economic factors and moral attitudes[2] this expansion of responsibility is the source of a most significant change in the meaning of welfare. At a certain level of general acceptance welfare emerges into the political sphere

---

[1]   Even "physical minimum" needs have been found in many instances to be culturally determined.

[2]   The growing inclusiveness of the feeling for the welfare of others is not a linear, constant, and uninterrupted movement. However, without assuming its expansion in the long run it would be difficult to explain a considerable part of social development.

In a generalized attempt, on the other hand, to interpret moral values in terms of expanding and contracting circles no clear one-way trend can be discerned: "It is more illuminating to think of differences among societies in moral values as consisting of differences in the areas within which certain types of behavior are commanded or forbidden, and to think of changes in a society's moral values as consisting of expansion or contraction of such areas" (Everett E. Hagen, *On the Theory of Social Change—How Economic Growth Begins* [Homewood, Ill.: The Dorsey Press, 1962], p. 116).

and is institutionalized in two main forms.

In the first of these forms welfare may be defined as an overall goal of the political community consisting in the optimal satisfaction of interests which the members of the community have in common. "Interest" is used here in the objective sense: a situation maximizing, for an individual or a group of individuals, a socially accepted value. Very large numbers of people, in principle even all members of a community, can be in the same situation relative to a value and can, therefore, share the same objective interest. The functioning of a given economic system, for instance, might imply certain risks common to all. To share these risks, to put the help given to individuals in cases of malfunctioning of the system on the stable basis of a guaranteed right, to alleviate for the individual the paralyzing insecurity created by the risk itself—this means to satisfy an interest which all have in common, even those who would rather be left to their own devices. To satisfy common interests by common action requires both a growth in capacity and an increase in understanding —the productive and organizational capacity to provide for the needs of the many and the understanding that these common concerns are more important than the isolated splendour of the few.

In its other dimension, welfare might be defined as a systematic activity meant to provide for the needs of those who cannot provide for themselves by methods considered normal in a community, such as the production of goods and services for consumption in the family, or by work for which the person receives remuneration.[1]

Earthquakes and floods, the breakdown of families, or the breaking of fundamental social norms, are, hopefully, not the rule in a community. Though relatively infrequent, they do happen, however, at all times and in all systems. They as well are becoming our common responsibility. In time, these two political meanings of welfare may meet and intersect at many points, as the first becomes more concretely defined and the second expands in objectives and methods.

Institutionalized social welfare activity for the relief of special needs is chronologically older than the political ideal of welfare for all. It has grown more inclusive through the influence of several factors:

The degree of deprivation an individual must suffer in order that

---

[1] The term "welfare" or "well-being" is usual for the first meaning and the term "social welfare" for the second. Their mutual convergence in development, however, does not help to maintain a clear terminological distinction.

the social welfare mechanism is set in motion becomes less extreme, with greater economic possibilities and higher standards of a "decent minimum" prevailing in the community.

The typical form of intervention by the social welfare institutions of society moves from repression of negatively regarded "social problem" behaviour, through attempts at regulation, outright assistance in different forms, efforts towards individual rehabilitation and restoration to "normalcy", towards systems of preventive measures.

The standards for the social evaluation of problem situations and ethical attitudes towards them vary from disapproval through compassion and various forms of social solidarity to rational detachment and the notion of individual rights to social benefits.

The possibilities of social welfare activity are part of the general capacities for action existing in a community at a given moment, and depend on the stage of development from face-to-face groups to large organizational systems.

The methods of coping with social problem situations include giving information intended to facilitate the orientation of the individual to social reality, assigning income and providing services, extending psychological support calculated to counteract different types of stress, regulating certain "problem prone" social relationships, as well as activities necessitated by the existence and the funtioning of the social welfare institutions themselves.

The professional character of social welfare activity varies from conditions where a general awareness of the existence of social problems is considered sufficient in order to participate actively in the performance of social welfare functions, through the differentiation of a body of knowledge and skills necessary to cope with them, to full professional status for the social welfare practitioners. Where specific knowledge and skills are required for the practice of social welfare they may be seen either as incidental to some other professional profile—doctor, nurse, teacher, etc.—or they are acknowledged as constituting a profession in their own right.

The type of institution carrying the largest share of social welfare activity includes the family, the local community, the State and its administration, inter-local non-governmental organizations, and networks of self-governing social institutions. Social welfare activity can be the only or the principal concern of an institution or it might be secondary to another main activity which the institution is performing.

A great number of concrete social welfare systems can and do result from the interplay of the various variables (economic possibilities, methods, required skills, institutions, etc.).

On the other hand, the ideal or goal of general welfare has become politically influential only recently. It is moving from a high plane of abstraction towards operational reality in the affairs of society. In this movement several forces coincide. Increasing productivity contributes directly to higher living standards and a better satisfaction of needs by the "normal" activity of the individual. Emerging possibilities to influence general economic conditions through rational planning and regulation tend to reduce the dysfunctional consequences of economic processes. The expansion of public services and the development of new forms of service, specially prominent in urban communities, contribute to the differentiation as well as to the satisfaction of needs. Political democratization transforms measures for the general welfare more and more into political objectives. Practical international collaboration in problems of development the world over has a very strong welfare aspect. As this activity emerges from token proportions and receives more weight in human affairs, the common aspects of welfare transcend national boundaries.

In measures like the establishment of social insurance and general social security systems it is already difficult to distinguish between the two concepts of welfare. These measures are aimed at individuals who cannot provide for their needs themselves in the traditionally normal way, but they are applied under conditions through which practically all individuals in the population pass at some time in their lives—childhood, old age, sickness—and they are aimed at risks to which a great number are exposed, such as accidents or disabilities. Here social welfare measures lose their subsidiary character and become normal methods to provide for normal and general needs.

The future of welfare in its new interpretation, general and concrete at the same time, is determined by the basic political alternatives and transformations in the world today.

With the attainment of a level of material productivity that brings within reach the possibility of meeting the material needs of all people, social welfare becomes the normal process of political and social responsibility for achieving what has been described as a "positive state of well being". The characteristics of this state are to be found in the full development of individual capabilities, the establishment and maintenance of satisfying human relationships, constructive participation in the life of the community, creative work and recreation, and in the constant re-establishment of the dynamic equilibrium between the drives towards new experience and towards security.

Activities cease to be economic in the sense that the performance by the individual of externally determined work is a condition for obtaining the material necessities of life. At the same time, social welfare is no longer subsidiary in the sense of assisting those who cannot provide for themselves. The juxtaposition of "productive" and "non-productive" activity is gradually losing its traditional significance.

In the affluent society, however, large concentrations of power-in-organization have become a present and grave danger to the very survival of humanity. The answer to that danger can only be a consciously planned process of social deconcentration throughout the institutional structure, a process corresponding to a growing dispersion of interests. New methods have to be evolved for the systematic satisfaction of a growing variety of human needs and the simultaneous handling of diverging interests. These processes and methods have a clear bearing on the concept of welfare.

The question is, what is the role of social welfare going to be in this new pattern? Is it any longer to be considered as a specific activity at all, or is it simply the sum of a great number of specialized professional performances, of attitudes and institutions, the most general aim and result of human interaction?

The attempt at an answer to this fundamental question has to proceed from the fact of non-uniformity of development. Development proceeds at various speeds in different places, reaches different stages at different moments, its thousands of elements fall into thousands of patterns resulting from the chances of history. What welfare is going to be and to mean to people and societies in all possible cases cannot be determined beforehand. Again only the most general variables of possible development can be investigated.

Even if the marginal character of social welfare is in the process of being replaced by a general political notion of welfare, marginal individual cases and marginal situations of groups are not likely to disappear at the same time. A society that did not produce stresses on its individual members would have to be a society completely without structure, which is a contradiction. In extreme cases existing structural stresses, whatever their nature, are likely to produce problem situations. By this I mean to describe those situations where the normal functioning of the social system does not lead to the expected and socially acceptable results.

With increasing productivity and changing institutional patterns the statistical frequency of different types of problems may change, but the fact of marginal situations will continue. Deviations and shortcomings from higher standards of need satisfaction might even become a much more general condition than the deficiencies relative to the physical minimum standards in epochs of scarcity. So that marginal welfare problems might really increase with a rise in expectations.

The activities involved in coping with these problems will retain the subsidiary character conventionally associated with social welfare. But at the same time they are likely to become more highly differentiated, and less the concern of just one type of specialist. It may very well be possible that the professional activity of social work will become further specialized and subdivided among a number of more specific activities based on knowledge and skill derived from the social and behavioural sciences. The present increasing subdivisions and special fields within the profession of social work, as well as the emergence of special types of applied sociologists, psychologists, psychiatrists, criminologists and penologists, urban planners, rehabilitation specialists, and many other professional varieties indicate the general trend.

Social change might be considered the one most general source of stress causing not only marginal but also universal problems. Whatever the future is going to be, change will be one of its outstanding features—change, for a time at least, with a tendency towards acceleration in the pace of change.

Forms of change and the resulting stresses depend on the stage of development of a given community. Modernization of work techniques, new materials, new sources of power, reorganization of institutional arrangements, changing occupational patterns, different location of economic and social activities, general movements and migration of people, developing population pressures, the transformation of family and community life, changing interest positions—all these general features of change have always been present. They influence the current social scene, and there is no reason to believe they will cease to be important in the future.

Change increases insecurity as old institutions are abandoned, as people lose status derived either from knowledge and technological skills that are now superseded or from traditional positions that have crumbled, as people move to unaccustomed places and occupations. As social controls break down, new situations tax to the limit, and beyond it, the capabilities of individual adaptation. People develop resistances against the forces of change and spend frustrating lives in hopeless battles against them. Whole groups are left in marginal positions, geographically and otherwise, and become a constant source of difficulties for themselves and for society.

To the familiar pattern new factors of the same kind are likely to be added: further transformation of the occupational structure through specialization, obliteration of the difference between manual and intellectual work in the wake of automation, disappearance of the contrast between urban and rural settings, dispersion of interests, deconcentration of organizational systems, and the gradual abandoning of the principle of hierarchy. All these are likely to produce modifications in human relations, roles, and status deeper than anything hitherto experienced; the corresponding stresses will necessarily be more tense and more powerful. It would be unrealistic to assume for the future that changes, however beneficient their expected functions, will occur without any dysfunctions, without their unavoidable dark sides. These dysfunctions, besides increasing the margin of problem cases, produce stresses falling generally on a great number of people and are therefore pertinent to the new generalized concept of welfare. These developments will probably result, among other things, in an even greater interfusion of social welfare with mental health thinking than exists today and has manifest general implications for the health services.

Welfare activities of whatever kind during a time of accelerated change will have to be much more versatile and adaptable than either social welfare or general welfare measures are today.[1] Neither a dogmatically held ideology of general welfare nor an academically hardened body of social work theories, rules, and precepts is likely to provide an answer to the quickly changing patterns of problems or to make readily available the potential resources to cope with

[1] Social policy will have to live up to the ideal of being "a policy which aims at a continual reform of society in order to eliminate weaknesses of individuals or groups in that society" (J. A. Ponsioen, "General Theory of Social Welfare Policy" in Ponsioen *et al.*, *Social Welfare Policy—Contributions to Theory* ['s-Gravenhage: Mouton & Co., 1962], p. 18). Social work as well has to fit into this framework, even if it stresses traditional values. It "must be an integral part of the national policy, aiming at arousing the nation's consciousness of its situation, at the readiness of the groups to accept a re-classification, at the acceptance of new patterns for traditional values, or of new values in the traditional hierarchy" (Ponsioen, *Social Welfare Policy—Contributions to Theory*, p. 34).

them. Programmes will have to be planned with a much shorter range of preparation, as well as a reduced period of social usefulness.

They will have to have greater adaptability as to place, since social development in different places on this earth will proceed in different ways, at different speeds, by different methods. And as responsibility increases internationally, it will be a very complex task to devise appropriate methods to deal with social problem situations and social regulating situations at different levels and in different varieties of development.

At the same time with accelerating social change, social programmes will have to be more adaptable in time—we will have to reckon with a shorter period of social usefulness for any single programme. Take, for example, community development. Even today we are often faced with the problem that where it has been initiated and has been a positive help in a given social situation, people press on with it—perhaps because certain structures have been built and certain vested interests created—even in situations where different structures, a stable system of local government for example, are needed. And often where we have a stable system of local government, we persist in it and become quite emotional in pointing out that it is the only democratic and only possible system, when already the development of metropolitan government, for example, would really call for completely different structures—for functional, vertical structures which are not compatible with the traditional structure of local government. We will have to adjust to the idea that all programmes which we invent have a certain limited span of social usefulness, and when this span is spent we should invent something new to meet new requirements.

This has important consequences for social work education, to mention only one implication. It will be less and less possible to give people a full kit for their practical professional performance during their whole professional careers. Much more stress will probably have to be laid on general improvements of personal development possibilities, general basic training in basic sciences, and leave all the rest to in-service training and development through practice.

Non-uniformity of development means inequality of levels of living and of chances of improvement. Moreover, increased expectations, besides causing a number of practical difficulties, also intensify the resentment caused by these inequalities. Sometimes new disparities—geographical, occupational, organizational, and others—compound old prejudices. Inequality and its consequences are probably the deepest and most important sources of tension and conflict in the world today, within individual countries as well as between them. Inequality sometimes results in different standards of value being applied to identical situations. Living conditions in a country, for instance, may be accepted by a part of the population as normal conditions of life, while they are regarded by others, applying values developed elsewhere, as unacceptable. Too great a discrepancy between goals and possibilities, between hopes and reality, instead of stimulating effort can lead to discouragement.

The new structures for cooperation, the collaboration of specialized individuals in working teams, coordinated flexibly and autonomously through specialized contact points and through decision-making bodies with general participation, presuppose much more general, pervasive, and motivationally efficient attitudes of equality than those prevalent today. The inequalities, internalized through the experience of long years of acculturation, and especially through the situation of hierarchical subordination and superordination in organizations, will be hard enough to unlearn. To these will have to be added the inequalities produced by the nonuniformity of development. The tension between the increasingly important standard of equality and the forces working against it is likely to grow.

The third field of development of welfare is what I would call social education, using that expression in the sense that we speak of health education—meaning not education of health practitioners, of doctors and nurses, but education of people to protect their own health. In this sense, social education will come to play an increasing and ever larger part in social welfare action. Even today, supposing that practical medicine would one day find itself robbed of the possibility of surgery, of the possibility of applying drugs, including antibiotics, we would find that not much more would be left of medicine than health education. In the social field we are not very far from a similar situation. The surgery and drugs which we apply sometimes have shown dangerous side effects—they have not in practice confirmed that we really know yet how to use them. So we will have to give greater place to social education. What I mean by social education is perhaps a little unorthodox. I would think that what was the standard education of the social worker twenty years ago should, twenty years from now, be the standard education for every person. Instead of teaching civics or some kind of ideological commitment to one side or another, we will teach people how they function in society, what makes them tick, what puts them under stress, what makes problems for them. This kind of general knowledge—and already today this is general knowledge —would have to be taught systematically to everybody, and this will be an important task of welfare.

The practical learning and acceptance of equality is a part of the new concept of welfare. The methods will tend to be composite. General measures promoting equality of condition, mass action teaching equality through actual cooperation, social education in a variety of forms, will go together with a patient building of the new institutional structures implying the solution of innumerable technical problems which are today difficult even to foresee. At the same time the "marginal" traditions of social welfare will possibly come to life again in the task of the treatment of offences and offenders against equality, or in specialized programmes to promote the well being of groups with a traditionally depressed status and, possibly, to develop a new and expanded ideology to correspond to the changing realities of the situation.

The stresses on a large number of individuals are increased by the political changes that are now unfolding. The traumatic impact of violent political upheaval, however progressive its results, the dangers of concentration of political power often inherent in efforts at accelerated development, and particularly the chilling experience of organizational society are among the main factors producing these stresses. Particularly the situation in large organizations demonstrates to people for the first time not only that cooperation at a technical task is possible without a corresponding community of interests, but that organizations can be turned into instruments of interest domination against their own members. Cooperation is no longer identical with interest-coalition, as it was with pre-organizational arrangements. The resulting feelings of loneliness and of being only a "cog in the machine" are among the principal strains of industrial society.

The political tasks of the future, however, are likely to exceed by far the stresses of the past. The problems of deconcentrating the dangerous agglomerations of political power, of breaking up the structures through which emotions aroused by conflicts of interests were brought to their highest points of intensity, and then of building the new structures for the constant adjustment of diverging interests, for social control without social domination, for free cooperative action — these are tasks which today can be glimpsed only in their barest outline. It will be the responsibility of welfare activity, even if not of social work in the narrow sense of the word, to help in setting up the self-regulating social mechanisms of the future. Take, for example, social security systems, which today are in their most primitive stages. They are based on a very primitive actuarial mathematical principle derived from social insurance systems, but this is completely inadequate to deal with the highly complex problems which, let us say, a national health service or any nation-wide insurance system poses. We have not yet solved these technical problems. To solve them will be a task for the future.

Today already, with social welfare as a subsidiary activity and general welfare as an aim of policy, the problem arises of the possible conflict between institutionalized welfare goals and actual needs of the individual. Welfare is "objectified", and the institutionalized pattern of welfare values is, in a way, imposed on the possibly varying pattern of human needs. This problem has been highlighted particularly by the various definitions of social welfare and social work as "adaptation". Even if the mutual character of adaptation is stressed — individual to society and environment to people — the question remains open: how far can institutions adapt people to their requirements without limiting their freedom in an unacceptable way? In the institutional structure of the future this will be a question of basic importance. The greater autonomy of freely cooperating individuals will make them less tolerant towards externally imposed values of whatever character.

Putting together what we have said about the institution of general welfare and about the perspectives of welfare as a professional activity, the full significance of welfare begins to emerge and its role in the construction of a society with higher levels of human dignity becomes apparent. Apart from furnishing in general welfare the material foundation of dignity, apart from introducing in professional activity dignity into the relationships with people under stress, welfare as a movement represents a non-violent method of individual and social change containing the seeds of a generalized approach to rationality in social processes.

In order to live up to this greater challenge, welfare cannot remain static. It must progress and grow as a profession, as a body of knowledge, as a commitment. Social welfare as the profession of social help and social planning will have to incorporate into one available body of skills all the various approaches to welfare developed everywhere in the world. It will have to establish and test a relationship between the various forms and the situations in which they can be most usefully applied. For this reason, welfare will have to assemble and systematize a body of knowledge of its own, knowledge about human behaviour in conflict and under stress, about human needs and interests. The sociology of welfare is the necessary scientific foundation of the practice of welfare. Above all, welfare will have to retain and greatly develop a feature which is for most of us its main attraction. More than ever, welfare will have to mean a firm moral commitment, a humanistic philosophy, a personal dedication to the universal values of man.

Beyond the level of any profession, finally, we see unfolding the drama of human development itself. Beginning in scarcity and extreme uncertainty, man has fought his way uphill against nature, both around and within him. From his initial successes in raising material productivity, his aspirations have expanded in all directions. Seeing today, proudly, members of the family of man make their first steps into space, we are no less conscious of the immense complexity of our task. The human condition is blessed with unending possibilities, but also fraught with many dangers. To make our achievements on the material level lead not to destruction but to growth, to freedom and equality, to the greater dignity of man, is the challenge of the times. It is also the profoundest meaning of welfare.

3

HUMAN RIGHTS AND SOCIAL WELFARE IN
A RESPONSIBLE SOCIETY

For the last ten thousand years or so, man has needed his fellowmen and, at the same time, has competed with them for survival. This deeply contradictory relationship has determined the basic patterns of human behaviour in a way analogous to the mechanism of genetic information regulating biological reproduction. But analogy is not identity. And that is perhaps our best hope for survival in the future. For the inherited social template, the basic information pattern regulating our behaviour in society during millenia, has actually become dysfunctional. Instead of contributing to survival it spells the gravest danger to survival. Can we change it before it is too late?

Even if at present we know too little for a conclusive answer, let us concentrate upon the question. Popper's saying that cognition begins not with collecting facts or constructing theories but with problems, is fatefully relevant in our present situation.

I

The exact nature of the processes in the tissues of the human brain — perceiving, memorizing, forgetting — is still largely unknown. The basic mechanism regulating behaviour in the individual is therefore a matter of conjecture, and sometimes simply of metaphor. It is pictured, apart from behaviour determined by the genetic code, as a pattern of concentric circles. Expanding circles when life-experiences of the individual jell into some sort of residues of increasing generality, or contracting circles when these residues function as switches orienting the individual's actions in real life situations in more and more specific ways.

The residues of conditioned reflexes, attitudes, values, beliefs, internalized norms, roles, etc., in the individual are established by associating tension or relief from tension with certain forms of behaviour. The more dependable the association in experiences repeated over time, the more stable, in general, the residues. The tensions, which are relieved by appropriate behaviour, stem from uncertainties in the natural and social environment of the individual.

It is here that the dilemma starts. Nature cannot be reasoned with. It is fight or flight as for any other animal, and this is the source of the deep-set patterns of defence and aggression. The human environment, on the other hand, is a more complex proposition. It can and does appear as nature, as a potential source of danger or of need-satisfaction, as the case may be, eliciting the same response of defence and aggression. But at the same time, it is society, the sheltering and protecting group, the main — in the beginning really the only — available form of insurance against towering uncertainty. This pressure of pervasive uncertainty is initially the most potent agent of socialization. Acceptance by the group is a condition of physical existence for the individual and he cannot see his existence as separate from the group. His whole life is subject to the rules of group-life in a measure which does not permit rational ends-means thinking to arise. Every action has to be sanctioned by a rule derived from the group. Aggression within the group is as unthinkable as it is normal between groups and in the extra-group environment generally.

In this way, the individual learns to seek relief from tension by two basically incompatible methods. Through defence-aggression in competitive affirmation of his interests, and through conformity-acceptance of the protective security of his group.

These were the basic boundary conditions established for human behaviour, and in this framework what we call progress was achieved. But at what price? As Lucien Lévy-Bruhl muses in his *La morale et la science des moeurs*: Maybe there as well, in social development, is boundless wastefulness, an unjustified expenditure — at least from the point of view of our reason — in suffering, in misfortune, in physical and moral pain, sacrificing in every generation the huge majority of individuals to the functioning of society as a whole.

Strangely enough, the price is increasing to prohibitive proportions precisely at the moment when the commodity bought for it is becoming less indispensable.

The development of the patterns determining human behaviour is one of growing complexity. An increasing number of values and norms creates alternatives for the individual. These alternatives are in the beginning experienced as conflict — and are so interpreted to the present day by humans conditioned to harmony as the basic prerequisite of social solidarity. Nevertheless, these very conflicts, the choices with which the individual is faced, the preference-orderings he has to establish himself, signal the birth of freedom. With the possibility of choice comes perspective. Alternatives create distances and the individual begins to see himself as different from his group, from society generally. Not all rules are necessarily accepted. They are seen as imposed from outside, as stemming from the expectations and requirements of society. As the pressure of uncertainty is reduced, social institutions are developed with the purpose of replacing diffuse environmental pressure with specific social constraints. Power as a peculiar form of concentrating the available instruments of physical violence in a community, of monopolizing the sources of uncertainty society-wide, comes into being. And though power in all its forms — patriarchal, patrimonial, governmental — tends in the beginning to be absolute and arbitrary, it is no longer completely identical with the individual's own internal programming. However large a part of society's commands and injunctions is internalized through the artifice of reward and punishment at the hands of the powerful, there is at least a remainder which is experienced as being imposed from the outside. And in revolting against this imposition, however mildly, however tentatively, however covertly, man lives his freedom for the first time.

In one sense history is the growth of freedom. The broader the span of requirements, the greater the variety of roles, the more bewildering the diversity of rules, the more confusing the contradiction in values — the better for freedom. The multiplicity of bonds creates choices, all these demands cannot but conflict. Man, conditioned as he is to acceptance, to conformity, tends to resent — at least with one side of his personality — this conflict and the freedom it implies. He sees it — in the words of the cautious conservative Durkheim — as anomie, the breakdown of security-bestowing law and order.

And well he may, to an extent or for a time. As long as uncertainty in the environment is not reduced below a certain threshold, there is no substitute for the safety and stability of society. It is this uncertainty which generates the dialectic of emerging curiosity, erupting activity on the one hand and defensive security, cringing avoidance on the other. In man's development, the fight for freedom and the escape from freedom are not the quaint self-contradiction they are sometimes made out to be. They are simply the consequence of a homeostatic information-processing and decision-making programme with originally very narrow boundaries.

But the boundaries are widening. Rising levels of productivity — understood as the ability to satisfy interests of any description — reduce competition for the satisfaction of organic existential needs. Expanding standards of rationality replace emotionally underpinned categorical norms with neutral hypothetical rules, derived from the regularities discovered in nature and behaviour. Social conformity, therefore, becomes gradually less important both for counteracting the consequences of unbridled competition and for ordering goal-oriented cooperative activity. Modes of both conflict and cooperation are subtly changing. Emphases are shifting away from the time-honoured social institutions of enforced regulation, the simple binary switchboards where the "yeas" and the "nays" were backed by appropriate rewards and punishments. Of these institutions, one stands out as particularly ominous: the political State. The threatening amplification of power achieved in the modern super-states is particularly frightening because this huge potential is the last form of power which remains basically unregulated. Ultimately, the competition between states is left to the maxims of the jungle.

The information-processing surface which a progressively more complex society provides for the individual is becoming larger. Alternatives of values, dispersed interests, membership in multiple coalitions, all these contribute to widening the leeway for the individual's orientation. But will he have the courage for his freedom? Will he know how to develop new forms of responsibility to replace the comfortable irresponsibility of obedience? And will he do all that in time?

II

What would have to happen in the reality of the world as it is today for the answer to these questions to be in the affirmative?

There are first, general preconditions. Uncertainty impinging upon man from his natural and social environment would have to be reduced considerably below the threshold that has been reached by now even in the most developed parts of the world. Let us affirm at the outset that this is technically possible. But it has to be done. And a mere technical possibility, with the prevailing patterns of behaviour being what they are, is by no means a certainty.

Technical productivity, available technological capacity to produce, when fully used and rationally distributed, is sufficient to remove, within a reasonable span of time, economic insecurity, uncertainty as to the satisfaction of basic organic needs, from the face of this planet. The actual achievement of this goal, even if only in a smaller part of the world, is already influencing significantly aspirations, hopes, and the temper of thinking across all frontiers. This most recent stage, when stark organic deprivation no longer constitutes a threat for the majority of members of a community in normal times, has been achieved in the greater part of Central and North-Western Europe as well as in North America. It has also been achieved, at a lower level of technological sophistication, in most East European countries. This is significant because it demonstrates the margin of productivity within which this achievement is possible for a country on its own by changing the ground-rules of distribution.

Uncertainty stemming from man's natural environment, however, is not the main problem today. The heavy and general pressures come from a social order in which — in Michel Crozier's words — control of the most important sources of uncertainty is still concentrated within comparatively small circles. We are living in power-societies, and the gradients of power — political, economic, organizational, even sometimes patriarchal power — run from the powerless to the powerful. The segregational influence of this stream of power is considerable. It splits society into unequal groups of the governing and the governed, the rich and the poor, the accepted and the tolerated, the honoured and the despised, along any of the lines of class, race, nationality, religion or belief which have been used during our long and painful walk towards humanity in order to separate people from each other. Groups which share unequally in the values and benefits which their common environment has to offer must necessarily be antagonistic. The more favourable position of one group can only be based on the relative deprivation of the other. And maintaining society partitioned into antagonistic groups means to preserve much of the social climate of primordial group-society where the relationships of absolute solidarity within the group and absolute hostility between groups created and reinforced the ambivalent patterns of conformity and aggression that bedevil man's desire for rationality to the present day.

This arrangement of roles and institutions is in the process of disintegrating anyway, at least in the more developed parts of the world. Possibly the process should be speeded up and rationalized. And it is important to understand that the reality of supremacy and subjection — however veiled in form and glossed over — has to be removed before even the attempt can be made to change the corresponding patterns of behaviour. This means to propagate and to generalize those structures which partake of the nature of coalitions. They already exist, even if only in very rudimentary form and in very small numbers. But there are organizations which, together with parts of their interacting environment, represent coalitions in the sense that every interest-group, and eventually every individual, engaged in the common undertaking has in principle the same amount of leverage with which to enforce its particular interest-demands. This leverage is based on its usefulness, on the contribution made to the joint purpose. The contribution can be positive, performance, and also negative, abstaining from interference with the collective operation when normally — in a factual and legal sense — in a position to interfere. Most advanced forms of work such as scientific research, higher education, complex engineering design, medical and social welfare teamwork, are carried on by coalitions which include not only the people actually engaged in the activity but also groups essential for the financing, placing of orders, licensing, reviewing results, developing methods, etc. To discover the ways in which such frameworks can be generalized is one of the most important tasks of social engineering.

To weave the network of cooperation out of the strands which now constitute the ropes of power is no mean task and it is not possible to see all the implications. One of them is the reappraisal of the ideology of efficiency. Efficiency as the demand for maximal rationalization of effort, at a comparatively low level of technological development, tries to transform people into parts of a quasi-machine. They must become cogs dependent on each other and ultimately on the purpose of the whole mechanism represented by management. The increase in productivity ascribable to greater efficiency is limited to a short, though very conspicuous, span in the ascending curve of growth. The advantages of a systematic division of labour at the level of the task are manifest in the time immediately after the industrial revolution before mechanization of work has got fully underway. In the longer run, however, decisive advances in productivity have all been achieved by transferring work to machines, fed by new and more abundant sources of power. It is science and technology that stand at the frontier of progress, not the "one best way" to perform manual work. But then it is perhaps not too great a price for establishing relationships of coalition-partnership, of equality at work, if we have to face the reduction in the machine-like efficiency of human work. Our productivity is likely to go on increasing even without transforming people into components of machines.

And now we come to the really difficult part. The third major prerequisite for reducing uncertainty to levels where the attempt to change prevailing behavioural information codes becomes a practical proposition is to replace the actual international disarray with some semblance of order. And order cannot mean hegemony of one power or a group of powers any more than it can mean world government. Not because that were impossible. Even if it is so today, it might very well become possible at some future time. But this would mean transferring the problem of power, with which we are now faced in every country individually, to the level of the world. And then it might really become unmanageable. What should be the countervailing mechanisms that could check and balance a world-wide monopoly of the means of physical violence?

We have to construct an international system with an in-built tendency opposite to the iron law of oligarchy, to initiate processes of equalization of influence at the same time that a growing interdependence would limit arbitrariness of decision in any part of the system.

One problem in this context deserves particular attention. The trend towards equalization must be world-wide. No third world, no "wretched of the Earth" must be left out if the seeds of violence are to be removed and not only transposed. But very many countries today are at a stage of development when the establishment of stable and effective national power is still a progressive goal. Normally it should be expected that increase in economic and military capability in these countries would result in more aggressive political attitudes within the national territory as well as in the international arena. How can these countries develop to more equal status with the rest of the world without having to repeat the philogenetic path through aggressive competitive national power-societies and without being controlled by a superior outside power? This is a problem which has not even begun to receive a solution.

There is some indication of possible approaches, but they are even more nebulous than the few existing types of coalition at the level of first-line cooperation at work. There are forms of activity on the international scene, organizations which, even when called "governmental", are essentially independent of power in the performance of their tasks. They number today about 2,000 and employ less than 100,000 professional people. If these international organizations — from ILO to the World Council of Churches and from the International Olympic Committee to the Red Cross — should number 100,000 and the number of people working for them could be counted by tens of millions maybe we should begin to get somewhere. The world-wide network of functional cooperation, in which people could work at tasks of common interest without being dependent on organized violence or other forms of imposition, should increase in density, quickly and acutely. There is no other way to displace the sway which governments hold over international relations than to crowd them out by other forms which would gradually take over all processes of constructive, useful international interchange and would, by contrast, clearly show the dangerous if ludicrous anachronism of present-day international politics.

III

If all these are only preconditions there seems very little hope left in our future. Obviously, the relationship is logical, not chronological. The achievement of more satisfactory directions in the processes of history can be attempted only simultaneously with the corresponding changes in our behavioral information code. And if this should still seem like a tall order, two thoughts are recommended for consideration:

— We have really no alternative. As long as we are genetically programmed to strive for survival we have to go on because there is no other way leading to survival. Karl Marx thought that humanity in its progression tackles only those problem at a certain time, which, at that time, it is able to solve. However, it is difficult to predict what can or cannot be solved without having tried. A more dependable maxim for action therefore seems to be that those tasks have to be assumed that cannot be left undone, however forbidding they may be.

— Also, we are not starting from scratch. Two institutions, still in their gestatory stage, particularly merit consideration:

1.   The emergence of human rights as a limitation of the unrestricted possibility of power holders to please themselves. Traditionally, the notion of right has developed as a regulated relationship between subjects of a power centre. Their claim upon the centre was at best a claim for protection against the infringement of their rights by other subjects, a claim for arbitration in the case of conflict, and a claim for implementing the settlements as pronounced. The wielders of power were above the rules they imposed on others. From time immemorial they did "as the Senate pleased", and in doing so they could do no wrong in any sense that would be practically relevant within their society.

The first time it was affirmed that the king *could* do wrong, that the ruler was not absolved from obeying the laws he promulgated, a genuine revolution was achieved in the human condition. The changes in the attitudes, feelings and acts of man which this reversal of principles effected from the moment it was first proclaimed testifies to the powerful logic inherent in a system of rules, even if these rules — and this is still their main weakness — were not and could not ultimately be enforced within an order where overwhelming force was concentrated in the hands of those against whom the rules embodying human rights should have been enforced.

2.   At the same time, the idea of an existential minimum level which would be guaranteed by society to the individual found expression in a number of new institutions and activities that go under the generic name of welfare in its widest connotation. While human rights were far-reaching in their abstract implications though in practical life honoured mainly in the breach, welfare measures were from the start practical and concrete although often woefully inadequate in scope and based on antiquated ideologies. While the proponents of human rights were often unable to translate their reasoning into reality, welfare achieved progress, even if small-scale, although frequently for the wrong reasons.

From its beginnings, welfare was independent of power for its functioning. Real welfare measures very seldom needed enforcing. It is therefore significant that most of the successful international large-scale organizations are in the field of welfare in its widest sense. WHO, ILO, UNESCO, UNICEF, FAO can operate on a world-wide basis in health, education, social security and social work, in child welfare and in the fight against hunger, in most cases without needing any enforcement machinery. This is why they function and produce results far ahead of anything that can be expected of the political machinery of the United Nations.

Given the actual though sporadic protection of human rights and the existing though not universal minimum welfare floor limiting the possible decrease of living standards, some might feel, with Bertrand Russell, that even today aggressive competitive behaviour exhibited nationally and internationally cannot be accounted for by prevailing pressures of uncertainty alone. Even today the embryonic institutions of equality are ahead of the inherited behavioural drives. If nothing else, this discrepancy should point the direction in which we should go: towards stabilizing the new institutional framework, reinforcing the influences which it must exert on values and attitudes.

That would mean, first, establishing minimum standards of welfare as a human right. Such a fusion of the two essential institutions preparing a new society would strengthen both. Welfare should obtain a stable threshold no longer subject to further discussion among interest-groups in society. This minimum welfare for all is a matter of elementary right, not involving any question of dignity, capability, self-reliance or any other device developed in order to lower the status of one individual or group in relation to others.

On the other hand, proclaiming the right to welfare would provide a human right with already perfected methods of practical implementation grown over the years in the field of welfare. How did welfare succeed in imposing a levy on the powers that be? To begin with, through two contradictory factors: through the threat, real or imagined, which mass destitution spelled for the existing order; and, on the other hand, perhaps through the feeling of pity which derives its existence from the deep solidarity of the primeval human group. After that the development of general welfare systems had four main aspects:

— With the increasing numbers of beneficiaries of welfare services, interests were mobilized which were too strong to be disregarded, let alone slighted.

— The increasingly professional character of welfare work in its many aspects created a powerful and well-organized pressure group whose interests largely coincided with those of the beneficiaries in expanding welfare benefits and services. The various professions of welfare have more than once functioned as social action groups in the struggle for progress in welfare.

— Potent existing beliefs and values were enlisted to reinforce the pressure for more welfare. The pertinence of welfare to the ideals of justice, equality and humanitarianism was established as self-evident.

— Finally, through the existence of a considerable network of non-governmental carriers of all kinds or through the gradual establishment of organizational forms independent of government, welfare was taken out of the hands of the power-establishment. This last achievement can demonstrate its advantages only after minimum standards of general welfare have been adopted and accepted. Therefore, for most of their past history, the relations between welfare and government have been ambivalent. Under the influence of democratic reforms government became more responsive to the interests of the masses, in this way becoming sometimes the most important agency in establishing welfare standards. On the other hand, the possibility of misusing welfare for purposes of power was never remote and remains present whenever welfare is dispensed only or chiefly through agencies closely allied with the centers of power.

IV

Further development of institutions of welfare and of human rights, together with other causes which help to reduce the level of un-certainty, should eventually result in a radical change in the matrices of behaviour. This change might be prognostically described as a new concept of responsibility.

In the power-societies in which we live, responsibility is based on power and flows from power. It is the principle of obedience to authority, based on the regular experience of punishment for dis-obedience. This experience is eventually and optimally internalized in the form of duty and the dictates of one's own conscience. Immanuel Kant has formulated the corresponding moral rule: to act in such a way that the maxim of one's action could be a princi-ple of general government.

In the functional society of the future, responsibility should be different in all its dimensions. It is the expression of a new social relation. Not of submission to the will of others but of cooperation in activities which can only be performed in common, of the necessary mutual respect for the interest-minima of each partner in the interest coalition emerging around the collective activity. In a coalition, each partner has the weight of his contribution, positive or negative, to the achievement of the common purpose. Respecting his interests is therefore not a question of fair play but a condition for the continuation of the activity. The penalty for deviance is not punishment imposed from outside. It is self-inflicted failure to achieve one's purpose resulting from the non-observance of technical rules by which the way to achieve the end in view is defined, or resulting from the exclusion from membership in the interest coalition without which the cooperative endeavor simply cannot start. This situation is likely to create its own moral rules. These rules, however, will not be rules of obedience, even to the internalized call of duty, but a morale of "rational instrumentality" and mutual respect of existing interests in relation to the chosen cooperative goal. The old rule could be paraphrased to suit the new occasion: "Act so that your action is likely to contribute to the achievement of the purpose of the activity in which you are participating, without detriment to anyone's essential interests".

V

Finally, what is the significance of all this for social work education?

Whatever social work education will develop into in the decades to come it will certainly not continue to be what it is today. But this is not a special feature of this field. Education generally, assuming paramount importance as the process of self-programming human behaviour, cannot remain what it has been: a process of imparting knowledge and conditioning behaviour by one group of people upon another group. The fundamental premises of this relationship of subjects to objects of the teaching operation are no longer tenable. Just as it is obvious that education cannot be limited to any particular part of the life-cycle. Not only because of the obsolescence of knowledge, but mainly because of the different functions in society, the increasing depth of understanding, the changing emphases in inter-personal relations which a human being can internalize and learn systematically only at given junctures of his progress.

Taking these momentous changes into account for the longer run, the question still remains: what are the probable next steps? First, the various professions of welfare, when turning to the future, converge towards one general task: to improve the ability of the people to stand the strain of steeply increasing requirements for elasticity and adaptation. This cannot be taught as a skill, as some kind of dexterity in handling people based on a few obsolete simplifications about "human nature". Understanding of change and social development, a "feeling" for the problems which the various development situations bring with them, cannot be taught in the traditional sense at all. It can be acquired only in discussion and observation. The optimal contribution from the "learning environment" for speeding-up this process has yet to be discovered. In the most progressive forms of education in the field we are just beginning to find our way towards these new learning communities. But to know does not always mean to know really, especially if the implications of the new knowledge run counter to inveterate habit and prejudice. To assist the process of acceptance, to assist the welfare workers to really take possession of what is new in our emerging image of the world, this should be the second immediate objective of the educational process. Only then can we think of preparing people for the transmission of new patterns of behaviour, by lived example, not by preaching to society at large.

In short, welfare workers will have to go on with what they are doing today, but with better awareness of the character of the transition which we are approaching. They will have to prepare themselves for the task of being an outpost in the tremendous reorientation of social education towards autonomous self-education of all people throughout their lifetime. And last but not least, they will have to organize for social action towards the establishment of minimum welfare standards, towards the independent and interdependent functioning of welfare services throughout the world. The idea that a profession has to be "neutral" in fundamental questions regarding its activity is a rule of every power-system, where power to decide the really important interest questions should be concentrated in the hands of the power-holders, and all others, including those most interested in the issue, should keep their hands off the game.

Assigning this piece of mystification with many others to where they belong, the museum of outlived prejudices, we must ask ourselves who are in a better position and more called upon to act collectively, politically and responsibly for the goals of welfare than those who have made welfare their profession, that is, the dominant occupation of their lives.

4

A THEORETICAL MODEL OF THE ROLE OF PROFESSIONALS IN COMPLEX DEVELOPMENT SITUATIONS

Social development in any society can be understood as a complex process of interaction between what I will call "total societal productivity" and the prevailing system of relationships which determines the availability, as well as the modes of apperception, interpretation, and utilization, of information. By "productivity" I mean the total creativity of people making up a society, that part of its total potential which is actually put to use, in all fields, from economics to morals, from science to religion, from arts to political organization. All the fields are interacting, and which one is more "important" for the total effect has to be decided in each case. Though it is probable that under conditions of scarcity the sector of economic production and distribution of goods and services will assume paramount importance, that does not mean that the same will hold in a society of abundance.

TECHNIQUES AND INTERESTS

Structures defining the use of information in a society have two aspects. One is the technical possibility of utilizing information for the achievement of results. The other is the question of whose interests are served by these results. Techniques and interests are the two poles around which a society and its informational capabilities are structured. The possibility of understanding and applying information needed for the performance of tasks, and the way information is handled to choose between interest alternatives and standardize behaviour in interest conflicts, interact with each other and are often so intertwined that it is only possible to separate them through an abstract analysis.

The total productivity and the complexity of information-structures tend to increase in response to the pressure of relevant uncertainty impinging upon man from his natural and social environment.

Increase in one variable depends on an increase in the other. Potential creativity can be realized only through existing information-structures. (These are distinct from the information-code of heredity; "culture is not a biologically transmitted complex".[1]) The greater the complexity of these information-structures the greater their capability for absorbing and utilizing information. Each level of social productivity has, as it were, a corresponding level of structural complexity satisfying the requirement of "requisite variety". Also, the more complex structures demand a constant and more abundant inflow of energy, which implies a higher average of continuously realized productivity, because the more complex structures consume a greater amount of social energy in the internal processes of linkage and coordination. The term "energy" is used here in a figurative sense, only alliteratively similar to John T. Dorsey's "information-energy model". Dorsey speaks about energy in the literal sense of calories or megawatts and relates the energy-level a society is able to extract and utilize to the amount of technical information this energy-conversion requires.[2]

The change in information-structures, the increase in their complexity proceeds along several dimensions, corresponding to two main aspects: techniques and interests. Increases in the span of social division of labour correspond to the increasing complexity of structures for the productive use of technical information. The increasing dispersion of interests reflects a greater possibility of satisfying basic material needs with a concomitant wider span of interests and greater number of interest-circles in which each individual can participate. Individual interest-preferences become, on the average, less compelling; the tendency of people in a community to split into interest groups with clearly defined positions and borderlines tends to decrease.

Most importantly, the role which *power* plays in society changes as structures become increasingly complex, and so does rationality. The nature of rules regulating behaviour in a society, their categorical or hypothetical character, becomes different, as does the transparency of given social situations for those who participate in them. It is interesting to consider in this context the relationship

[1] Ruth Benedict, *Patterns of Culture* (New York: Penguin Books, 1934), p. 13.
[2] John T. Dorsey, Jr., "The Information-Energy Model", in Ferrel Heady and Sybil Stokes (eds.), *Papers in Comparative Public Administration* (Ann Arbor: University of Michigan Press, 1962), pp. 37-57.

between the prevailing span of social division of labour and the pressure towards uniformity, postulated by Durkheim. His notion of "pressure towards uniformity" can be interpreted as an expression of power relationships aiming at the restriction of the free flow of information, in its technical aspect as well as in its interest aspect.[1]

THREE STAGES OF SOCIAL DEVELOPMENT

Societies can be classified into three stages.

Stage 1:   Group Society

In the first phase, of relative helplessness, man is on the defensive. The very heavy pressure of uncertainty coming from the social as well as from the natural environment creates a sort of defensive solidarity within comparatively small groups with simple structure and without bridges between them. Absolute loyalty to the group corresponds to irreconcilable opposition among groups; a small span of division of labour, to a high concentration of interests upon a few objectives; great transparency within the group, to almost complete opacity in relation to the environment. Though the rules regulating behaviour are mostly categorical, there is relatively little emphasis on systematic and society-wide application of power. Existing structures are too simple for this task. External pressures supply the binding element holding the community together.

Stage 2:   Power Society

In the next phase, greater social productivity permits more complex structures which serve mainly to check uncertainty arising from the social environment. Comparatively small and isolated groups are integrated into larger structures through the systematic application of power at the level of the community. The institutions of power — from property to political sovereignty — make the social environment more amenable to control and so more predictable. But this gain is bought at the price of significantly greater tension within

[1]   Erik Allardt, "Emil Durkheim—Sein Beitrag zur politischen Soziologie", *Kölner Zeitschrift für Soziologie und Sozialpsychologie*, No. 1 (März, 1968), p. 3.

communities because power operates mainly as an instrument of domination in potential or actual conflicts of interests.

Power-holders and power-subjects tend to become the main opposed interest groups, power being at the same time the main binding agent and the chief divisive force. In this second phase, the span of division of labour is increasing slowly. There is comparatively little dispersion of interests. All possible interest-orientations of the individual are still subordinated to the satisfaction of basic existential needs. A minority able to satisfy these needs more amply than the mass has to concentrate on upholding the power structure guaranteeing their preferential position. Rationality is narrowly circumscribed to those areas where technological expertness had developed. Thus in social relations rationality is more widespread among the rulers than among the ruled. Transparency increases but is inhibited in social relations by the rulers who need to rely on secrecy and misrepresentation of social reality as an instrument of power.

Stage 3: Functional Society

In the third phase of his social development, man perfects instruments which permit him to control a significant proportion of the uncertainty stemming from natural causes, chief among them material scarcity. The common denominator of the technological and social revolutions implied in this change is the transformation of existing structures into structures of a considerably higher degree of complexity. The new patterns have to accommodate, on the one hand, the rising flood of technological information — in the widest sense of the term — and on the other to permit the socially meaningful expression of a widening span of interests by an increasing number of people.

This more intricate system of relationships exists only on the condition that the flow of productivity in a society has been stabilized on consistently higher levels. The production, handling, and use of information claim more and more of the available social energy. This is the reason why large-scale bureaucracy as a specialized information-handling structure is a relative late-comer in the development of a culture. And the same reflection lends weight to Max Weber's contention that "monocratic-bureaucratic administration" is a product of comparatively recent history.

The greater equality in chances of interest-satisfaction is possible only if these chances are realistic for a very large majority of the population, meaning more abundantly available means of gratification. The complexity of structures is expressed in a wider span of division of labour, as well as in greater dispersion of interests. Potential interest conflicts become more numerous but individually less compelling as motives for behaviour because their preference ordering is less general and less absolute and because more and more conflicts are intra-personal. There is less motivation for favouring the method of interest-domination over all other possible solutions of conflict situations. This has important consequences for the application of power-as-coercion on a society-wide basis. The reason for establishing a monopoly of the means of physical constraint as a social institution, that is, the domination of a given aggregate of interests in all conflicts over time, is losing its urgency.

A decrease in uncertainty permits a greater prevalence of rationality as the underlying mental attitude of the individual. Categorical rules as means of regulating behaviour are displaced by hypothetical prescriptions of the "if... then" type. Increasing transparency of social situations is paralleled by a "compartmentalized transparency" of the technological information flow.

At present, the world is in transition from stage two to stage three. The new structures permitting a wider flow of technical information and implying greater equality of chances in the expression and realization of interests are already in existence. But they are limited to narrow areas of high productivity or confined to a shallow upper layer where the structures are shared on a world-wide basis. But the unity of the world, even if it is at present only communicational, influences significantly the development process in each individual country. The transformation, the seeming overlapping of stages, are characteristic of the situation we professionals have to cope with.

PROFESSIONALS AS RELATED TO THE STAGE

People form the central element of the information-structures in any society, as well as the main source of its productivity.[1] Professionals are people in a special social role. In order to analyze

---

[1] See Bertram M. Gross, "Social Systems Accounting", in Raymond H. Bauer (ed.), *Social Indicators* (Cambridge: MIT Press, 1966).

their possible impact on development, one must understand how their role is related to a stage in the development of the productivity and information-structure of a society.

Some of the characteristics of the professional role seem to be fairly universally accepted. In most parts of the world, it is agreed that professionals are people who: (a) perform an activity on the basis of specialized training and, usually, higher education; (b) work full-time for (c) a remuneration which is their main source of income. Professionals subscribe to some sort of ethical code or value-scheme, but the content of these values may be different in different cultures. The same can be said about the trait of professional solidarity, which receives various interpretations and limits in different cultures.

There is, however, a list of characteristics considered essential for the role of the professional in some societies but not in others. The term "professional" is sometimes used restrictively for people performing their highly specialized activity under conditions of relative independence, who "work for themselves" and not in an organization or for an entrepreneur. Often the activity of the professional is understood as the application of knowledge, not its creation. Thus the teacher in an art school falls into the category of professional but the creative artist does not; the doctor in a hospital does, but not the scientist in fundamental biology. Or the relationship of the professional to the client for his professional services is stressed and interpreted as a relation of dependence and trust on the part of the client. Or, more generally, the orientation of the professional toward the performance of service is considered essential. (It is possible, however, to observe a service orientation in given activities even at pre-professional stages, as with the cameralist bureaucracy in Germany and Austria in the seventeenth and eighteenth centuries.)

Some of these characteristics are defined by the prevailing span of the social division of labour and the corresponding level of productivity. People cannot work full-time at an activity which is not immediately productive and live from it, without using coercion, before a certain general level of productivity is reached permitting the span of division of labour to extend to pursuits which contribute to survival only in an indirect way.

Specialized training and higher education require an even more advanced stage of development in which complex technological information is available and can be used for practical purposes.

Other aspects might be expressions either of a given level of general development or of a stage in the transformation of a special culture. The list of existing professions is lengthening, and they almost defy classification. Some are related most directly to material production, among them engineering, agricultural economics, architecture, forestry management. Others combine the production aim with an integrative function; among these are urban planning and the consulting systems specialty. Still others are mainly integrative: for example, the law, public administration, business administration, applied sociology. Another group combines integrative purposes with a mediative role, such as education, or social mediation with a restorative effect, for instance, social work. There is a group of professions, for example medicine or criminology, in which the accent is chiefly on restoration of impaired productive capacity and structural integration.

Like any other social institution, the role of the professional is a product of social development. It is a part of it and, to a certain extent, also the contributing cause of development. By following the tangled links between these two concepts we can attempt to better understand the whole phenomenon.

The Professional: Transitional

On the whole, the professional seems to be characteristic of the transition from stage 2 to stage 3 in the development of social productivity and the corresponding information-structures. Professionalism tends towards the expansion of the intellectual, informational element.

Even in the older professions such as the army and the crafts,[1] despite the great manual skill required, the tendency is toward greater expertise, meaning a more important informational content. In this sense the crafts were clearly a progressive, propulsive sector of social development, particularly at the beginning of the industrial era.

In his famous "Parable", Henri de Saint-Simon includes the craftsmen among the constructive, valuable, essential population of France:

[1] Both were certainly considered to be professions at certain times and in certain places: The mercenaries and their leaders, the condottieri, had all the characteristics of professionals in Italy and other parts of Europe in the Renaissance, and craftsmen in the German-speaking countries of Central Europe were, even at the beginning of the twentieth century, called "die Professionisten".

Let us assume that France should lose unexpectedly fifty of its foremost physicists, fifty of its first physiologists... fifty of its first joiners, fifty of its first woodworkers, that is about three thousand foremost scientists, artists and craftsmen of France.

As these are the Frenchmen who are productive in the most essential sense... really the bloom of French society, those without whom the nation cannot live, the nation would become a body without a soul; losing them it could not exist, it would perish[1].

Similarly, today the military in developing countries has also a progressive aspect. It has been pointed out particularly that:

(a) the armed forces include technical experts;
(b) they play an important role in the process of socialization;
(c) they increase stability;
(d) they represent, on the whole, a rational approach;
(e) they contribute to development by building roads and railways and undertaking other useful investment projects.[2]

The proliferation of professions in developed countries in our times is an expression of the "information explosion", the vast increase of the importance of information for productivity and the significant growth in the capability for information-handling. In this sense the professions increase their social influence by creating higher levels of productivity and more complex information-structures.

On the other hand, the technological profile of the professions themselves changes under the impact of further developments of the social division of labour. As the span of division grows, there is less possibility for any socially meaningful activity to be performed by an individual working in technological isolation. The group, the team, the collective setting replaces the individual as the smallest technically meaningful unit of work. Without reducing expertness, these developments are transforming the doctor, the architect, the social worker into a member of a team; there are other professionals, for instance the administrator, the planner, the systems specialist, — who could never conceive of their work otherwise.

The social context in which the professions first emerged was one of power institutions. Normally, the older professions — adminis-

---

[1] Henri de Saint-Simon, *L'Organisateur*, Vol. IV, p. 17; quoted by Georges Gurvitch in "Les fondateurs français de la sociologie contemporaine: Saint-Simon et P. J. Proudhon", *Les Cours de Sorbonne* (Paris, 1955), p. 32.
[2] See H. Daalder, *The Role of the Military in the Emerging Countries* (The Hague: Mouton & Co., 1962), pp. 18-20.

tration, the law, the church, education, the army — were born as instruments of an existing social power centre. At first the professional's orientation is toward the support of the established order, a subservience to power which goes beyond personal attitudes into the realm of ideology, communication, and organization. Professionals depend on the power elites and, sometimes, are members of these elites. But even in this early phase, the professionals bring a certain rationality to the exercise of power, a reasonableness and systematic approach which in itself *limits the essentially arbitrary nature of power.*

And from the beginning there is another side to this picture. There are the would-be professionals, the intellectuals who for one reason or another are not employed in the professional roles to which, by their education, they aspire. These are persons with intellectual training but without professional commitment, with the capacity to understand the reality of social relationships but without the economic position and security the social system provides those who are professionals. This intelligentsia belongs, more often than not, to the disaffected part of a power-society, highly critical of the established order, producing the prophets of new ideologies and providing the kernel of movements for social change. Educated elites are in fact sometimes thought to induce social change by their very existence. "There seems to be general agreement that groups which have wider orientation in terms of education or travel are often focal points in efforts at induced change."[1]

Professionals as Propulsion for Change

As development goes on, however, the professions themselves evolve a critical attitude toward things-as-they-are. Social welfare workers, applied sociologists, planners, public health specialists are naturally led to look for the underlying causes of the problems they have to cope with. If they find them, as often they do, in the existing power system, changing this system — however gently and gradually — will tend to become part of their broader professional goals, and the corresponding behaviour will receive a positive evaluation in the professional code.

---

[1] United Nations, *1965 Report on the World Social Situation* (New York: United Nations, 1966), p. 6.

This professional goal of social action towards change tends to overshadow the original stress on professional expertise. But this shift is not easy, and it leads to the question: Is it permissible for a profession to overstep the limits of its technical knowledge and yet remain a profession? The problem appears in highly developed countries as well. "Social work in America faces the alternative of confining itself to well-defined areas where its technical knowledge and skill are well established and respected, or of varying its single standard of preparation and extending its efforts to new problem areas where it has special concern and commitment, but where it cannot at this moment assert superior knowledge and skill."[1]

Professions by their very existence tend to work, in a certain sense, for equality. They confront the established ascriptive criteria of social status with new and prestigious achievement standards and so loosen the old patterns of inequality. Also, the majority of professions tend to incorporate the ideal of equality into the codes governing their relations with the users of their services. This attitude is reinforced by the increasingly collective character of professional performance, its dependence on work-groups, laboratories, and other auxiliary units. It is enhanced by more impersonal methods of financing the professional services. It is sanctioned by spreading democratic ideologies.[2]

In the course of the emergency of industrial society, the work performed by the professions has the very important characteristic, and indeed the privilege, of not being amenable to the prevailing industrial method of dividing the work-process itself into progressively smaller and simpler particles. The work of the professional remains whole, even when the profession itself subdivides into new and more narrowly circumscribed special fields. The cardiologist is not related in the same way to the general practitioner as the mechanic on the conveyor-belt is to his general supervisor. In an era of technological alienation the professions gain the added attractiveness of un-alienated, "complete" work. In this they are the precursors of a work-situation of the individual which tends to become more general as automation and new control techniques

---

[1] David G. French, *Objectives of the Profession of Social Work* (Bangkok: United Nations Economic Commission for Asia and the Far East, 1967), p. 17.
[2] Higher education has been bound to be correlated with more egalitarian attitudes (lowest education has also, but not the middle level). Cf. Charles C. Moskos, Jr., and Wendell Bell, "Some Implications of Equality for Political, Economic and Social Development", *International Review of Community Development*, 13-14 (1965), p. 230.

tend to shift repetitive routine operations from man to machine. Even in an organizational and collective setting the professional retains the personal independence which flows from the necessary inner completeness of his professional work. Professionals tend to be less affected by the stereotype of the "Organization Man" even in a time when the power of organizations is at its maximum. As "cosmopolitans",[1] professionals always retain a part of their personal independence and, in a way, prepare the way for a greater independence for all.

Technically, the professions are a source of progress in productivity. They do require higher levels of general productivity in a society, but they also tend to produce such levels by performing in the more complex productive processes, by creating the necessary orderliness in the general environment and building the system of the productive undertakings themselves, and above all by being the carriers of the growing pool of information on which the modern expansion of productivity is built.

But politically, the professions are the most promising new institution for the integration of a society not based on coercive power. Their influence is derived from knowledge and tends toward functional specialization, not toward overall domination. Their political claim is for participation, not technocracy; in terms of David Apter's classification of claims for participation into "popular", "functional", and "interest" claims, the claim of the professionals belongs definitely to the "functional" category.[2] The professions can be integrated only in a collaborative setting, and their total social influence depends on the recognition of equality among information-sources. By becoming conscious of this situation, the professions as a whole can develop movements for social action. David French has noted, for example, that "social workers... have to accept the fact that at this point in history social work is closer to the 'social movement' end of the continuum than to the 'professional' end, and act accordingly. American social work was a social movement long before it was a profession."[3]

---

[1] Alvin W. Gouldner, "Cosmopolitans and Locals: Toward an Analysis of Latent Social Roles", *Administrative Science Quarterly*, No. 2 (1957-58), pp. 281—480.
[2] David E. Apter, "Political Systems and Development Change", Proceedings of the International Political Science Association 7th World Congress (Brussels, 1967), p. 6.
[3] David G. French, *op. cit.*, p. 18.

PROSPECTS

What is the perspective for the future? The burst of technological productivity in the developed parts of the world is so powerful that it represents a potential source of change for the whole world. As these changes begin to interact more intensively with each other, the stages I have abstracted from history will probably be less applicable than they are to the past. Parts of the world which are still at stage 1, "group society", or in transition from stage 1 to stage 2, "power society", will necessarily be affected by other parts which are already on the threshold of stage 3, "functional society".

It is possible to imagine that the stages will be accelerated and even be telescoped into one in each society. Thus, in any case, at some point in the future the world as a whole will certainly present a single picture of development. It is in this sense only that one can speak of the world as one.

The decisive front-line on this strategic map of development is the advance from power society to functional society. This seems to be our most realistic chance to avoid a cataclysmic clash between the existing power systems. But this advance depends today on the total situation in the world. The weight of all the world's societies still in transition toward integration into power systems is holding back progress in the most forward sections. These countries, with their necessarily positive attitude toward coercive power — which to them must appear as the specific condition for leaving their own dismal past behind — are natural allies of the conservative forces in the developed power systems which are opposing and counteracting their transformation into functional information-structures corresponding to the levels of productivity already reached in these societies.

It seems, therefore, crucial to establish a world-wide network of institutions and social processes which could make more effective the oneness of the world and which would be, in its operations, as independent as possible of the existing political power systems. To try to by-pass governments seems, at least today, to offer better possibilities than to strive for a world government. Some first steps have been made already. One of the most urgent tasks in this context would be to integrate the less developed countries into the world's development without necessarily strengthening and solidifying their internal political power systems.

Within this broad perspective the potential role of the professions is important.

The professions, though very significant as a part of a community's total social productivity, are unlikely to emerge by spontaneous process during the early stages of development. If the professions are a useful contributing factor in raising productivity and influencing structural development in the direction of functional instead of power relationships, then a principal professional contribution to countries below a certain level of productivity will have to come from the outside.

The present levels of effort along these lines are plainly inadequate, not only because far too little is done in quantitative terms, but more fundamentally because the role of adviser entails responsibilities and raises expectations which the average professional cannot satisfy.

To "advise" implies knowing better, and this, in the majority of instances, is simply not the case. The advantage in professional knowledge and technical skill which the adviser has, possibly, over the people he works with is more than balanced by the disadvantage of not knowing or misunderstanding a practically unlimited number of specific and topical factors essential for the accomplishment of the task. This relationship is, probably, particularly unfavourable for professions in which the existing technical knowledge and skill is not much more than a theoretical generalization from everyday experience in a given cultural setting, as in social work or public administration. The stories of "experts" stumbling over blocks which are obvious to every child in the country are assuming the proportions of a literature. The social problems of advisers — becoming discouraged, apathetic, opinionated, or aggressive, or retiring into a personal limbo as a result of lack of recognition or success — tend to get as serious as the problems they are sent to help solve.

Advisers are frequently put into a position where they must go beyond their field of expertise. The narrower span of division of labour in the developing country draws the adviser, willy-nilly, into contiguous fields; the expectations of the host induces him to make proposals for broad policies and plans which transcend not only what he knows but also what can be properly called technical advice. These broad plans are, as often as not, rather naive and utopian speculations of the adviser which he himself would see differently in his own country. Measures which, at home, he would perceive clearly as matters of political struggle and conflict of interests are presented to his hosts as technical problems, with technical solutions which he draws from his superior expertness and which can be implemented simply on the condition that this knowledge be acknowledged and acquired. So advisers blithely advise centralization or decentralization, the introduction of a merit system, of social insurance schemes, of land reforms, of equality for women and other far-reaching transformations of the institutional and social system of a country as if the transformation were only a matter of know-how. This is certainly not to say that advisers are superficial and irresponsible people. On the contrary, the more thorough and responsible they are, the harder they will try to fulfill the obligations of a role which is beyond the scope of the professional as specialist.

The people of the country with whom the advisers are working have from the beginning a highly ambivalent attitude toward them. On the one hand, the adviser is for them a person embodying all they know or assume about the superior achievements of the country he comes from. They are prepared to vastly exaggerate his knowledge and importance and expect from him more than any average good professional can give. Moreover, they are equally prepared to resent being put in the position of people receiving advice or assistance. They will watch for the first mistakes the adviser cannot help making, or for the first signs of his disorientation, and sometimes they will be unable to suppress their glee. This means that the more ambitious programmes of advising will almost certainly foster movements toward all kinds of isolationism; they will strengthen tendencies to "go our own way" even in matters where it would be manifestly more profitable not to do so. This has been observed even in settings where strong ideological bonds of solidarity bound together the advisers and the people they were advising. The collaboration of professionals across national boundaries is easier where the difference between the professional's home country and his host country is less pronounced. But with the decrease of the difference, resentment at accepting "advice" will tend to increase.

This does not mean that advice is not needed and should not be given. But advice should grow out of a massive long-term programme of professionals working in other countries at tasks within their special field of competence. The fundamental approach should be not to advise, but to do. And instead of the present trickle, there should be a steady stream directed to the strategic points of development. Out of these larger numbers the successful advisers would be selected by a largely automatic process. These would be people who happen to have the necessary capabilities for understanding and empathy, who for one reason or another fit better in the new milieu, who are more easily accepted, and who have in the course of their activities in the other country developed ideas which can be useful and seem convincing to the people of the host country. To give any kind of useful advice the professional has first to learn much himself about the host country. And he can only learn by working and living there for a time, not as an adviser from the beginning, but as a professional expected to do a professional job. He will teach more by being successful at his profession than by any number of reports, suggestions, or conclusions.

In this operational role the largely neutral attitude of the outside professional toward those conflicts of interests and emotional tensions that move the nationals of the country would be an asset, instead of the liability it is in the role of adviser. He would demonstrate by his own behaviour the possibility of professional objectivity, which is one of the important conditions of success in most professions.

Also, in action it would be easier for the professional to adjust to the more restricted span of specialization than it is in giving general advice. A case worker or a specialist in community organization will adjust with less difficulty to the practical task of including the administration of a children's home in his weekly round of work than he will to abstract talk and writing about institutional care. The organization-and-methods specialist will be able to perform without further preparation simple personnel work or elementary financial administration. My main argument is that one must think in new ways. The concept of advisers does not work well. New institutional mechanisms must be created to allow professionals from one society to be integrated into the working structure of the institutions where they are expected to function; to set them apart and provide them with a "counterpart" reduces by 50 per cent their chances of achieving anything. Their integration can, of course, never be complete. And it should not be. Just by being outsiders they can perform the stimulating and innovating role of "marginal men", in the sense introduced by Stonequist. But they should not be artificially isolated. Of course, world-wide programmes of professional inter-country mobility will also have to overcome the well-known practical problems, such as language difficulties and differences of basic habits and standards of living. But these problems are not new. And they were and are tackled successfully by a number of agencies and organizations when it was, or is, in their economic or political interest to do so. There is no doubt that it can be done on a more massive scale when it is in the fundamental interest of the world.

These programmes would have to be planned in such a way that they could be reduced parallel with the growth of professional capabilities in the developing countries. This raises the important problem known under the journalistic nickname of "brain-drain". A great share of the effort at training professionals in developing countries is lost for their country of origin by their emigration to countries with a higher standard of living, where better opportunities exist to apply their professional expertise with all the auxiliary and supporting services they were taught to consider indispensable. A report by the UN states also that "lack of professional freedom, a feeling that there is insufficient esteem for the work performed, and the paucity of contacts with persons in similar specialties may be contributory factors."[1]

It is essential to understand that for a considerable time to come this process is unavoidable and should be accepted. But one of the reasons a massive movement of professionals to developing countries is necessary is precisely to offset the "brain-drain" and organize the migration of professionals as a two-way street. The attraction of working in a location which is novel and exotic, without ultimate loss of the standard of living available in the home country, would be as great for professionals from developed countries as is, today, the hope of newly trained professionals from developing countries of bettering their lot by going to the richer parts of the world.

Equally important as supplying professionals for developing countries is the need to improve the informational micro-structure of the professions in all countries. Today, in the most developed countries (economically speaking) the influence of the professions in creating functional institutions and relationships can make itself felt. But it is in these countries also that the professions still carry with them past traditions of serving power systems and still have an orientation toward material gain as a primary goal. Changing these sometimes deeply ingrained attitudes is a precondition if the professions are to grow into their ultimate social role and become important structural elements of the functional society of tomorrow.

[1] United Nations, *1965 Report on the World Social Situation, op. cit.*, p. 62.

5

POWER, PLANNING, DEVELOPMENT

If plurality of meaning could be quantified, it would be a challenge to anyone to find three words exceeding those of the title in compounded ambiguity.[1] And yet, how much of our world and its most pressing problems is contained in these three words.

Power, or organized violence, surging from the past as the harsh dominant in the symphony of history, the *ultima ratio* of human relationships, looming over our present-day world as its most real and apocalyptic danger. Planning, on the other hand, as the reasonable alternative, the rational quest for a social optimum; reducing, by conscious action, the entropy originally inherent in human affairs; substituting, in the last analysis, the management of things for the government of man. Finally, development, reminding us that only change is permanent, change which we can hope to influence but can never stop; reminding us, also, that nearly all history is present today, that all situations are possible, all problems pertinent, all solutions conceivable somewhere in the world, but not everywhere.

Ideal projections apart, however, planning and power co-exist

[1] At one end of the scale, "power" can refer to the purely passive possibility of being influenced, as in Locke's definition of the power of wax to be melted by heat. At the other extreme are the specific meanings of power which restrict the use of the term to the field of human relationships, particularly in its application to politics as in Max Weber's understanding of power as the possibility to assert one's will against opposition.
Two extremes of planning are found in Ponsioen's general definition given in "Planification et politique sociale" (Planning and Social Politics), *Revue internationale des sciences administratives* (No. 1/1959): "Planning is the systematic ordering of the near future", and the very specific meaning given by Bičanić in "O monocentričnom i policentričnom planiranju" (On Monocentric and Polycentric Planning), *Ekonomski pregled* (Vol. XIV, Nos. 6-7): "Planning is the institutionalized and rationalized, *ex ante* quantified and periodized economic development achieved by the conscious effort of people in a given territory, through previously established instruments, for the purpose of economic gain."
Finally, there is no need to emphasise the ambiguity of "development". The very essence of its value content is controversial. Is development necessarily change for the better?

and in a sense have always co-existed. Political power, as the possibility of imposing one's will continuously over a territory on the basis of a monopoly over coercive instruments, cannot be established without some modicum of planning. On the other hand, an entire school of contemporary economic and general societal planning is based on the notion of the plan as directive, as legal command, implying political power as the basis of its validity and the condition for its implementation. According to this view, the foundation of power is the specific characteristic which distinguishes "real" planning from the probabilistic prognoses of indicative economic forecasts, binding no-one and committing only the professional reputations of the authors.

The relationship of power, especially political power, to planning, particularly society-wide planning, and the probable trends which this relationship will follow as social development progresses, would seem to offer an interesting subject of study.

In the amazing multitude and complexity of facts related to this problem, the starting point should presumably be some kind of hypothesis about development. The hypothesis to be put forward here is naturally related to my experience of development in Southeast Europe and developing countries elsewhere. But this is of secondary importance. Any experience which is filtered into a theory must be highly selective and subjective. And almost any theory will do as a starting point, its main objective being to be disproved and replaced by a better theory.[1]

I

Development as a complete, undivided process, can be interpreted for analytic purposes as the dynamic interaction between the structure of a society and the level of productivity it has attained. "Productivity" here is the total potential of the members of a society to satisfy possible interests in all fields from economics to religion, and from aesthetic expression to moral significance. "Structure" denotes the sum total of relatively stable relationships established among people in the course of their social existence.

---

[1] Let us acknowledge our debt to Karl R. Popper who influenced so much of contemporary social science when he said that "a hypothesis can only be empirically tested—and only after it has been advanced". *The Logic of Scientific Discovery* (New York, 1965), p. 30.

The mutual influence of productivity and structure shows a regularity reminiscent of the second law of thermodynamics. Rising productivity supplies the energy necessary for the gradual reduction of the relevant uncertainty impinging upon man from his natural and social environment. The effect is achieved through a more and more complex social structure which permits the perception, storage, transmittance and use of increasing amounts of pertinent information. The drama of development is provided by the unevenly rising line of productivity. The moment when, for one reason or another, actual productivity is insufficient to sustain the level of complexity reached by existing social structures, the inherent entropic influences will cause their disintegration and replacement by simpler relationships. On the other hand, a spurt in the rise of productivity will bring about other tensions. The existing social structures will be unable to accommodate rising productivity and its need for information, and may not be sufficiently elastic to adapt promptly to the new situation. Antiquated structures are sometimes broken and destroyed in violent conflict.

Social structures which channel information and selectively define the possibility of access to information and the checkpoints that permit control of areas of uncertainty, can also be considered from two aspects. On the one hand, relationships which determine the allocation of resources and products for the satisfaction of interests; on the other hand, links that bind people at work, technically organizing the necessary cooperation, but neutral as to the interests involved.

For clarity of exposition, the continuous and uninterrupted process of development can be divided into three stages.

1. The stage of the "group society", in which relatively small and isolated human groups live on a low level of productivity, permitting only the simplest social structures. Cooperation is organized on the basis of face-to-face contact and an *ad hoc* division of tasks. An almost complete solidarity of interests within the group is balanced by the almost absolute opposition of interests between groups. Divergencies of interest within the group are either controlled by an intensive process of socialization under the pressure of uncertainty from the environment, or adjusted by means of compromise. Only in exceptional cases do they lead to reorientation, signifying the splitting-up of the group. Interest conflicts between groups are not adjustable. They lead to a quasi-permanent state of war, or per-

haps to reorientation in that the groups avoid each other.

In a developing situation, group society structures are no longer adequate either as modes of cooperation or as means for the allocation of interest satisfaction. The face-to-face group is incapable of dealing with the conflict between the necessity for a more efficient assignment of tasks — a condition for any larger undertaking — and that for greater elasticity caused by the increasing speed of social change. Isolated groups cannot survive the greater mobility and frequency of contacts. With rising productivity and more abundant products, the risks implied in these encounters tend to become psychologically and socially unbearable to them. More complex structures have become the order of the day, both from the technical and the interest point of view.

2.   The stage is now set for the emergence of the "power society". Power — possession of authority over others — has become the central institution in a society in which conflicts of interest are principally solved by the domination of certain categories of interests over others.

The primary form of power is political. It is power over people in relation to a territory, based on a concentration of physical force which is clearly superior to any competing force and therefore monopolizes coercion over all inhabitants of the territory. Political power is power in its social dimension. In its individual dimension, the most important form is economic power. The surplus of goods over the requirements of immediate consumption brought about by greater productivity, leads to ownership, i.e. the concentration of goods and productive instruments in the hands of the owners. All others are thus excluded from participation in the use, distribution and consumption of sources of interest satisfaction.

At first, the development of power structures follows one of two dimensions: a territorially extensive but shallow pattern in which subjects are dominated intermittently, most of their daily lives remaining outside the influence of the power centres; or an intensive but territorially restricted form in which the influence of power on the interests of its subjects is more pervasive but its action radius shorter. The older empires and the class of governments which Wittfogel calls "oriental despotism" fall in the first category; city states during millenia of Mediterranean history or feudal units of ownership and government are examples of the second.

As the main principle of cooperation, in its technical sense of the way in which people work, the face-to-face type prevalent in group society is replaced by hierarchical organization. Hierarchy is power translated into a cooperative arrangement. It combines a maximum of definitiveness in the assignment of tasks with a relative maximum of elasticity, thus solving the apparently contradictory requirements which had overtaxed the pliability of the face-to-face group.

Examples of historical discontinuity in the transition from group to power societies include, on the one hand, the revolutions associated with Clisthenes, Solon and Servius Tullius in the City States of Athens and Rome, and on the other, the almost complete disappearance of many political organizations established during the Great Migration from Asia to Europe from the fifth to the tenth centuries, and as late as the disintegration of the Mongol Empire established under Genghis Khan and Tamerlane. In the first category, a sudden leap in productivity breaks the old tribal social structures and replaces them, violently, with a territorial society in which scions of ancient tribes and resident "aliens" are subjected to the same power centre under a new system of classification that substitutes the yardstick of wealth for the old criterion of birth. In the second set of examples, the power structures which had been established in an extraordinary spurt of energy could not be maintained by the societies concerned at their normal level of productivity: they fell apart, reverted to their previous form of society, or merged with the conquered population without leaving significant cultural traces.

The fact that most of recorded history coincides with the stage of power society is decisive for the current view that power is a permanent fixture within the social fabric.

The last century has seen the approach of a crisis in power society, comparable in depth and intensity to the dilemmas which preceded the supplanting of group society.

To all appearances, hierarchical organization has reached the point of diminishing returns. Based though it is on intensive supervision and control, it seems unable to solve the conflict between operation and supervisory coordination within the same period. As organizations grow in size and complexity, more of the working time of their members is taken up in coordinating activities, writing and reading instructions and reports and general communications, leaving less time for the basic service or productive activity they are meant to perform. At the same time, the main line of the social division of labour is shifting back to the method of dividing and subdividing fields of interest instead of splintering the entire individual work process into an ever larger number of simpler and more senseless, uniformly repeated, miniature operations. Whenever such splintering is at all possible, automation indicates the machine as being the cheaper and more rational method of performing the resulting "work crumbs", as Friedmann calls them. Specialization by dividing fields of interest, on the other hand, does not imply simpler and less skilled work for the specialists. It leads gradually to an equalization of skills within the organization, stripping hierarchy of its chief justification that it corresponds to the actual differences in skill and difficulty of tasks among hierarchical levels. This trend towards equalization contradicts hierarchy in two ways: it is more time-consuming to exercise intensive supervision over people of greater knowledge and skill, thus aggravating the dilemma between operation and coordination; and people who fail to see any significant differences between their own skill and that of their superiors, begin to resent the differences in authority and rewards.

On the interest side of the social structure, rising productivity permits better satisfaction of basic interests for an ever increasing number of people. The result is a process of interest dispersion. Each individual develops more new interests and many conflicts of interest become intra-individual. Basic needs being more or less satisfied, the individual's numerous new interests compete for his attention, each by itself having less motivating power than the few necessities in simpler and poorer societies. The divergencies of interests between individuals become possibly more frequent but each interest by itself is motivationally less decisive than before. The influence by which interests, with an iron logic of their own, used to align man into one or other of a few large and distinct camps, becomes less compelling. Structures tend to become more diffuse and less stratified. Domination, as the main method of solving conflicts by the systematic use of power, seems less necessary and also less acceptable. Power, on the other hand, grows more powerful as advancing technology supplies it with an increasingly abundant inflow of energy; it is also more dangerous, deflecting the stream of progress towards purposes of destruction.

3. In trying to conceive the features of the third stage, the "functional society" of a possible future, we have no choice but to start with the extrapolation of existing trends. Hierarchy starts to be

replaced by more complex structures in which a more ramified interdependence produces wideflung networks following the logic of the main functions of each of the confederated units. The links between the units — relatively small teams and work groups — are horizontal and specialized instead of the enforced vertical subordination of the monolithic hierarchical pyramids. Even today, the university, the hospital, the research institute and other more advanced forms, begin to show some characteristics of these more complex patterns of cooperation in functional society.

With respect to interest relationships, a twofold process is under way. On the one hand, the structures of political power become interspersed with expanding service networks. The state, in its development from a police to a service state, assumes a growing number of activities which by themselves are independent of power. In relation to the service activities performed under sponsorship of the state, the primary aim of the individual is no longer to be protected by isolating his private sphere from encroachment by government agencies, but rather not to be excluded from his rightful participation in the benefits and services dispensed. From being subject to the state, the individual becomes a user and consumer of its services, eventually a participant in its decisions, i.e. a citizen.

But this is the individual's perspective in times of peace. At the other pole, power is swelled by the growing level of resources in developed societies. It is allied with the most progressive science and technology which depend on governmental financing, primarily military. However, this growth is much less visible than the expansion of the service state. It is shrouded in military secrecy. There is less discussion about military budgets in popular and representative assemblies than about other items of the public household; there is less readiness to discuss power, its holders and its mechanisms than other and less important public issues.

Under conditions of interest dispersion, which obviates the need for domination, power as a social institution is becoming obsolete. But power institutions are actually becoming both more influential and potentially more destructive. This is obviously the catch in the transition from power society to functional society. It gives us cause to pause and direct a more attentive look at the institution of political power.

II

Power has been with us since the dawn of history and is very much with us today, making it difficult to examine it from a distance. In this respect, our hypothesis about development gives us a starting point in emphasising the change in the social role of power, its historical ambivalence.

In its beginnings, power serves the all-important purpose of cheaply and simply reducing the almost unbearable uncertainty stemming from man's social environment. It is difficult to see how the basic integration of small groups into larger societies, indispensable for progress of any kind, could otherwise have been achieved. Given the prevailing level of productivity, it was almost impossible to solve the interest conflicts developing within larger social aggregates in any other way.

During the evolution of its historical role, power has exhibited considerable versatility in the refinement and diversification of its methods. It started in the crude form of applied or threatened violence, of direct enforcement. Then the many situations of deliberately created dependence, economic or psychological: the conditioning process which continued for generations, reinforced by organized religion, ideology, charisma, moral rule, simple drill; diluted by many varieties of association of the power subjects with the interests of the power holders; the many attempts to camouflage power, to make it socially less transparent, less personal, its exercise less blatant.

From its beginnings, however, power as a social institution has its social costs. By enabling some interests to dominate and repress others, it creates frustration and emotional tension which cause the general atmosphere of society to deteriorate noticeably. The nostalgia for the "good old days", the golden age of the past, paradise lost, so prevalent in the literature and general culture of all historic societies, clearly shows the feeling that power society, at least in its human relationships, is a step backwards as compared to the lost human climate of group society with its primitive democracy, egalitarianism and solidarity.

Power structures show a rigidity, a staying-power, a perseverance in defence of vested interests, beyond anything known in group society. Power began very early to exercise a negative influence on development, retarding necessary changes and discouraging new social ventures whenever these seemed a possible hazard for existing power interests, foreshadowing the situation with which we are faced today when power stands in the way not only of progress but, ultimately, of survival.

As long as there is more than one power centre, the inbuilt competitiveness does not concede defeat or recognize final victory. Other interest conflicts can conceivably be adjusted by compromise, de-fused by reorienting their carriers to different interest goals, removed from the focus of attention by other events or simply by geographical distance or the passage of time; finally and most notably, interest aspirations can be satisfied, thus bringing the conflict to an end. But the existence of more than one power desiring, by definition, security and therefore absolute superiority and monopoly, is a logical impossibility; by the same token, permanent conflict between them is a logical necessity.

As time goes on, the social costs of power increase, whatever the refinement of method. The growth of power structures in size and effectiveness of influence enhances all the negative characteristics of power. Its might presses more heavily on the individual, there is increasingly less possibility to escape, to preserve a free area, literally or figuratively, beyond the reach of its tentacles. The conservative attitude of power becomes more pronounced and its effects more reprehensible as the rate of social change steadily increases and adjustment of structures becomes more and more necessary. The competitiveness of power assumes pathological proportions in the largest structures of political power, the states, with their security syndromes, which eventually come to imagine that the existence or even potential existence of competing power centres might endanger their security.

Two new factors in the situation increase the tensions created by power, even at its most useful, to the point of serious reappraisal of the whole institution. With rising productivity, greater capacity to satisfy the basic interests of an increasing number of people, and the resulting dispersion of interests, power begins to lose its main historic justification of being the only method by which permanent open clashes about interest conflicts can be avoided through instituting a system in which some interests are continuously and as a matter of course dominated by others. When interests can be satisfied they no longer have to be dominated. And this is what current developments in productivity in the most advanced countries make possible, or at least foreshadow. The obstacles standing in the way of a society of abundance are now manmade rather than natural.

While the original social utility of power thus dwindles and its initial functions tend to disappear with the emergence of functional society, its costs in one particular context are becoming prohibitive. The existing structures of political power, the states, have used technological inventiveness and scientific advances to perfect their instruments of coercion, and have thus accumulated a destructive potential which cannot safely be entrusted to anyone. It can least of all be entrusted to people in whom the exercise of power induces necessarily pathological deformations of personality, reducing the effectiveness of normal human inhibitions resulting from the process of socialization; neither can it be put at the disposal of structures whose very existence generates unlimited competitiveness and aggressiveness, whatever the human qualities of their members.

And this is where we stand at present with the problem of power. Our task sometimes looks depressingly like the situation of the mice confronted with the question of who should tie the bell to the cat. But the task is there, and we can no more avoid it than we can shed our skins. If it is true, as Marx said, that humanity tends to assume only the charges it can carry, it is equally true that it sometimes has to confront questions which cannot be left unanswered.

III

In this context, planning is essentially a thing of the future. It is the activity by which the complex functional networks and manifold diverging interests in society are optimally integrated into an ongoing process, meaningful both in terms of the increasing technical interdependence and of the prevailing interest positions of the participants. The devising of changing criteria of optimality is a constituent part of the planning process itself.

Planning is for a functional society what power was for a power society, i.e. its main method of integration. The techniques and methods, the whole institutionalized structure of planning are yet at their very beginnings.[1]

---

[1] The extraordinary prudence and dogmatic hesitation with which the development of planning methods is sometimes treated, reminds us of the cramped behaviour of the novice driver clutching the steering wheel. But there is a difference. Even the poorest of drivers sits in a machine which has some material solidity and an in-built

Indeed, there are few features of this future activity of planning, understood as integration of functional society, of which we can be sure today.

The classical distinction between political decision and administrative implementation is obliterated in planning. If politics beyond power is concerned with interests, divergent interest positions and interest conflicts, then planning is clearly politics. On the other hand if, in the techniques of cooperation, the rigid articulation of hierarchy is to be replaced by a more supple arrangement, planning will have to play an important role in the processes of functional integration. In this way, planning is an activity which combines techniques with interests, assuming the heritage of two lines of development: from the face-to-face groups by way of hierarchical organization in the methods of cooperation, and from small group solidarity by way of interest domination in the modes of behaviour in interest conflicts. Generally speaking, planning operates by removing interest conflicts from the cycle of direct action. These conflicts have to be considered and a position taken on them, long before the interests involved are actually contacted in action. This reduces the emotional impact of conflict, increases the weight of rational argument and permits easier adjustment, but nevertheless a decision about interests must still be made.

Technically, planning can also dispense with the notion of a centre. As Bičanić points out (*op. cit.*), planning is essentially polycentric, the various functional lines of action being interdependent, related to each other, but without any clear criterion by which to assess their intrinsic importance or status, their position of mutual superiority or inferiority in any acceptable technical sense. From the point of view of interests, these functional lines represent coalitions in the sense of horizontal interest-associations in which the overall positions of the members are the same, and the concrete position of each in every moment in time depends on the significance

---

functional logic of its own. But in relation to the new social structures needed for the society of tomorrow, only questions have so far been asked. The "machine" has to be built as we go, and this is an immensely intricate task, It requires an attitude quite contrary to a timorous and conservative dogmatism, a readiness for the boldest experiment and a complete lack of reverence for tradition of any kind.

Here again, the less we can foresee, the more we must adhere to the rules and, paradoxically, the less we are free to adapt to the unforeseen. Lack of effective control causes hesitant behaviour in situations where the opposite approach is most needed. (Cf. Eugen Pusić, "Social Planning—Interests and Techniques"; Social Planning Conference, University of Puerto Rico 1966, p. 30).

of his specific contribution to the total function.

Teams and work groups form such coalitions on the micro-level. Representatives of coordinating networks may be members of the coalition but can never form the only relevant factor. On the macro level of society, similar coalitions form the institutional framework of planning, for instance:

— information-producing systems, e.g. planning institutes, statistical agencies, meteorological services, research institutions;

— rule-producing systems, corresponding to popular and representative assemblies, agencies for establishing technical standards of quality, etc.;

— rule-enforcing systems which operate chiefly by withholding benefits and services and by differential allocation of advantages;

— interest-adjusting systems, e.g. self-governing boards and councils, courts, arbitrating commissions;

— operating systems, with representatives of rule-enforcement and interest-adjusting organizations as coalition members.

The maximum available information about the state of the society, the matrices of the manifold interconnections, must be given to each system in order that it may initiate activity within the framework of the plan, but sole control is not placed in the hands of any particular system. The changing fabric of the plan is the product of the coalition process.

The objective must be to make coalitions at all levels participate as effectively as possible. Functional planning is based on participation, both for the technical reason that essential skills are widely dispersed, and in order that the many divergent interests involved may be safeguarded. This presupposes the general accessibility of information and the general ability to understand the issues involved. It also requires that the rule-producing and interest-adjusting bodies, whose role is particularly important in the planning process, be numerous enough to offer sufficient individuals the chance to participate. However, in order not to overtax everyone's time budget, thus undoing the advantages of a developed division of labour, participation must be selective as to cases and systems represented.

IV

Only the most advanced parts of the present-day world have reached the threshold of functional society. Their planning is no more than an activity of transition, which coexists with institutions of power in various characteristic relationships.

Planning means acting on the basis of understanding complex interconnections. In the transitional stage, while understanding is still meagre, the accent is on acting. What is called planning is purposeful action based on voluntaristic assumptions which later become more defined. This is possible to some extent on two conditions. Firstly, that the relevant relationships in society are still sufficiently simple to allow for rather primitive methods of goal-setting and comparison of aims and resources, and for the repercussions of forcible intervention not to be disastrous. Secondly, that there is sufficient centralized power to back up the largely arbitrary assumptions of the plan directives and to react correctively to the negative feedback from the environment. Power is essential because the arbitrariness of the planning assumptions is related mainly to the prevailing interest situation. A harmony of interests is assumed; all differences or conflicts of interests are swayed by the exercise of power to the benefit of those served by the planners — more often than not, the interests of the power holders. Power must be centralized; if this were not so, conflicts would probably arise among power centres and deprive the plan of its orderly appearance.

In fact, this is the greatest danger inherent in the symbiosis of planning and power. Planning based on power tends to become subservient to power, and to give the self-justification of rationality to the essential arbitrariness of power.

But what are the alternatives? To some extent, the various mechanisms of the market, taking the term 'market' in its wider connotation. Just as a 'plan' can mean purposeful action on the basis of arbitrary decisions by power centres, 'market' is initially used simply in the sense that conscious control over economic or other socially important processes is lacking; on the hypothesis, amply disproved by experience, that some kind of automatic regulatory process will take care of all problems. This negative experience leads to corrective interventions by power centres, which either proudly use or assiduously avoid the term 'planning' to describe such interventions.

As their initial naïve assumptions regarding the self-sufficient automatism of the market or the interest-harmony and rationality of the plan become invalidated, the two systems of thought converge. In doing so, they finally discover the potentiality of both power and market in the transition towards a functional society.

A feasible reaction to feedback is a necessary complement to planning even at its most advanced. While political power exists in its present form, one of its more innocuous uses is undoubtedly to function as a generalized feedback mechanism in the technical sense, complementing the forecasts, reacting to the unforeseen. Power is socially problematical in its interest aspects when it serves purposes of domination and tends to walk over opposing interests, not when it is used as a technical corrective of technical shortcomings.

Also, if planning is coloured by power, power is to some extent constrained by planning. Just as a general rule or system of rules binds even its initiators, so the systematic picture of the future laid down in the plan imposes rules on the unruliness of power, restricts, to whatever small degree, its freedom of maneouvre.

On the other hand, in a qualitatively new sense as an instrument consciously introduced within the framework of planning and power, the market can be a perfectly progressive and useful criterion with which to measure at least one dimension of social usefulness: the relationship between the costs and results of a particular activity. In this sense, and within these limits, the market is the first realization of the polycentric nature of advanced planning in actual day-to-day practice. Polycentrism, in turn, is the first step towards reducing the centralism which is essential if power is to dominate over competing interests.

Obviously, the development of planning and the emergence of the functional society is going to be a long, hard and uneven process. To study the general direction of the movement and all its possible pitfalls, from all imaginable angles, would seem to be the primary task of the social sciences during the next decade or so. In facing up to this challenge, they would not only aid the advanced countries in their institutional engineering. As our planet becomes more united, at least in a technical sense, planning in an increasing number of networks will have to become global. Short of the unlikely triumph of one centralized political power over the entire world, global planning cannot be based on centralized power and must therefore develop the features of advanced polycentric planning in a functional sense. This situation, again, would necessarily influence the development of all parts of the world, for once obviating the need to live history as the superfluous repetition of generally recognized mistakes.

6

SOCIAL PLANNING — INTERESTS AND TECHNIQUES

I INTRODUCTION

Discussions of social planning often compound Don Quixote with Sancho Panza. The windmills of existing difficulties are transformed into giants of principle. Then, instead of fighting them we declare them invincible or else lazily point out someone else who should have fought them in the first place. At best some word-magic is used against them.[1]

The argument, suitably compressed, usually runs as follows:

In social planning — as distinguished from economic planning — we lack uniform standards and units of measurement; various goals cannot be significantly compared with each other, and the decision among them is a matter of free choice based on value-orientations and unfathomable personal criteria.

Therefore, social planning is not really planning in the technical sense; it is political decision-making. As such it is not the responsibility of planners but of politicians.

Even in its over-drawn form, this is a persuasive argument. What makes it persuasive is the portion of truth it contains. It is easy to overlook the distortion of perspective, the partial irrelevance, and the exaggeration which go along with the partial.

It seems worthwhile to try to define our basic assumptions about the relationship between the two concepts, "economic" and "social".

Hardly anybody wants factories or railways, coal mines or oil wells, tobacco plantations or banks for their own sake, because they are beautiful or good or desirable in any essential and ultimate sense. Our attitude towards them is as a rule, instrumental-rational

---

[1] Such as, calling "the complementarity method" the process of reflecting if we have enough money to do what we want to. When proved wrong in our guessing and forced to cut our objectives or to find additional resources we speak, with handsome understatement, of "serial approximation".

("zweckrational" in Max Weber's terminology). We see them as sources, direct or indirect, from which to satisfy our wants and needs, to get food and shelter, protect or restore our health, build cities; communicate with each other, pay for the education of the young, provide for our old and helpless fellows, and realize the thousands of other interests which man has acquired in modern society. It seems, therefore, misleading to speak of "economic" and "social" development or planning as if they were in any sense parallel.

The maintenance and improvement, individually and socially, of our human condition, as we see it, is the *end* of most of our efforts and activities, social as well as individual; it is the development of our society, it is social development. In order to achieve this, as a *means*, we must manipulate and expand scarce resources and use them to the best advantage; this we might call economics and economic development. In a world of scarcity most social ends have an economic or means-aspect.

This fundamental relationship implies a number of considerations and distinctions which make up, at least in part, the problem of "economic v/s social" with which we are concerned.

People might disagree about ends and objectives, about the society they would prefer. They might disagree about the relative importance of various goals, about the sacrifices they are prepared to make for their realization, about the aptitude of any means to bring about agreed upon ends, or about all of these. Disagreements are difficult to handle. We sometimes prefer, therefore, to start with the assumption of universal agreement and to see planning as a purely technical activity, the realm of the specialist, the professional.

Some resources are more and some less amenable to quantification. It is, for instance, easier to treat quantitatively investments expressible in monetary terms than to treat the mobilization of the will to work in a similar manner. We are reluctant to regard people as commodities or "capital", and think, therefore, of the production of drugs as an economic activity while we would not so consider the training of physicians. In short, we sometimes designate as "social" the activities directly concerned with people, and sometimes similarly designate fields where we encounter difficulties in setting up comparable units of measurement.[1]

---

[1] "The term "social" is sometimes used in planning and programming with reference to objectives (direct protection of the living conditions of the population at large or

The scarcer the resources the more important it seems to increase them. In these situations attention tends to concentrate on capital formation, on expanding the total product, so that anything which costs money and is not transformed, visibly and immediately, into further marketable material goods or saleable services, comes to be regarded as somehow secondary, "residual" or "social". "Profitability" becomes an ultimate criterion in its own right, parallel to "need". At the same time diseconomies on the spending side — which are exactly as important — escape attention.

Improvements in health and education, for instance, are practically ultimate values. Their translation into increased earning power or productivity is certainly an interesting side-issue. However, to look upon them exclusively from this point of view is a rather surprising consequence of the "economic fascination", which is characteristic of the epoch.

Planning practice and theory are concerned with the optimum realization of human ends. They have to start, simultaneously, from the objectives chosen and from the resources available. Planning therefore includes ends as well as means, it is social and at the same time economic,[1] it is a political as well as a technical activity all the way.

Planning is an essentially new form of human behavior. The gaps in theoretical knowledge and practical skills in planning are considerable. As in other fields, progress seems to come from concentrating on the gaps, directing efforts towards the points of least knowledge. Some of these gaps are, in my opinion, particularly in the field of social planning:

1.   What is the role of the existing interest situations of individuals and groups and how do these situations influence the possibility of social improvement?

2.   What technical procedures might increase the chance that the

---

of disadvantaged or vulnerable groups); at other times it is used with reference to methods (school education, health services, social work, community development etc). *Methods of Determining Social Allocations* (UN Publication E/CN. 5/387—1965) p. 5.

Cf. also Rafael Kafisov, "Concepts of Social Planning: Social Planning and Economic Planning, Similarities and Differences", in *The Problems and Methods of Social Planning* (UN Publication SOA/ESWP/EG/Rep 4-1963) pp. 21 ff.

[1]   "In other words, the economic criterion is nothing but a pattern of behavior which may be adopted under different conditions..." Goffredo Zappa, "Concepts of Social Planning: Social Planning and Economic Planning—Similarities and Differences", in *The Problems and Methods of Social Planning*, p. 36.

expenditure of resources would bring optimum returns in terms of social objectives?

3. What is the interrelationship between certain social structures and conditions on the one hand and the chance to realize given social objectives, including the expansion of resources, on the other?

4. What are the probable future development trends of interests and techniques and what are the possible consequences of this development for planning?

II   NEEDS AND INTERESTS

A frequent approach to planning, especially social planning, is through the assessment of needs. But equally frequent is the evidence of difficulties when trying to define the concept of "social needs". We read, for instance: "Social needs... are — by definition — needs that are not adequately met by the market process (or by home production)". And on the same page of the same text: "While the literature often speaks simply of meeting "needs", as the basis of social policy, that formulation from a psychological point of view is ambiguous since individuals may experience acute needs for objects (jewelry, sport cars) that are quite outside the scope of public concern. The expression "social needs" is used here to refer to needs related to the basic components of the level of living and judged to be a matter of national and international concern."[1] The two definitions do not cover the same range of phenomena. Or "...social need has to be seen as a somewhat relative concept. It may perhaps be defined in a negative sense, i.e. as a lack of social well-being of people, groups and communities, who do not get any real satisfaction of their need for a wholesome life to be conducted of course along socially approved lines." After pointing out that "it is not easy to assess the standard of well-being in a community", and that it is "much more difficult to get to grips with immaterial social needs", the author concludes that "social needs" are "elusive and relative social facts."[2]

These difficulties seem rather surprising in view of the considerable literature devoted to the concept of "need" in economics, psychology, sociology, even in philosophy (let us think, for instance,

---

[1]   *Methods of Determining Social Allocations*, p. 43.
[2]   Willem A. C. Zwanikken, "Measuring Social Needs", in *The Problems and Methods of Social Planning*, pp. 38 ff.

of Hegel's "system of needs"). The trouble with "social needs" can be reduced, in my opinion, to the following points:

a.   Needs are not conceptually problematical as long as they are understood as subjective, sometimes called "wants"[1] or, not without ambiguity, "felt needs".[2] The problems are practical: how to find out what the subjective needs are, what to do about them if they appear unreasonable, untimely or in any way deviating from the standards laid down by the beholder. The difficulties begin when we start to speak of objective or "real" needs. The fundamental question is: who sets the standards, who says what are the objective needs of any individual or group?

b.   As long as they are subjective, needs are individual. They can be experienced only through the individual consciousness. What is the meaning of "group needs", or of the "extensity of need"?[3]

c.   As long as they are subjective, needs are attached to the person and, therefore, essentially incomparable. Their size, or "intensity",[4] cannot be rated on a general scale. The phenomenon of differential elasticity of needs — pointed out by Engels and others — relates to their motivational improvisibility. Classifications of needs have to be made with the explicit reservation that they do not imply prognoses about the motivational effect.[5] At each step motivational inconsistencies are noted, such as the tendency to purchase "non-essentials"[6] or the phenomenon that supply creates demand.[7]

d.   Needs of individuals and of groups are not necessarily compatible. The assumption of harmony, implicit in concepts such as Benthamian utility and much of the current welfare thinking, conceals a vital dimension of the ends-means complex.

As they are a matter of definition, these difficulties are certainly not irreparable. The basic concept requires careful determination, so that it retains the present scope of "need" and adds the objective

---

[1]   *The Problems and Methods of Social Planning*, pp. 22-23.
[2]   Zwanniken, *op. cit.*, pp 40 ff.
[3]   *Methods of Determining Social Allocations*, p. 43.
[4]   *loco cit.*
[5]   Paul-Henry Chombart de Lauwe and Marie-Jose Chombart de Lauwe, "Changing Needs and the Dynamic Concept of the Family", in *Social Policy in Relation to Changing Family Needs* (UN Publication SOA/ESWP/1961/3-Geneva, 1962), pp. 45 ff.
[6]   Ellen Winston, "The Contribution of Social Welfare to Economic Growth" (93rd Annual Forum, National Conference on Social Welfare, USA, 1966), p. 8.
[7]   Planning of Social Development in Yugoslavia", in *The Problems and Methods of Social Planning*, p. 100.

and conflictual aspect. Terminologically, we might keep "need" and give it this wider connotation. I am suggesting another term simply in order not to get involved with the acquired meanings and overtones of the word "need".

This term is *interest*. I define objective interest as a situation of the world — independent of anybody's consciousness — which tends to maximize a socially accepted value in relation to an individual or a group of individuals. Subjective interest is understood as a state of the mind, consisting in the belief that a real-world situation exists which tends to maximize an individual value of the subject. Subjective interest would coincide with the notion of "want" or "felt need". The criterion of objective interest is the currently dominant scale of values in a given community, a notion to which we shall return presently.

Group interests are defined by the number of individuals who find themselves in the same objective interest situation or share the same subjective interest belief. The importance or size of an interest can be determined objectively by the place of the respective value on the social scale of values together with the distance between the actual situation and the socially accepted standard, and subjectively by a given level of correlation among answers by a plurality of respondents.

Conflict of interest is defined, objectively, as a real-world situation where an interest cannot be realized or protected without prejudice to another, and subjectively as a belief that an objective interest-conflict exists.

The decisive concept of this system, the social scale of values, can presumably be found by content-analyzing relevant public utterances in a given community. I submit that there is to-day increasing convergence, internationally, in the social scale of values, that a general objective, such as "maximizing human well-being",[1] is gaining internationally comparable operational significance. As an illustration, the following list of items, taken from UN publications and similar sources, is suggested (not implying that the various general fields of the examples within each field are ordered by importance):

---

[1]   Jan Tinbergen, "Social Aspects of Economic Planning", in *Social Progress Through Social Planning—The Role of Social Work* (Proceedings of the XIIth International Conference of Social Work, Athens, 1964), p. 63.

General living standards
— Steady and stable improvement of living standards as measured by real family incomes,
— Stable decrease of the number of families whose income falls under the current "poverty line";

Security
— Achieving increasing stability of main economic indicators concerning standards of living,
— Achieving full employment,
— Achieving general security in relation to the common risks of existence, such as losses through disease, accident, loss of family breadwinner, old age, etc.,
— Steady and stable increase in the quality of services given in cases of social emergency, such as disaster, breakdown of families and individuals, etc.,
— Stable improvement in the climate of international relations and the achievement of peace;

Liberty and Equality
— Increased protection against arbitrary infringements of the individual sphere and of human rights by any individual, organization or power,
— Increased opportunities for active participation of people in the affairs of the community,
— Steady improvement in equality of condition and in the universal sharing by members of a community of its resources and benefits;

Health
— Steady improvement in life expectation,
— Progressive reduction in infant mortality,
— Stable improvement in nutrition (as measured by calories consumed per day, animal protein and poor protein food per day etc.),
— Decrease and eventual eradication of preventable disease,
— Steady and stable improvement in health standards,
— Improvement of health facilities, as measured by physicians per 1000 population, maternity beds per 100 births, hospital beds per 1000 population, etc.;

Education
— Stable reduction of illiteracy,
— Stable improvement of educational and cultural standards,

— Improving school attendance,
— Increasing percentage of corresponding age group in higher education,
— Improving vocational training,
— Improvement of educational facilities, as measured by number of places in classrooms, in training workshops, in boarding schools and students' hostels, etc.;

Conditions of work
— Progressive improvement of the conditions of work,
— Steady and constant reduction of the number of accidents at work;

Housing
— Steady reduction of overcrowding,
— Stable improvement in housing conditions, as measured by percentage of population living in dwellings, average number of persons per room, percentage of dwellings with piped water and with toilets, etc.,
— Stable reduction of rent and of the costs of building;

Social Welfare
— Reduction and prevention of neglect and destitution among children,
— Steady and stable reduction of criminality and delinquency,
— Improved care for the aged,
— Improved care for the handicapped and other vulnerable groups, as measured by the number of places in creches, kindergartens, homes and institutions, etc.

The general acceptability, and actual wide acceptance, of such a list is, however, deceptive. The social scale of values is an instrument of measurement, not a declaration of harmony. Given scarce resources, it happens in actual experience that the things postulated by the social list of values are not achieved equally by all.[1] The age-old question "who gets what, when and how" is answered in the contemporary world, roughly in three main ways: (1) by self-regulating mechanisms such as the market, (2) by conscious inter-

[1] "This inexplicitness of economic 'Welfarism' is liable also to encourage another weakness to which democratic governments are inevitably prone. This is a reluctance to face the fact of conflicting interests, and the temptation to fend off awkward political choices and decisions by trying to get experts to produce 'objective' answers." T. W. Hutchinson, "*Positive Economics and Policy Objectives*" (George Allen and Unwin, London, 1964), p. 167.

vention through such means as a central plan, or (3) by any combination of the first two methods.

Historically, initial extreme solutions have manifested serious shortcomings. The market mechanism is open to all kinds of artificial obstructions, creating favored positions for a minority of actors. It sometimes tends towards the concentration of consumption, but under some circumstances, especially in the transition from "Agraria" to "Industria", it inhibits the process of concentrating productive forces.[1] In developed countries it is usually the values of social justice and social security that motivate movements towards the limitation of the market.[2] In developing countries the argument is more often its impracticability or inefficiency from the point of view of sustained accelerated growth, although voices that "development should not be for a minority only", are not infrequent.[3]

Conscious intervention, as a rule by the State, can correct the shortcomings of the market, but the extreme forms of such intervention tend to develop defects of their own. Often accumulation or saving is overstressed in relation to consumption, economic and social initiative is inhibited, and there is a tendency toward bureaucratic overconcentration of political power.

In an attempt to avoid the defects of extreme solutions, an increasing number of measures are being introduced and developed. All these measures, from income tax to workers' self-management, are calculated to correct the socially unacceptable consequences of a "free play of forces" and, at the same time, to restrain as little as possible the activities and the initiative of individuals and groups. A coherent system of such measures certainly implies planning in the technical sense. On the other hand, it also implies politics,

---

[1] The negative influence of the market on the human personality is often described as alienation, in the technical, legal, social or political sense. But it seems that certain phenomena such as that "the performance of working activities, as far as their pace and content are concerned, becomes increasingly independent of the worker's personal characteristics..." stem from the traditional structure of industrial organizations and are independent of the market. On the other hand, it is certainly true that "the most different needs and requirements of the individuals can only be satisfied by the system when they can be expressed in terms of effective economic demand", which means that no needs can be satisfied in the market for which the subjects cannot pay. (G. Zappa, *op. cit.*, p. 32).

[2] Cf. Elizabeth Liefmann-Keil, *Oekonomische Theorie der Sozial-politik* (Springer Verlag, Berlin-Gottingen-Heidelberg, 1961) p. 2 and p. 13, where the author argues that justice cannot be defined once for all but that it is concerned with equality of treatment.

[3] *Methods of Social Allocations*, p. 9.

understood as the social behavior related to conflicts of interest.

In an attempt to adjust potential conflicts of interests, these measures aim at redistributing existing chances of interest satisfaction. The redistribution occurs:

— between different groups of the population,[1]
— between different types of expenditure,
— between units of time,
— between units of geographic space.[2]

The instruments of redistribution are measures of:[3]

financial policy, such as direct and indirect taxation, contributions, social security and other benefits, the manner of appropriating public funds, special levies and appropriations etc.,

economic policy, such as minimum wages legislation, price support, indemnities and export premiums, sliding scale arrangements, price maximization, minimum inventory regulation etc.,

social policy, (in the restrictive sense) such as maximum hours, protection of vulnerable groups in employment, social welfare services, reductions and privileges for certain groups on public facilities etc.

The smaller the total national income to be redistributed, the less the importance of measures of redistribution. Real progress in the satisfaction of all interests existing in a community can be obtained by increasing the outlay for publicly managed services accessible to all. In this context, it is important to know if the resources allocated to the financing of these services are used to the best advantage, and if the outlay as such is likely to help or to retard general improvement and the growth of capabilities.

But in turning to these questions we should keep in mind that

---

[1]   Of particular importance in this context are the categories of "private" and "public" consumption of "individual" and "social" allocations. By transferring a portion of the real income of the population from individual money income to social outlays, it is possible to influence the composition of family budgets in a direction thought more consonant with their objective interests.

But besides reducing the "non-essential" items in family budgets and channelling expenditure towards more essential goals, social outlays can be used in a number of socially dysfunctional ways, as for bureaucratic ostentation, and particularly in the pernicious cause of war and armaments.

[2]   Cf. Liefmann-Keil, *op. cit.*, p. 19.

[3]   Cf. E. Liefmann-Keil, *op. cit.*, pp. 94-95, and *Methods of Determining Social Allocations*, pp. 33-35.

they are meaningful only in the framework of the solution for, or rather of the continuous solving of, the constantly arising conflicts of interest.

III   OBJECTIVES AND RESOURCES

Planning is, technically, a procedure to achieve the optimal relationship between objectives and resources, including the results of future activity.[1]

This is not an effort to add another sample to the myriad existing definitions of planning. The intention is rather to indicate the belief that our present planning techniques are, essentially, only the elaboration of very simple basic ideas practiced traditionally — from the individual peasant household to military strategy — in all known cultures. In planning we live apparently still a pre-Newtonian era, though, if I read the signs correctly, at its outer edge.[2]

The present moment in the development of planning techniques is characterized by a convergent movement: from the general to the

[1]   Definitions of planning usually list various steps, in logical or chronological order. These steps can invariably be related either to the heading of what is to be achieved, or to the other "by what means". As an example, two rather marginal forms of planning, social policy planning and development planning.
The following steps can be distinguished in the planning of social policy:
1. estimation of the future development of population;
2. estimation of the future development of national income;
3. estimation of the future cost of the social policy schemes now in operation;
4. decisions with regard to the size of the share of social income transfers in national income;
5. allocation of the share of national income available for new social security schemes among different purposes.
Pekka Kuusi, *Social Policy for the Sixties—A Plan for Finland* (Kuopio, 1964), p. 104.
"In a summary way, development planning can be said to imply:
a) analyzing the economy, its endowment with capital, labour, national resources, institutions;
b) identifying structural difficulties, bottlenecks etc.;
c) setting objectives or targets for the entire economy and per sector;
d) determining policy instruments, including a development strategy to achieve these targets; and
e) setting up the machinery for the execution of the plan.
Methods of Determining Social Allocations, p. 16.
[2]   The methodological elaborations and refinements of the basically elementary effort at adjustment have not reached the same level everywhere. Sometimes we are even cautioned not to move too far too fast in the direction of sophistication, especially in view of the time factor, the pressing need for action. "... rough assessment may be the most sensible policy in many circumstances". *Methods of Determining Social Allocations*, p. 44.

specific and in the opposite direction, from the detailed to the inclusive. Methods developed from the planning of social macro-relationships and those that started from micro-planning of single projects move towards a middle ground where the two levels meet and complement each other.[1] This convergence is due to negative experiences with the application of either method to the exclusion of the other. In macro-planning mistakes in details tend to aggregate, and not to cancel each other out, to the point of vitiating the global prognosis. Micro-planning alone is blind as to the general direction of development and events at more general levels can deflect the purpose of the individual project.

I

Objectives are in practice often less problematical than they appear in theory or when speaking about them generally.

Basic objectives in a community are implicit in its socio-economic structure and in existing conditions. Rarely if ever is a conscious decision taken about them. In a country, for instance, where a firmly entrenched class of big landowners maintains itself at the top of the social pyramid, a plan starting from the assumption of a radical land reform may have a very great significance as a political manifesto but hardly as a technical instrument.

This conclusion holds equally for objectives whose returns are more immediate and easier to measure, usually called "economic", as well as for those where the results take time to become manifest or where only costs can be measured in obvious money units. The

---

[1]   The same idea is often found in texts on planning. In my opinion, it coincides, for instance, with Tinbergen's distinction of two main planning methods: the complementarity method and the project appraisal method, though he speaks of macro- and micro-complementarity. This seems to me already the results of the convergence mentioned. Cf. Jan Tinbergen, *op. cit.*, pp. 65-67. I understand in the same sense Warren's classification of planning methods in abstract and rational on the one hand and concrete and social on the other, though this distinction appears contaminated by a generalized value judgement. Cf. Roland L. Warren, *Two Models of Social Planning* (Brandeis University, preliminary draft).
This is meant, as well, by the distinction between "global and specific" analyses of utility. "Planning of Social Development in Yugoslavia", in *The Problems and Methods of Social Planning*, p. 113.
It is a problem in itself, how far given objective conditions can play a role in making one or the other method appear initially more useful. The notion of social and economic density is an attempt to explain differential attitudes in this respect. Cf. Pusić, "The Interdependence between Social and Economic Planning, with Special Reference to Yugoslavia", in J. Ponsioen et al, *Social Welfare Policy: Contributions to Theory* (Mouton & Co., The Hague, 1962).

emphasis on immediate consumption, as compared with postpone-
ment of satisfaction in order to save and invest, can be brought
about, at various levels of development, by pressures too strong to
be ignored. Such situations can obtain at low levels when the hungry
masses, or the "hungry" new and aggressive ruling classes, are too
impatient and all surplus is channelled into consumption, plan or
no plan, by fair means or not-so fair. It can happen at medium
levels when dysfunctional consequences of over-investment and
over-concentration have produced strong strains and begun to
defeat the fundamental social purposes of development. Finally,
when the total product has grown sufficiently and the momentum of
necessary productive investment can be maintained without special
conscious effort and restrictions on other sectors, more long-term
interest preferences can assert themselves.[1]

At other times priority is given to the expansion of resources,
usually termed "economic". The reason may be the correct assumption that projects must be backed by capabilities if they are to
be realistic, or the incorrect assumption that economic expansion
with concomitant industrialization and urbanization are unmitigat-
ed blessings. In fact, development can be started, it seems, at any
point. Present evidence does not exclude any assumptions in this
respect. The selfless efforts of the partisans of educational enlightenment and general social betterment in Europe and particularly in
Eastern Europe during the 19th and the beginning decades of the
20th century are not an overly encouraging example. Their
campaigns to spread literacy, hygiene and cultural activities were

---

[1] The dependence of planning on the time dimension, i.e. on levels of development,
and on the fundamental facts of structure and conditions in a community is now all
but universally recognized. The point is made for "social planning" by Dankowski,
"Analysis of Costs and Benefits of Social Programmes", in *The Problems and Methods
of Social Planning*, p. 63: "It is now beyond dispute that the general tenor and scale
of social programmes and measures differ from country to country, *depending on the
degree of economic and social development* and existing *socio-economic and political
conditions*".
At the same time, it is often pointed out that "social plans" tend to be geared to longer timespans than "economic plans". Cf. Dankowski, *Ibid.*, or *Administrative
Aspects of Social Planning* (UN Publication No. 64-40342, Paris, 1964) p. 5. The
impression of longer duration is created, in my opinion, chiefly by the uncertainty
as to measuring results. I am confirmed in this opinion especially by the
theoreticians of "unbalanced growth". Cf. Albert O. Hirschman, *The Strategy of
Economic Development* (New Haven, 1958). As soon as the automatic relationship
between investment in "social overhead capital" — which includes transportation and
power—and direct production is not assumed, the investment in an electric power
system, a system of roads and railways or an irrigation system is just as "long-
term" as the establishment of a school of languages or a physical research institute.

unable to achieve a fundamental change in the way of life of the poor peasant masses. Their emphasis on the social morals and values of this life did not change appreciably the social position of these classes nor their status in the socio-economic pyramid. Critics of the "enlightenment" approach like to point to the spectacular achievements of "primarily economic" development in, for instance, Japan, the USSR or the USA. The obvious retort to this is to ask the philosophical question of who is really better off and the not so philosophical one about the social costs of explosive industrialization. The real argument, however, seems to turn around the true character of accelerated growth. Is it possible at all without an initial social breakthrough, a traumatic experience of expanding geographic or social boundaries which mobilizes masses of people to extraordinary efforts and sacrifices. The fact is that the "social" and the "economic" aspect of development cannot be separated even for purposes of analysis.

Often also objectives seem obvious because they are legitimated by the socially accepted scale of values — as can be judged from the example of such a scale given above. The question is more often how and how quickly they can be realized than if they should be striven after.[1] The decision among them can be political in the true sense of being the outcome of an interest-position or -adjustment but sometimes it is "political" in the sense only of being based on impressions which cannot be too well substantiated.[2]

In time, however, a number of refinements were worked into the

---

[1] "However, I believe, in the reality of most countries alternative choices are relatively limited and the choice is more related to the relative pace with which to move in a direction determined by political, economic, and social conditions than to the alternative directions in which to move." Gerhard Colm: *Certain Aspects of Planning as a Tool for Social and Economic Development* (UN Publication No. M-7849, 4/13/64, Paris, 1964), p. 18.

[2] This, of course, is again true irrespective of the character of the values and the character of the project in question. Even if it might be conceded that "social allocations are less easily derived from technical data and formulas than are economic allocations" (*Methods of Determining Social Allocations*, p. 37), it does not follow that they "involve a larger number of non-technical value decisions" (*ibid.*), as the text quoted seems to imply. A conclusion from facts to values is logically inadmissible. If our technical data are poor our judgement will be unsupported but it will remain a judgement of fact and will not, for that reason, become a judgement of value. Value judgements are made, explicitly or implicitly, in any decision, and the more general the level the larger the value element tends to be. In this respect the fundamental decisions about investment, industrialization, emphasis on heavy industry, imports and exports are not only more value-laden but certainly also more possibly controversial than decisions related directly to the realization of accepted social interests, such as to extend free health services etc.

technical assessment of planning objectives, in response to new problems appearing in practice.

a. The problem of *information* became increasingly important with the realization that objectives acquire concrete significance in planning only in comparison with the actual situation. Data to judge the situation will, by definition, never be sufficient for the planner. Apart, however, from this psychological propensity, the lack of essential data often bedevils precisely those countries where a country-wide planned coordination of efforts towards development would be most necessary and where it is, in fact, most widely accepted as a *modus operandi.*[1]

b. The translation of objectives into concrete *targets*, which are derived from the comparison of the actual situation with established *standards and norms*, represents a further step in methodology of planning. The problem is in establishing a valid empirical relationship between objectives and targets, and a further problem to keep the standards and norms within existing possibilities and at the same time elastic enough that they can be revised upward as capabilities improve.[2]

c. The problem of *comparability* of situations and aims arises when

[1] Cf. *Preliminary Report on Targets of Social Development* (UN Publication No. E/CN. 5/394-1965), pp. 19 ff. In most less-developed economies, viz. pre-entrepreneurial "competitive" (but with significant discontinuities in pricing) or "project planning", and in all socialist economies, the information problem is of capital importance because of the price inadequacy just described and the need to amass data on individual projects. Michel C. Kaser, "The Analysis of Costs and Benefits of Social Programmes", *The Problems and Methods of Social Planning*, p. 52. Cf. also "Planning Social Development in Yugoslavia", *ibid.*, p. 111.

[2] Much damage to development can be brought about by social standards set so impossibly high that nothing is done to achieve them. This does not mean that people in poorer countries, in any absolute sense, need fewer doctors, schools, housing facilities etc., than do people in the richer countries. (In fact, they may need more doctors because they have more sickness.) It means only that, for the practical purpose of developing programming and policy, social standards of adequacy, and related planning targets, must be formulated in manageable terms. *Methods of Determining Social Allocations*, p. 47.
Experience seems to point to the conclusion that targets should be fairly clear-cut in relation to objectives. To try to hit too many flies with one stroke usually leads to missing them all. "In so far as social programmes are seriously guided by economic considerations, they may not be able to realize simultaneously the ideals of social justice... At the same time, particular economic projects that are directed towards immediate social objectives can —and sometimes do—fail for the same reason." *Ibid.*, p. 11.

attention is turned from one country or region to the larger national or international scene. A level of realization of a given objective established by inter-regional or inter-national comparison represents a certain guarantee of the realism of the adopted standard. On the other hand, it can be objected that what is compared in these comparisons is not comparable at all. For instance, the same percentage of national income spent on education does not mean the same thing, obviously, in a rich country and in a poor one where the total income is smaller and the educational needs greater. Also, the fact that the international average of expenditure for preventive health services has attained a given, low, level should not be decisive for a country where the eradication of malaria is the first condition for a take-off to anywhere.

Comparing objectives internationally is even described as a separate method of planning in its own right.[1]

d. The problem of *priorities* is inherent in choice among value-objectives and even more among instrumental targets leading, supposedly, to the same objective. It became pressing and increasingly significant at the same time when indirect relationships between objectives and targets came to be better understood. The charting of second and higher order influences of activities aimed at one objective made it possible not only to appreciate more fully what one was about to do but also to choose among alternative starting points on the strength of the comparable side-effects.

From the initial crude alternative between "economic" and "social", planning techniques are moving increasingly towards the appreciation of secondary and further removed consequences of any course of action on any set of objectives. There is better knowledge of the stresses created by over-investment or by inflation due to over-strained programmes of expansion, and of the positive influences of security on the productivity of labor.[2]

---

[1] Cf. Donald V. McGranahan, "Problems of Target-Setting in Planning for the Needs of Children", in *Planning for the Needs of Children in Developing Countries* (UNICEF, 1964), p. 178.

[2] "The first and weightiest argument is that social policy is capable of mobilizing new human resources for the purposes of production... Second, social policy tends to stabilize economic activity... Since it tends to increase and stabilize consumption, social policy also contributes to stimulating the replacement and expansion of productive machinery... Social policy generally tends to increase consumption, and appears to be one of the contributing factors in the gradual extension of the sphere of public investment." P. Kuusi, *op. cit.* pp. 86-89. On the other hand, social outlay may have negative consequences for the economy as well. On the whole: "Social policy is

Anyway, when priorities are once established the initial haziness about objectives corresponding to needs or ultimate values disappears and planning gets really technical. Now, the planner is faced with requirements, i.e. with the task to sum all the tasks which flow from the direct or indirect consequences of the initial choices.

e.   Finally, there is the discovery of *difference*. No lesser expression will do, as planning with its inbuilt inclination towards harmony had real difficulties to accept, at the level of technical planning operations, the fact that, first, there were more than one objective and these not necessarily compatible, and then, what was even more troubling, that various people engaged in the planning process or intimately concerned with it could have different views on the objectives to be pursued. Not because they differed in technical opinion but because they were on different sides of existing interest fences.[1] This discovery seems so important because it forced the planners to think of operating with more than one preference scale and still get technically usable results.[2] Starting with the still rather dogmatic assumptions of economic theory on market be-

----

capable of mobilizing human resources and making for stabilized consumption; but at the same time, the propensity to save may slightly decline and the value of money fall to some extent". *Ibid.*, p. 90.

There is nearly general agreement that increase in real personal consumption raises the productivity of labor. On the other hand, increased productivity is the prime condition for the realization of the accepted interests of a community.

Any activity, productive or otherwise, has fundamental requirements as to the quantity and quality of people who are to undertake it. "Various measures planned in the course of development are sometimes interrelated in the sense that the feasibility of one is a condition for the success of another." Eugen Pusić, *Reappraisal of the United Nations Social Service Programme* (UN Publication No. E/CN. 5/AC. 12/L. 3/Add. 1, New York, 1965).

[1]   Even at the level of the most abstract theory there is considerable difference among the authorities, though objectives such as "freedom", "peace", "justice", "security", "economic growth", "progress", "democracy" tend to recur. Hutchison (*op. cit.* pp. 168-169) has listed quite an impressive array of these opinions. The point, however, is not how far people agree or disagree. The essential discovery is that these various values, as far as they can be given operational meanings, can and often do contradict each other. "Economic growth" might be bought only by a risk of security or a restriction of freedom. And one man's justice might be another's breach of peace. And so on.

[2]   "In fact, starting from 'pluralist' sets of objectives may stimulate the exploration of policy in empirical, piece-meal or 'incremental' terms from the starting point of actual conditions, and bring out the costs of each improvement in the fulfillment of one objective, in terms of the forgoing of others. That is, it would be useful to elicit, where it is practically possible, preference functions, at least roughly indicative of marginal rates of substitution". Hutchison, *op. cit.*, p. 178.

havior under conditions of perfect competition, oligopoly, monopoly, social scientists and planners in their wake were forced from the prescriptive and normative into the indicative mode and the empirical language. Up to now their results seem more reliable and useful in comparatively closed systems such as organizations where behavioral theories appear to correlate not too badly with observed facts.[1] In the more open fields, such as social planning, we are only at the beginning of the experimental stage with game theory and derived devices. The limits, to-day, might be about that point.

2

Resources in the meaning of our definition of planning imply all means. They include raw materials and other resources "in the state of nature" as well as those expressed in actual and potential human activity. What the planner proposes to do can, therefore, for practical purposes and logically, be accommodated within the same term.

The adjustment of resources and objectives is done, traditionally, by two elementary methods, corresponding to the two initial orientations of macro- and micro-planning:

One is the method of comparing macro-flows of resources in a community, called variously from balancing to national accounting. What were at the outset very rough comparisons is being gradually refined and made more complex by introducing detailed sectoral planning, through the use of models, matrix theory and electronic calculating equipment.

The other is the method applied in order to assess the resources needed for an individual project, designated as project or programme appraisal and in its more advanced forms as cost/benefit analysis.[2] In this method the same movement from rough to fine can be observed, as better operationalizations of the concept of utility are achieved and as whole systems of cause-effect and functional interrelationships are coordinated within input-output tables.

As the two methods converge — input-output is a good example

---

[1] Cf. for instance, Richard M. Cyert and James G. March: *A Behavioral Theory of the Firm* (Prentice-Hall, Englewood Cliffs, N. J. 1963).

[2] "The scope of cost benefit analysis may thus be defined as the logical arrangement of benefits accruing from some economic activity and accruing from any other feasible activity where neither group or benefit is subject to randomness or competitive strategy". Kaser, *op. cit.*, p. 49.

— and levels of sophistication grow, awareness of problems increases at the same time; the difficulties, not suprisingly, are parallel to those on the objectives-side:

a.   The availability of *information* and data at the right time seems even more crucial in relation to resources than for appraising the "zero-situation" at the beginning of a planning period. Planning is understood more and more as foresight combined with elastic preparedness to adjust to the unexpected. For the functioning of the feedback, data at the right time are essential.[1]

b.   The problem of *comparability* in relation to resources is both more complex and more concrete than in respect to objectives. Instead of one category of items to be compared, there are two classes pertaining to resources: the outlays and the profits from any given commitment, or the costs and benefits.[2] That means that the comparison is, first, between costs and benefits for any given alternative, and then among various alternatives, and after that possibly along other dimensions as well.[3] On the other hand, the comparisons are much less conjectural than with, often largely putative, objectives. In order even to begin to compare, the various magnitudes must be substantially present. The main trend of effort in order to achieve and facilitate comparability is in the direction of standardization. The standards are expressed in absolute numbers, calculated on an average or for an "ideal type", or in the form of percentages, especially in the apportionment among various classes of typical expenditure for each project.[4]

[1]   "In less developed economies of the system mentioned, the lack of knowledge of resources, of expert survey, of technological knowhow and of pressure by beneficiaries, present limitations to the validity of opportunity cost". *Ibid.*, p. 52.
[2]   "By benefits and costs in the widest sense we mean the positive and negative contributions to general welfare along all channels; this presupposes a valuation system for the various influences exerted." Tinbergen, *op. cit.*, pp. 65-66.
[3]   "All [activities] should be at a level which maximizes the nation's welfare over a time period. This means that the net marginal utilities they bring about must be equalized between time units and between these activities. Another consequence is that, for instance, the level should be such that marginal benefit and marginal costs are equal." *Ibid.*, pp. 64-65.
[4]   Dankowski states for Poland: "Statistical analysis of the cost of social programmes has shown that, of the total amount expended in the period 1955-60, outlays for peronnel fluctuated between 48.0 per cent and 44.8 per cent, running material expenditure between 35.2 per cent and 37.9 per cent, and other items such as capital repairs, scholarships and various grants between 17.3 per cent and 16.8 per cent. These figures do not, of course, represent any hard and fast principle; but they may be taken as a rough guide for other countries in situations similar to that of the Polish People's Republic." *Op cit.*, p. 71.

As a rule it is easier to define costs than benefits. This leads to the fallacy of disregarding all benefits but those that are readily expressible in comparable units, usually money, and to the further misapprehension of speaking of projects where benefits are not comparable in these terms as "unprofitable".[1]

c. The problem of *measurement* is closely associated with comparability and is usually treated together with it. The progress achieved in this field comes from the insight that measuring is not restricted to *prima facie* quantitative magnitudes. The concerted judgement of impartial arbitrators or judges can give results which are for all practical purposes equivalent to measures (in figure skating or high board diving, for instance). This method has the additional advantage of making it possible to aggregate measures on quite different scales.[2] Mathematical set theory has provided a

---

[1] Speaking about the definition of benefits, Kaser compares them along two dimensions of which he calls the first "the perspective of the beneficiary" and distinguishes three forms "in which the benefit is seen by the decision-maker": "1. Real empirical social benefits", "2. Benefits assumed by policy makers", and "3. Real empirical private benefits". The second dimension is "the time of consumption of the benefit" where investment and consumption are understood as different points on the same continuous time-scale. (*op. cit.*, pp. 54-56).
Authors understanding benefits in the unjustifiably narrow terms of monetary profitability often speak, in a general way, of the "unprofitability of social projects". This seems mistaken in at least two ways. Disregarding non-monetary benefits in a project which has also returns that are readily measurable in money, distorts the situation in the same way as considering only "feasibility" and "economicalness" in projects where the monetary measure cannot be used at all. To consider only the returns on capital investments in a factory and not the effects on the social structure, the change in patterns of occupation, the increased mobility etc. is the same as speaking of a school, a museum, or a research institute as "pure outlay" without any profit. And then, comparability is not the result of the existence of a criterion but of its correct application. In this respect no project is proof against faulty judgement. A steel-mill without appropriate markets for its products is in no way better off than a school training people for unwanted jobs.
[2] "That is, the measuring instrument must be the human individual, who is quite capable of comparing items and values that are technically non-comparable and reaching choices and decisions. This is done constantly in every-day life; it is a familiar aspect of public administration, as in recruitment to the civil service where such disparate variables as intelligence, experience and character are taken into account in reaching a decision on appointment at a given salary level. It is essential that such judgement in the planning field be a) informed, and b) disinterested." McGranahan, *op. cit.*, p. 182.
It is quite customary to see comparisons of costs and benefits such as the following: "In 1961, the national income amounted to 53 thousand zlotys per employed person. If we compare this figure with the cost of training fully-trained workers from certain types of training establishment—including the cost of training in the secondary school for fully trained workers from higher educational institutions—it appears that once they start work, fully trained workers repay in the form of national income

powerful tool for extending the range of measurement.

Here again it is almost traditional to equate the "social" with the immeasurable. And the same answer that was given in the case of comparability goes here. To measure only what can be measured readily and to declare everything else, explicitly or implicitly, as non-existent because there is no measure that meets the eye, seems not much better than not measuring at all but going by impressions. Anyway, what can be measured and what cannot is a question of fact and no general pronouncements will get us anywhere in this context. As the range of measurement gets wider, the truculent assertion that "not everything can be measured" reminds of R. H. Tawney's dictum: "It is like using the impossibility of absolute cleanliness as a pretext for rolling in a manure heap."[1]

d.   At the limits of present development in planning techniques is the problem of *probability*. Assessing the probabilities of various outcomes has first been used, as far as I know, in military operations research but it is spreading to other fields of planning as well.[2]

The uncertainty and lack of control in planning operations makes for rigidity. The less we can foresee the more we must stick to rules — in order to "absorb uncertainty" — and, paradoxically, the less we are free to adapt to the unforeseen.[3]

---

produced, the funds expended on their education. Those trained at vocational training schools repay the sum in five months, at secondary training schools in ten months, and at higher educational establishments in something over two years." Dankowski, *op. cit.*, p. 73.
This type of measurement seems to me mistaken not only because it operates with largely meaningless averages, which is usually conceded, but also because it conceals possible incongruities in the training-pattern (training too many of one type and not enough of another), because it inhibits the assessment of the quality of training, because it sidesteps the issue of the total social and individual benefits from training, and finally, because it implies the dangerous principle that the individual getting training is because of that in some way indebted to an abstract entity, the community.
[1]   Quoted after Hutchinson, *op. cit.*, p. 192.
[2]   "The planner or decision-maker cannot act rationally unless he has prognoses on the development to be expected in his line of planning." *The Problems and Methods of Social Planning.*
"The use of projections is an indispensable aspect of any of these methods [of determining social allocations], particularly when allocations are made in the context of planning." *Methods of Determining Social Allocations*, p. 41.
[3]   "Eckstein points out that lack of control leads to several different types of adaptive behavior by the planners: 1. The use of routine and stereotyped rules, 2. Oversimplification, 3. Rigidity and inertia, 4. Political, rather than rational decision-making, and 5. Centralization of administration. He points out that these adaptive behaviors either involve decreasing the area of rational decision-making or resorting to non-rational modes of behavior." R. Warren (*op. cit.*, p. 12), referring to Eckstein's analysis of the British Health Service.

IV   PERSPECTIVES

In the course of history methods of cooperation have undergone several radical transformations and modes of behavior in situations of conflict have changed in an equally fundamental way. Two main perspectives on this development seem relevant. One is the phylo-genetic view of the development of the human species generally, and the other the "polito-genetic" outlook on the emerging individual community. As in biological philogenesis and octogenesis, the second is, to an extent, the repetition of the first, and the present, therefore, a sample of cross sections of the past. It might stimulate a discussion to take a brief look first at the one and then at the other.

1

Man's associations started on a *personal* basis: the family, the horde, the clan, the tribe. The decisive social fact was always the individual belonging to the group, the main bond of loyalty to the group, and the principal way of functioning of the group was in the face-to-face contact of its members. The opposition among groups was natural and an authority who could arbitrate conflicts among them did not exist.

Fundamental changes in the technological conditions of man's life called, later, for new social institutions. As land became the decisive source of livelihood, the principal means of production, the basis of social structure became the *territory*, a clearly limited complex of land, over which a group claimed exclusive authority, a relationship that later became known as sovereignty. The group itself became more and more identified with the territory, the former personal bonds lost gradually their importance.[1] Territorial limits by themselves, however, were not enough to ensure the necessary cohesion of the community. Political power, i.e. a legalized monopoly of coercion, of physical violence in a given territory, was the new social institution that provided the binding material for the group of comparative strangers included under the same territorial sovereignty.

---

[1] "There has been a tendency... to break up or re-cast various institutions in which social and economic functions have been closely integrated, under a system of "paternalism" (e.g. the feudal-type agrarian estate, the trading company with a territorial grant, the industrial company town)." *Methods of Determining Social Allocations*, p. 7.

At the same time, face-to-face contact, as a technical means of cooperation, became too small in scope and insufficiently adaptable for the expanding tasks of the larger territorial community. It was replaced by the *organization* which, combining the systematic division of labor with the equally methodical construction of a network for coordinating continuously people in action, is one of man's most remarkable inventions. In the territorial and organizational society, however — which we have, through one-sided experience, come to identify with society as such — territorial groups though larger and more inclusive, continued to be opposed to each other and to refuse to recognize a binding verdict in their conflicts other than superior physical force. Political power, in that way, came to be the fulcrum around which, in territorial society, turned the possibility of internal conflict-resolution by domination of one among the conflicting interests over the others as well as the chance of survival in the jungle-area of inter-State relations.

The social phenomenon of conflict has changed very little through all these times; when one interest cannot be satisfied without prejudice to another the alternatives are: to dominate all opposing interests, to abstain from satisfying the interest in question or to reach an understanding on the basis of a partial satisfacton of the opposing interests. Improved techniques of social action have hitherto contributed chiefly to enable the continuous and systematic domination of all interests in favor of some, those of the political power holders.

It seems that this situation is today neither acceptable nor any longer really necessary. It is not acceptable because the weapons of conflict have grown so destructive that we cannot afford to pay the price of clashes between territorial powers. At the same time, the economic productive capacities have grown to such a level, where the meeting of basic needs for all people comes, technologically speaking, within the range of rational discussion. With it the main source of conflicts throughout history, the principal cause of the existence of groups with irreconcilably opposed interests, i.e. the competition for scarce resources, tends to lose ground.

The new fundamental change in the fabric of society, which is under way today, has been inaugurated by the industrial revolution. Land lost its place as the all-important means of production it had been before, and came to be replaced by the functionally-oriented organization: the factory, the shop, the institution, the agency, organized around a function, a goal, an objective, logically independent from the land on which it stood. With the demise of land as the principal economic factor, territory as well ceases to be the compelling structuring criterion of human society. Other overall forms of human association than the territorial community with political power as its common denominator are becoming conceivable.

Organization, however, also faces a crisis. The increase in specialization causes greater costs of coordination, in time and personnel, with the point of diminishing returns clearly in view. Also, the necessary working independence of the specialists becomes more and more difficult to reconcile with hierarchy, the essential principle of organization.

All these developments point to a time when more loosely structured work-groups of equals will have to be integrated into progressively more complex groupings around ever more comprehensive social objectives. In this process technical problems should be solved along with questions of interest, cooperation arranged simultaneously with the adjustment of conflicts. One does not include the other but neither are the two mutually exclusive. They are part of the same, consciously analyzed and ever-changing social situation. The structural institutional unit of the new system might be the functional task-oriented work group, its method of operation — planning.

2

Development, however, is not unidimensional. Countries develop, or stagnate, in many ways. Within the general tendencies outlined above, several variables can be identified that might be significant for planning.

a.   The first is the level of *rationality*. The dichotomy of "organic" and "mechanic" forms of society — from Maine's status and contract and Tönnies' *Gemeinschaft und Gesellschaft* to Mendeta y Nunez' mechanization and Parsons' pattern variables — is so often encountered in thinking about society that its corresponding to a quasi-universal social fact is very strongly suggested. More recently the idea of a continuum is more often mentioned, a succession of changing forms of interaction with more emotional and connotative elements emphasized during the early stages and more informational and rational factors coming to prevail later. Increasing rationality, and the accompanying "disenchantment of the world" — in Max Weber's words — are, by and large, a function of time. With two important reservations, however. The process proceeds at very unequal speeds, depending on various influences difficult to systematize — for instance, the development of religious ideas, contingencies of local history etc. And second, frequent relapses into an earlier stage of development can be observed, under the influence of intensive social action or otherwise emotionally turbulent social atmosphere.

b.   A second variable, already mentioned and called *social density*, can be defined as the incidence of organized secondary group activity in relation to total available potential resources.

In situations of low social density, and in order to speed up its increase, measures of direct intervention, centrally directed to strategic points (e.g. power, steel, transportation) will tend to give quicker and larger results. As density increases, direct intervention will tend to give way to indirect regulation and centralization of decision-making will probably appear less indispensable.

Here as well variations in speed are frequent and "irregularities" in the sequence of stages often encountered. A very low organizational density will sometimes make decentralization the only alternative, because more inclusive attempts at control seem unrealistic (e.g. community development). Also, whole systems of social control can come as it were too early and be superseded by another system which, logically, should have come earlier.

c.   A third variable related to the applicable methods of planning might be called *transparency*, defined as the number of people and the amount of relevant information to which they have access; access meaning availability as well as possibility of understanding.

Effectiveness of participation depends on transparency. Besides, transparency is essential for reducing time- and energy-consuming "false" interest conflicts, stemming from a lack of information as to the actual situation, as well as reducing the uncertainty element in decision-making generally.

The development of transparency is atypical. In the early stages there is great transparency because of the comparative simplicity of relationships. On the other hand, in these stages transparency is often obstructed on purpose by the power holders, in recognition of the fact that privileged access to important information can be a decisive instrument of power. Later, there is perhaps less reason for withholding information, as — and if — power centers become more numerous, "countervailing" and controlled, interest clusters more diffuse, and participation more general. But the number of relevant data and the complexity of situations have at the same time increased so much that actual transparency does not manifest a clear trend in any direction. This remains one of the great socio-technical problems and tasks of our time.

d.   The fourth important variable of development is *interest dispersion*, defined as the average number of interests of one individual that are, in principle, of roughly equal motivational significance.

Interest dispersion is increasing as a consequence of the increasing possibility of satisfying basic material needs and as a secondary consequence of a greater complexity of relationships and the larger number of situations which are seen as potentially satisfying for a proliferating and ever more varied list of needs. The consequence is less polarization of communities into clearcut and opposed interest groupings, the expansion of intra-personal situations as compared with situations of interest-divergence; the intra-personal situations being more complex, less fixed, of smaller motivational potential.

In conclusion we might return to the fact of inseparable association between objectives and resources in planning, of what we want to achieve and what means we have to achieve it. This association holds, probably, for all phases of development and is not permanently influenced by the constellation of the variables. Progress in planning seems, therefore, to depend on clarifying our purposes as well as the possible consequences of our actions.

7

PATTERNS OF ADMINISTRATION

What changes in administrative structure and function can be expected to accompany the general social and political development of a society? This question is becoming increasingly important to students of administration. It is worthwhile, therefore, to exchange ideas on this problem based on empirical data collected in societies that have different historical backgrounds and that have developed according to different doctrinal models. The theoretical position of monocratic bureaucracy, related to the corresponding stage in the actual development of administrative patterns, has been stated, classically, by Weber (1921: 111, ch. 6). Theoretical approaches transcending Weber's position, and taking into account new directions of social and political development go back at least to Saint-Simon (1951). Since then the interest in the dynamic relationship between administration and its social environment has become more widespread and there is also more awareness of some fundamental administrative values, of the interplay between technical considerations and human needs and interests in the administrative process.

ASPECTS OF ADMINISTRATION

It is assumed here that administration is concerned simultaneously with two aspects of activities involving people at work: (1) the technical problem of how to achieve optimal results in the overt goal of the common undertaking, and (2) the question of interests motivating people to participate in it.

Technical Processes

The size of the hierarchical superstructure and its demands on the total time budget of the organization tends to increase with the level of complexity of the tasks of the organization. And since communicating through hierarchical channels tends to reduce the time available for actual production, a point of diminishing returns is eventually reached at which hierarchy ceases to be a technically acceptable means of administration.

With a higher level of technology, proliferating specialization of knowledge and skills, and particularly the spread of automation, there is a fundamental change in hierarchical relationships. Initially, hierarchy is the structural result of dividing and subdividing a task into progressively smaller and simpler components until the level of direct operations is reached. The fragmentation of the work process as a main characteristic of industrial operation in the first half of the 20th century is discussed extensively by Friedmann (1956). The lines of subordination and superordination reflect, at least roughly, the differences in responsibility and intellectual difficulty of the work involved. However, higher levels of skill required by greater professional specialization now bring to the lower strata of the organizational hierarchy, to the line of immediate performance, more and more workers who are not inferior in knowledge and skill to their hierarchical superiors. Job ranking ceases to be even a rough indicator, not only of the importance of the incumbent professionally, but even of the relative importance of the position for the overall objective of the organization. To coordinate high-level specialists by hierarchical relationships is technically inefficient, because it is too time consuming, as students of the span of control have already pointed out. Furthermore, hierarchical position is resented by specialists as a means of allocating status and other rewards. Similar ideas about trends of development are expressed by a number of contemporary authors in various countries. The differences among them are the inferences which they draw from their observations. As an example, Hage (1965: 318, N. 75) points to the *exponential growth in occupational specialties* and *the trend towards professionalism*.

Interest Relationships

In the development of interest relationships and in the development of methods for handling conflicts of interest, the classical organization more or less imitates the relationships in its society. Management claims the same kind of authority that power groups exercise in society. In social institutions based on power, conflicts of interests are resolved by the domination of one interest or group of interests over others. In the same way management, purporting to represent the power of ownership or political control — depending on the prevailing economic system — resolves potential or actual conflicts of interests by securing the domination of the interests fundamental to the power system.

With the changes associated with the industrial revolution and the present technological explosion, the territorial systems of sovereign states and their governments face a gradual process of decentralization of power, since increasing numbers of people participate in a larger multiplicity of interest groups as a result of the growing technological and economic opportunities. Therefore, each single interest has less motivating power for the individual than his former paramount concerns of sheer existence. Society is less likely than before to divide itself into clear-cut fundamentally opposed interest camps, and domination will have to make way for compromise and more pluralistic approaches to conflict resolution.

In organizations, this means pressure towards increasing equality of chances for individuals and groups to realize and protect their interests. This pressure is based not only on the growing functional equality in the relationship of the individual jobs to the whole task of the organization, but also on the dispersion of interests just described.

Egalitarian demands stimulate wider participation of all members of the interest coalitions in an organization, Cyert and March (1963) have indicated. This increasing participation does not necessarily nor directly contribute to better technical decisions, but at present, it is the only alternative to solutions enforced by hierarchical power.

MODELS OF ADMINISTRATION

It seems useful to set up a model of administration to study the development from organizational hierarchy and interest domination towards new forms of cooperation — such as teams and work groups — with the equal participation of all members. The model might be represented as a continuum with the traditional structure, *territorial* administration, at one end, and the new tendencies, as far as it is possible to project them into a systematic picture, *functional* administration, at the other. Administration can be defined as the continuing coordination of socially accepted activities aimed at the realization of possibly diverging interests.

Territorial Administration

Territorial administration, named after its most characteristic example: territorial systems of political power, tends to be multi-functional in that it encompasses a number of technically unrelated tasks. Territorial systems are based, technically, on a division of labour; the overall goals of the system, understood as tasks, are divided and subdivided into progressively smaller and simpler parts, subtasks, assigned to individual positions. The resulting pyramidal network is then used to lead and coordinate the whole enterprise through a *chain of command*, a *ladder of advancement*, a *line of reporting and subordination*. These expressions indicate the principal method used to achieve coherence and unity in territorial adminis-tration — by the power of and, ultimately, the monopoly of the means of coercion by the territorial state. Even the most legitimate hierarchical authority depends on the availability of overwhelming force to political governments.

This necessary dependence on power introduces an arbitrary and authoritarian element into the process of defining the various tasks of the territorial system. Furthermore, the system serves the interest of its owners, the political power groups, the providers of funds, and so on, and rewards are distributed and interests satisfied in strict subordination to the dominating interest and according to hierarchical rank. In this type of system, it is assumed that the higher the rank the higher the rewards. In case of conflict of interest within the system or with the environment, the method of resolving conflicts most frequently resorted to is domination based on power.

Functional Administration

Functional administration is at the other end of the continuum. The term refers to the administration of enterprises and institutions organized around a given social function. Such systems tend to be mono-functional; that is, having a single function or a group of technically interrelated functions. Technically, the functional system starts not by dividing the overall task, but by integrating the individual specialists and their expert knowledge and skill into progressively wider and more complex combinations of technically determined functions. The individual and the immediate work group are more important than in a territorial system. Linkage is achieved through mutual technical interdependence of the individuals and the work groups; and the relationship of individuals and the technical activity itself tends to be defined by technical rules, and therefore less subject to arbitrary decisions. Necessarily the level of professional skill and knowledge of the participants in functional organizations tends to be significantly higher than in territorial systems.

Since the determination of technical tasks in functional systems is not arbitrary, there is a much closer link between the technical performance of the system and its possibility to satisfy interests; therefore, the danger of displacement of goals is reduced. This close linkage should make interests more stable and homogeneous than in territorial systems because the possibility of the functional organization to choose among ends as well as among means is limited technically. The theoretical framework sketched here has been partly elaborated in English (Pusić, 1966) and also Pusić, 1964, 1965.

The two models represent the limits of a continuum along which present-day administrative organizations are situated. It seems important, therefore, to find some way of measuring the extent to which the various characteristics of territorial or functional administration are present in concrete administrative organizations. It would then be possible to characterize organizations more suitable for functional relationships or to understand the causes and forms of power and its persistence or reappearance among people at work. The main problem is to find quantifiable indicators for the various dimensions assumed for territorial and functional administration. At first these indicators must be found in relation to a relatively homogeneous administrative system of a single country, then the more difficult problem of making the indicators comparable between countries can be approached. The present study is an attempt to find reliable indicators of the various dimensions of the territorial and functional model as they apply to the administrative system of Yugoslavia.[1]

[1] I would like to acknowledge the work of my colleagues Marija Branica, Ema Derosi-Bjelajac, Ivo Dujmović, Sonja Dvoržak, Ivo Golušić, Ladislav Horvat, Stipo Ivanišević, Željko Pavić, Inge Perko-Šeparović, Stanko Petković, Milan Ramljak, Boris Sorokin, Eugen Zadravec. The project was a common enterprise and all participated in the research work as well as in the theoretical discussions. The author is responsible for writing about the work in a language which is foreign to him. I would also like to thank Professor Jack C. Fisher of Wayne State University and his colleagues for reading the draft of this article and for their useful comments.

DEVELOPMENT OF ADMINISTRATIVE STRUCTURES IN YUGOSLAVIA

In Yugoslavia, governmental policy in the past 20 years has been calculated to speed up the transformation of traditional forms of economic and political administration into new patterns of relationships at work and to promote general participation in decision making.

The fundamental institution to implement this policy is the system of workers' self-management in economic enterprises. Since 1950 all economic enterprises comprising more than five workers have been managed by the workers directly or, if the size of the enterprise is large, by bodies elected by the workers. The basic policy decisions are made by the workers' council, which is elected by all workers. Day-to-day management is by a smaller management board, elected by the council but not necessarily from among its members. The method of choosing the director of the enterprise has varied. Since 1963 he is appointed by the workers' council on the proposal of a commission composed of members of the council and of the communal assembly, the representative body of the local government.

Since 1952 the same system has been introduced, gradually and with various modifications, in the management of institutions in education, health, welfare, social security, culture, communications, science, to name only the most important. Also since 1952 the powers of the communes, the local government units, have been gradually expanded, and their organization has been changed, with the purpose of developing self-governing local communities having a high degree of independence from the central government and functioning as associations of citizens, groups, and organizations. The idea of the commune as a free association and the basic unit of society goes back to Marx (1960). The communes are now governed by a communal assembly, composed of the commune chamber, with members elected by all citizens over 18; and the chamber of working organizations, with members elected by all members of enterprises and institutions within the commune. The assembly elects a number of executive councils and the main officers of the commune — the president and one or two vice-presidents — and appoints the secretary. The day-to-day local administration is carried on by administrative departments and agencies under the policy direction of the executive councils and the general supervision of the secretary. The commune is conceived of as combining the traditional role of local government with the new task of a platform where the various self-managing organizations as well as individuals meet on an equal footing. The importance of the different roles of local units might vary from country to country and within the same country at different times. For a stronger emphasis on the influence of central agencies in an otherwise similar system, see Ostrowski and Przeworski (1965) and Wiatr (1965: 3).

Finally, with the Constitution of 1963, the employees of central governmental agencies participate in decision making within their agencies. In each agency, the employees elect a council to the working community, which has three kinds of responsibilities: 1. decisions for which the council alone is responsible, mainly employee relations and the pay plan; 2. decisions which the council makes in collaboration with the head of the agency, such as internal organization and personnel (in case of disagreement the government, that is, the Executive Council, arbitrates); 3. decisions reserved for the agency head, in which the council can only give consultative opinions. More detailed descriptions of Yugoslav government and administration can be found in Bilandžić (1965), Milivojević (1965), Fischer (1966), Bjeličić (1962), Dordević (1958) and Meister (1965).

Of the four units in the system of self-management, two represent opposite ends of the continuum. Self-management in economic enterprises has the longest history, and here the regulating mechanisms of the market make it easier to dispense with government intervention. Economic enterprises therefore closely approach the functional model of administration. At the other extreme, agencies of government remain largely what they were before: hierarchical organizations and instruments of political power, examples of the territorial model of administration. Self-governing employee councils are only beginning to modify the traditional structure.

The other two units, communes and service institutions, are nearer the middle of the scale. Each has some background of comparable experience: one, the traditions of local self-government in cities and rural areas; the other, instances of earlier institutional self-government — in social security, higher education, non-governmental health and social services, and so on. The significant difference between them is that communes are territorial units, and institutions are defined by and organized around specific functions.

To compare communes and institutions in Yugoslavia from the

point of view of the theoretical models of territorial and functional administrations, beside testing the theory, could have the important practical result of offering guides for future policy in developing self-management systems. *If the commune, in spite of its structural and functional modifications, has retained the characteristics of the territorial model and differs in this respect significantly from institutions practicing self-management, then its anticipated role as an integrated part of the self-management system might well have to be critically reappraised.*

RESEARCH DESIGN AND RESULTS

The objective was to compare the process of administration in communes and in institutions from the point of view of characteristics derived from the theoretical models of territorial and functional administration. Communes and institutions were identified by their legal definitions. Legally, both are determined by prescribed procedures in their formation or the modification or termination of their activities.

Eight conceptual dimensions were derived from models of territorial and functional administration related to their technical as well as to their interests aspects, and indicators were chosen to measure each of these dimensions. Table 1 summarizes the dimensions and indicators.

TABLE 1

Dimensions and indicators for models of territorial and functional administration

Territorial model	Functional model
Technical processes	
Authoritativeness: the prevailing method of settling technical differences	Activity defined by technical rules
Technical differences resolved by hierarchical authority	Tasks defined by technical rules
Authoritative methods used to achieve discipline at work	Perception of difficulty of changing tasks and activities
Dependence on centers of political power	Professionalism and skill
Number of decisions influencing the work process originating outside the organization.	Educational background of personnel
Intensity of outside influences	Level of professional skill of personnel

Interest relationships

Heterogeneity of interests	Satisfaction of interests based primarily on technical activity
Number of interest groups	
Number of conflicts of interest	Perception of influence of various interest groups
Domination: the prevailing method of resolving conflicts	Perception of influence of technical process on interest relationships
Conflicts resolved by domination	Stability of interests
Decisions based on formal authority	Change of interest orientations
	Change of influence

The indicators were tested in 10 communes and 10 institutions of the Zagreb area. The communes were selected from the city, the sub-urban area, and the rural area of the Zagreb district. One institution was selected from each commune and the sample included schools, health centres, social insurance agencies, a theatre, a museum, and a workers' university.

The following instruments were used in the test:

1.   A questionnaire of 25 questions was administered to 210 members of communal assemblies, councils, officers and administrators, as well as to members of councils, management boards, and employees of service institutions. Where more than one member was chosen from one group, no randomizing procedure was applied.

2.   A total of 103 minutes of assemblies, councils, management boards, and workers' meetings, with a total of 770 analytical units was content-analyzed.

3.   Case studies were made of two complex decisions, one in a commune, the other in an institution.

4.   The annual work programmes of the ten communes and the ten institutions were analyzed in order to discover the relationship between tasks determined by technical rules and tasks not so defined.

5.   The legal norms prescribing the responsibilities of the communes were examined for the relative importance of the various sectors in local administration.

In territorial administration, it was expected that even in purely technical decisions, there would be more reliance on the authority of hierarchical position than on technical expertise, and that authority would be used in achieving the necessary cohesion within the organization. This dependence on power would tend to make the individual organization within a territorial system, for example, a commune, more subject to outside influences. It was also expected that both the number of interest groups implicated and the number of interest conflicts within the system, would be greater in territorial systems than in comparable functional systems, and that the organization would rely chiefly on domination and formal authority to terminate conflicts of interests.

TABLE 2

Data on some indicators for models of territorial and functional administration

Indicators	Communes	Institutions	Chi²
Territorial administration	(% of all cases)		
Technical differences resolved by hierarchical authority	27% (277)	18% (201*)	27.69; $p < 0.001$
Methods of achieving discipline			
Authoritative methods used to achieve discipline at work	76%	61%	14.69§; $p < 0.01$
Nonauthoritative methods	19%	36%	14.69§; $p < 0.01$
Other methods	5% (217)	3% (151)	14.69§; $p < 0.01$
Number of decisions influencing the work process originating outside the organization	64% (262)	34% (274*)	48.04§; $p < 0.001$
Intensity of outside influences	35% (322)	17% (289*)	26.16§; $p < 0.001$
Differences in hierarchical rank are not causes of conflict	23% (105)	57.9% (95†)	26.17; $p < 0.001$
Domination in resolving conflicts			
Conflicts resolved by domination	37%	7%	
Conflicts resolved by compromise	56%	70%	
Other methods	7% (129)	23% (100†)	33.48§; $p < 0.001$

Decisions based on formal authority	37%	7%	
	(129)	(100†)	28.12; $p < 0.001$
Functional administrations Tasks defined by technical rules			
Questionnaire	35%	45%	
	(415)	(365*)	8.09; $p < 0.01$
Analysis of minutes	29%	42%	
	(584)	(186‡)	10.01; $p < 0.01$
Analysis of work programs	73%	91%	
	(2841)	(69‡)	11.38; $p < 0.001$
Perception of difficulty of changing tasks and activities	77%	64%	
	(415)	(365*)	15.37; $p < 0.001$
Change experienced as *easy*	7%	15%	
Change experienced as *difficult*	63%	44%	
Undecided	30%	41%	
	(266)	(276)	16.73§; $p < 0.001$
Perception influence of technical process on interest relationships	35%	31%	
	(584)	(186*)	0.73; $p < 0.3$
Change of interest orientation			
Inside groups	75%	83%	
	(493)	(468*)	8.58; $p < 0.001$
Outside groups	63%	61%	
	(655)	(542*)	0.33; $p < 0.8$
Change of influence			
Inside groups	70%	76%	
	(515)	(461*)	4.42; $p < 0.5$
Outside groups	59%	52%	
	(629)	(530*)	4.99; $p < 0.5$

* Number of cases mentioned by respondents in questionnaire
† Number of respondents
‡ Number of items analyzed in minutes and work programs
§ Degree of freedom in computing Chi^2 equals 2

In the functional model, technical activity would tend to be defined by technical rules, therefore changing this activity would be expected to be more difficult than in the more versatile territorial organization with its power potential. This is the same assumption made by Thompson and Bates (1959: 179) that the possibility to change from one goal to another decreases with increased technological specialization. Also the functional system can be expected to have personnel with higher levels of education and skill because the work is more technical.

TABLE 3

Active Interest for the Organization shown by Members

Groups*	Communes N = 246 %	Institutions N = 268 %
Employees	8	19
Leading employees or professionals	11	18
Secretary or director	8	23
Officers or management board	23	12
Elected members or councils	7	10
Citizens or clients	21	9
Members of political[+] organizations	6	2
Members of committees of political organizations	13	3
Members of professional organizations	—	1
Members of higher government units	1	1
Other groups	1	2

* Where two groups are named, the first applies to communes, the second to institutions.
[+] League of Communists of Yugoslavia.
"N" indicates the number of responses. The two columns indicate the percentage of responses stating that the corresponding group *was* showing active interest for the organization (the columns sum to 100% each).

In interest relationships a clearer link can be expected between the technical activity and the satisfaction of interests and greater equality in access to means of interest satisfaction. Also, it is expected that greater dependence of interests on a stable, technically defined activity will result in greater stability of the interests themselves. There would be less frequency of change in interest orientations and the possible directions of change will be constrained by the more restrictive technical framework.

The results are presented in Tables 2-6. Table 2 gives the data on most of the indicators; Tables 3-6 refer to individual indicators.

TABLE 4

Percentage of Conflicts Originating in Opposition of Interests (not by Differences in Technical Opinions) as Perceived by Respondents

Conflicts	Organization*				
	Communes			Institutions	
%	N 106	%		N 93	%
I	II	III		IV	V
100	—	—		1	1
90	5	5		4	4
80	7	7		4	4
70	9	8		4	4
60	12	11		10	12
50	7	7		8	8
40	15	14		8	8
30	10	9		15	16
20	21	20		10	12
10	14	13		20	21
0	6	6		9	10

* Chi² equals 10.83, dif. $= 9, 0.20 < p < 0.30$.
"N" indicates the number of respondents. Columns II and IV indicate the number, and columns III and V the percentage of respondents estimating that the corresponding percentage of conflicts originated in opposition of interests.

TABLE 5

Education and Skill of Employees in Communes and Institutions.

Training	Communes %	Institutions %
Education (N 1.401)		
Higher	13.0	20.0
Secondary	35.2	49.7
Elementary	51.8	30.3
Skill (N 147)*		
Highly skilled	0.4	3.2
Skilled	1.1	9.2
Semi-skilled	0.5	1.0
Unskilled	8.6	8.2

* Blue-collar employees.

TABLE 6

Influence of Professional Groups within the Organization as perceived by Respondents

Influence	Organizations*				
	Communes			Institutions	
%	N = 106	%		N = 97	%
I	II	III		IV	V
0	2	2		3	3
20	33	31		16	16
40	28	26		17	17
50	13	12		18	19
60	22	21		22	23
80	6	6		18	19
100	2	2		3	3

* $Chi^2 = 13.62$, dif. 4, $p < 0.01$
"N" indicates the number of respondents. Columns II and IV indicate the number, and columns III and V the percentage of respondents estimating that in the corresponding percentage of cases influence was exercised by groups within the organization rather than by outside groups.

DISCUSSION AND CONCLUSIONS

The over-all result of the test seems to confirm the hypothesis that administration in communes is nearer to the territorial model and administration in institutions nearer to the functional model. Except on the perception of the difficulty of technical change and the change of interests, where results run counter to expectations; and the inconclusive result on the number of conflicts of interest and the influence of technical processes on interests, all other indicators corroborate the difference hypothesized between territorial and functional administration. Discussion of methodological problems and possible sources of error are omitted for the sake of brevity.

The results might appear obvious, particularly to an observer from a traditional system of local government accustomed to institutions administered by private citizens or nongovernmental organizations. In the Yugoslav system, however, where until 1953 institutions were all administered by the government, administrative independence is comparatively recent. What is even more important, the commune, according to prevailing Yugoslav doctrine, should be different from traditional local government. In the transition to a classless society, the commune is conceived as the first basic unit of a system of self-governing associations. In the commune, just as in service institutions, shops, and factories, citizens should express their interests directly and participate in all the basic decisions affecting themselves and the system as a whole. It was mainly this assumption which was tested in the present research.

In the service institutions, for such indicators as change or stability, heterogeneity of interests, and definition of task, significant differences were found between health centres at one extreme and the workers' university at the other. The first is bound to a given activity by the specificity of the skills, by the kinds of the instruments (X-ray, laboratories, dental units, etc.); the other is free within a very wide general goal, but is constrained by the necessity of negotiating its programmes and the price to be paid for its services by the various clients (factories, institutions, communes, etc.). (The staff of the university consists of a small nucleus of managers employing specialized educators on a part-time basis as the programme may require.)

Several dimensions were identified along which service institutions can be classified to relate them to the functional model:

1. The technical character of the basic activity, such as the relation between the value of fixed assets and number of workers, the degree of specialization, susceptibility to change and innovation, and so on.

2. Frequency of interaction among all members or various groups of members. Members of a university might meet only when meetings are called, whereas members of a planning bureau work and can work only in constant contact with each other. Groups with a higher frequency of interaction can be expected to have a greater influence regardless of the hierarchical position of their members. Smith (1965) thought that the higher frequency of interaction within the wards, as compared with other units of the organization, might be the source of their greater influence. The same inference can be drawn from the results of recent research of integration in the Yugoslav local system. Mlinar (1966: 4) indicated that local communities, subunits of the commune, were better integrated into the commune if they were different in size and composition, because

otherwise the greater frequency of interaction within the local community made them independent of each other and less dependent on the commune.

3. The relationship between production and the nonproductive units. In the Yugoslav system of bookkeeping, productiveness is calculated for each unit, and participation in the distribution of the total income of the organization is based on it. The extent of participation in producing revenue is a constant source of tension between units of higher and lower productivity, especially between line and auxiliary units. These conflicts are similar to those studied by Dalton (1956; 1959: 75ff.). In some organizations, there is a formal difference between units that participate directly in the revenue-producing activity (for instance, teaching in a school, or medical work in a hospital) and those that do not (research, administration, etc.), resulting in the greater influence of the former in decision making.

4. The territorial radius of activity, that is, the location of the users.

5. Technological interdependence with other organizations.

6. The position of the institution in its market, that is, whether it is monopolistic or competitive.

The study indicates that the analytical distinction between the technical aspect and the interest aspect of administration is fundamental. Both the classical school of management (Taylor, Fayol, Gulick, Urwick, etc.) and many authors starting from Weber's frame of reference seem either to ignore this distinction or to proceed on implied assumptions about some uniform interest position of all members of administrative organizations.

Eisenstadt (1959: 303) has pointed out the shifting point of view that results from disregarding this difference, but his own view is restricted in considering only the interests of the political power holders or the organization itself. He does not make it clear that every administrative decision implies some interest, which is not necessarily the interest of those in power or of the bureaucratic organization itself.

For the technical aspect it seems important to distinguish between the work contributing directly to the achievement of the formally accepted objectives of the organization, and the coordinating activities understood by the term administration in its classical sense. The distinction between basic work process and administration corresponds to the categories of programmed and nonprogrammed decisions used by Walter (1966). When the activity is programmed, decisions which remain to be made about it are a matter of administration, and therefore decisions of hierarchical superiors. In nonprogrammed choices, the technical expertise of the subordinates carries greater weight but, probably, only in decisions related to the basic work process, not necessarily to administration. It seems important to distinguish between the two categories of activities when speaking about *proportion of jobs that participate in decision-making* (Hage, 1965: 293). Does the *proportion of administrative jobs* mean those jobs participating in the coordinative decisions of administration, or the proportion of all jobs participating in the technical decisions relating to the direct performance of the basic work process?

Although it is to be expected that eventually administrative activities will depend on the basic work process, discrepancies and lags in the development of one or the other are likely to be common in the change from territorial to functional forms. The characteristics of the basic work process and the administrative process and the relationship between them can be expected to change during development from predominantly territorial systems to mainly functional systems of administration. The relationships, however, between the various characteristics and between their respective rates of change, especially the relationship between the characteristics of administration and those of the basic work process, are a matter for research.

Interests can be related to the basic work process or to the administrative process, and will probably follow a different course of development in the two cases. It is likely that interest allied to administration will, on the whole, tend to be conservative and to exert a retarding influence on the movement from territorial to functional patterns. The relationship is, however, complex enough that almost any combination might be obtained at a given place and time. Crozier (1966) reports about the technical conservatism of lower technical personnel afraid to lose their expertise through the technical progressiveness of the highly educated administrators.

In considering the specific problem of the commune it appears that the idea of the commune as a component part of the self-management system might have to be reappraised. It is possible that the commune, even with most radical measures of decentrali-

zation, remains an integral part of the traditional system of government based on the systematic wielding of political power over people
and therefore intrinsically in opposition to a society-wide system of
self-management.

This answer is tentative partly because of the nonrepresentative
sample in relation to the entire population of Yugoslav communes.
Though the communes and institutions investigated were chosen to
include three different settings — urban centre, urban fringe, and
rural — the sample is not representative of Yugoslavia as a whole.
This limitation must be kept in mind in interpreting the results. But
the main weakness of the research is that it does not take into
account the very important dimension of time. The transition from
the old pattern of government to the new institutions of a self-
governing society might be expected to take some time. It might be
that self-management structures and methods can be adopted more
quickly and more easily in an institutional than in a territorial
setting and that territorial self-management is simply farther off in
time.

There are also other questions that might be considered. Territorial units of general government have a tendency to grow in size
all over the world, a consequence of the increase in the cost of their
services, which are thought to require a constantly broadening
economic base; and of advances in the technology of communication in the widest sense, which makes it possible to service larger
areas and populations. Increasing the size of local units is not likely
to improve conditions for cooperation among their inhabitants.
Creating smaller subunits seems not to be a solution, because
these subunits can have so little influence that people are not
particularly interested in them. Furthermore in an urban setting,
spatial proximity in itself does not necessarily create links among
people; modern man gets more and more used to classifying his
interests and to pursuing their satisfaction in a functional context.

On the other hand, there seem to be obvious territorial aspects to
social life which are not necessarily associated with territorial
centres of political power. Human settlements of any form create
certain types of spatial needs, which require territorially defined
services, local public utilities, etc. If all activities oriented towards a
given group of consumers are conceived as a kind of service, it is
unavoidable to organize institutions for the protection of their
consumers, and one of the requirements for the functioning of this
protection might be its territorial proximity to the activities control-

led. Also, even if political goals and interests might become less local in the future, local association might still be the necessary starting point of political action. Considerations such as these indicate the probability of persistence of territorial forms of organization.

Adapting the research to the complexities of the setting will mean including the stratification of communes and institutions according to several differentiating criteria as well as adding new dimensions to the model. Only then can the characteristics be operationalized, criteria of measurement constructed, and instruments chosen to test them. It would be interesting to have a discussion of the theoretical bases of research efforts among the contributors to this journal.

REFERENCES

Bilandžić, Dušan
  1965 "Social Self-government", *Medunarodna Politika*, 1.
Bjeličić, Sreten
  1962 *Le Système Communale en Yougoslavie* (Beograd: publ. Co. "Jugoslavija").
Crozier, Michel
  1966 "Pour une théorie sociologique de l'action administrative", In George Langrod (ed.), *Traite des Science Administrative* (The Hague: Mouton) 759-780.
Cyert, Richard M., and James G. March
  1963 *A Behavioral Theory of the Firm* (Englewood Cliffs, N. J.: Prentice-Hall).
Dalton, Melville
  1956 "Conflicts between Staff and Line Managerial Officers", *American Sociological Review*, 15: 342-351.
  1959 *Men Who Manage: Fusions of Feeling and Theory in Administration* (New York: Wiley).
Dordević, Jovan
  1958 "Politique ét technique sociales en democratie socialiste", *Politique et Technique*.
Eisenstadt, S. N.
  1959 "Bureaucracy, Bureaucratization, and Debureaucratization", *Administrative Science Quarterly*, 4 (December): 301-320.
Fischer, Jack C.
  1966 *A Multinational State: Regional Difference and Administrative Response* (San Francisco: Chandler).
Friedmann, Georges
  1956 *Le Travail en Miettes: Spécialisation et Loisirs* (Paris: Gallimard).

Hage, Jerald
1965 "An Axiomatic Theory of Organization", *Administrative Science Quarterly*, 10 (December): 289-320.

Marx, Karl
1960 "Der Bürgerkrieg in Frankreich", in Karl Marx and Freidrich Engels, *Ausgewählte Schriften*, I (Berlin: Dietz Verlag), 446-518.

Meister, Albert
1965 *Socialisme et Autogestion*: *L'Experience Yougoslave* (Paris: Editions du Seuil.)

Milivojević, Dragoljub
1965 "The Yugoslav Commune", *Medunarodna Politika*, 8.

Mlinar, Zdravko
1966 *Social Participation of Citizens in the Local Community*. Information Bulletin No. 20 (Ljubljana: Inštitut za sociologjo in filozofijo pri Univerzi v Ljubljani).

Ostrowski, Krzystof, and Przeworski Adam (eds.)
1965 *Local Political System in Poland* (Warsaw: Institute of Philosopy and Sociology. Polish Academy of Sciences).

Pusić, Eugen
1964 *Upravljanje Društvenim Poslovima* (Zagreb: Zbornik Visoke upravne škole).

1965 *Mehanizmi Integracije u Funkcionalnom Upravljanju* (Zagreb: Zbornik Visoke upravne škole).

1966 "The Political Community and the Future of Welfare", in John Morgan (ed.), *Welfare and Wisdom* (Toronto: University of Toronto).

Saint-Simon, Henri de
1951 *L'Organisateur* (Paris: Editions Sociales).

Smith, Dorothy E.
1965 "Front-line Organization of the State Mental Hospital", *Administrative Science Quarterly*, 10 (December): 381-399.

Thompson, James D., and Frederick L. Bates
1959 "Technology, Organization, and Administration", in J. D. Thompson et al., *Comparative Studies in Administration* (Pittsburgh: University of Pittsburgh).

Walter, Benjamin
1966 "Internal Control Relations in Administrative Hierarchies", *Administrative Science Quarterly*, 11 (September): 179-206.

Weber, Max
1921 "Die Bürokratie", in: *Wirtschaft und Gesellschaft, Grundriss der Sozialökonomik*, III (Tübingen: Springer).

Wiatr, Jerzy J.
1965 "Socialist Industrialization. The Political System. The Local System", in Krzystof Ostrowski and Adam Przeworski (eds.), *Local Political System in Poland* (Warsaw: Institute of Philosophy and Sociology, Polish Academy of Sciences).

8

AREA AND ADMINISTRATION IN
YUGOSLAV DEVELOPMENT

The relationship between the size of governmental units and the quality of the administrative process in them appears sometimes as the dilemma between efficiency in the abstract and usefulness from the point of view of the individual citizen. The argument runs, roughly, as follows: the larger the territory of a governmental unit the better, on the average, its position with regard to resources. Other things being equal, more territory means more fiscal and other income immediately translatable into increased administrative capability.[1] There is also a pronounced factor of economy size in administration, so that territorially small units are uneconomical or even outright incapable of performing the administrative functions required of them.[2] On the political side as well larger units have advantages derived from their more abundant resources. They provide a larger pool of political talent and will be less likely to fall under the excessive political influence of a few people.[3] Also, being richer, they can be politically more independent of central government which exercises its political influence through financial grants and assistance.

On the other hand, from the point of view of the individual, in smaller units government is more accessible to the citizen. He is within a short distance of the town hall; the local council—as the political arm of the citizenry—can better control local services when these are small and overseeable, and there are specific services involving proximity to the 'consumer'.[4] Also, any real participation of citizens in the local political process is decisively limited by the territorial factor. As a local unit becomes larger so the political

---

[1] Arnold Köttgen, "Wesen und Rechtsform der Gemeinden und Gemeindeverbände", in: Hans Peters, *Handbuch der kommunalen Wissenschaft und Praxis*, I Band, p. 228, Berlin, 1956.
[2] Harold F. Alderfer, *American Local Government and Administration* (New York, 1956), pp. 14 and 18.
[3] John Stuart Mill, *Representative Government* (London, 1957), p. 352.
[4] J. Herwald Morris, *Local Government Areas* (London, 1960), p. 107.

interest of the inhabitants further from the centre tends to decrease, their image of the political process to become hazy, their actual ability to be present at various political functions and activities in the centre to diminish. People are always more ready to identify politically with the traditional small, unit, so only the small unit can perform the role of a "school of democracy".[1]

The dilemma between the tendency towards administrative enlargement of scale[2] and the opposite demand for keeping local units small cannot be solved, so the argument continues, by finding the ideal compromise size. The standard remedies recommended are various tiers of local government—an upper tier for carrying the main burden of local services and a lower tier for keeping close contact with the citizens, or associations of small local units for the common organization of services which are too costly for each of them individually.

All these arguments are plausible enough at first sight. The problem is that they are difficult to test, to start with, because local government areas, as a rule, change slowly, haphazardly, and not many at a time. Such changes do not depend exclusively, or even mainly, on rational consideration of the dilemma of size. They are the result of history, are influenced by political expediency, and subject to innumerable coincidences of personality and other specific factors of time and place. And so traditional administrative science continues to move in the world of prescription and counter-prescription which is essentially timeless, whereas administrative development proceeds in a different dimension of pressures and counter-pressures, of push and inertia.

The development of local government areas in Yugoslavia during the last twenty years is, in this context, a case apart.

The special form of partisan warfare which armed resistance in Yugoslavia assumed during the Second World War resulted in a large number of small local units, comparatively independent of each other and of the central government, which constituted the political background of, and gave logistic support to, the operating military units. A year after the end of the war there were still over 11,000 basic local units, local people's committees, responsible for

---

[1]   H. F. Alderfer, *op. cit.*, p. 20.
[2]   H. A. Brasz and Gerard J. Heyne den Bak, *The Regionalization of Public Administration in the Netherlands: Fact and Failure* (Amsterdam, 1968), p. 12.

an average area of just over 20 square kilometres and an average population of some 1,300.

During the first phase of public ownership, local enterprises (small factories, shops, catering and service undertakings) were controlled and managed by local government. Local government bodies and officials appointed the directors and managers of such enterprises, provided the resources and took the main decisions as to capital investment, production and sales. In a later phase, when workers' management was introduced as a system, local bodies and officials remained responsible for the control of economic enterprises, and planning local economic development. This was accomplished less by administrative interference and more by cooperation in the provision of the infrastructure necessary for the growth of such enterprises. It is important to note that these special responsibilities given to local units at a time of economic dynamism tended to overshadow their more traditional functions and to distract them from their role of providing local services for the population.

Actually, Yugoslav local government found itself faced with the task of providing local services in a situation of accelerated urban development and parallel rural deterioration, with the additional handicap that the economic resources of the country were strained to the utmost by capital investments in industry. In spite of considerable, and sometimes imaginative efforts, city administrations were often unable to deal adequately with the rising tide of demands made upon them. Standards of service declined (for example in road maintenance, street cleaning, upkeep of parks). On the other hand, local governments in rural areas found themselves drained of resources and personnel, and unable to improve the rural environment and thereby help to reduce the flight to the cities.

These pressures brought about a vast movement towards expanding the size of local governmental units. At each step the well-known rationale of increasing administrative and political efficiency by maximizing territory was invoked. The rather startling results are shown in Table 1. The average size of the basic local unit—the local people's committee until 1952, the commune after that (cities having lost their separate administrative identity in 1955)— has increased more than twenty times in twenty years to some 500 square kilometres with about 40,000 inhabitants.

TABLE 1

Year	Region	Districts	Cities	Communes	Local People's Committees
1946	2	407	81		11 556
1947	2	338	85		7 886
1948	1	339	88		7 967
1949	23	344	198		7 782
1950	20	360	236		7 101
1951		360	236		7 104
1952		327	265	3 811	
1953		327	264	3 904	
1954		329	268	3 912	
1955		107		1 479	
1956		107		1 479	
1957		106		1 441	
1958		95		1 193	
1959		91		1 103	
1960		75		839	
1961		75		782	
1962		75		759	
1963		40		581	
1964		40		577	
1965		40		577	
1966		23		516	
1967		17		510	
1968		—		501	

Source: *Statistical Yearbook of the Socialist Federal Republic of Yugoslavia*, 1968, p. 62.

Whatever the other consequences of this expansion—unique in numbers, speed and proportion—may have been, it made the problem of testing the current assumptions about the dilemma of size both more pressing and easier to tackle.

Several questions relating to the dilemma of size were singled out for research, among them the following:

1. Does increase in size of local units result in an increase in revenue and, consequently, in better local administration?
2. Is distance from the centre of the township or commune a factor

in the citizen's interest in local affairs and the activities of local government?

3. Is distance from the centre a factor in the personal composition of the various decision-making bodies in the centre of the commune?

4. What is the actual pattern of the various activities of the governmental unit in the commune as compared with the image of this pattern held by local officials?

The methods employed were chosen with a view to obtaining in a minimum of time, maximum information for the orientation of research underway.[1]

An analysis of the principal components of twenty-five variables for 514 communes in Yugoslavia and of fifty variables as well as a factor analysis of the same data for all communes in the Republic of Croatia—one of the federated units of Yugoslavia—was made. The data for all communes in Yugoslavia were virtually those published in the official statistical yearbook of Yugoslavia for 1967, while for Croatia additional data were obtained from special publications by the Institute of Public Administration of Croatia for the year 1966.

A total of 825 citizens of a predominantly rural commune in Croatia were interviewed on the basis of a questionnaire containing nineteen items. The citizens were divided into three experimental groups ($N=244$, 243, 217) and one control group ($N=121$). The three experimental groups were the total population of three villages comparable in all features except distance from the central locality of the commune, the respective distances being 6, 11 and 20 kilometres with similar roads and transport facilities. In contrast with the predominantly rural character of the experimental groups, the control group was chosen from among the workers in an industrial enterprise situated in the central locality of the commune.

The addresses of 574 officials (elected members of the communal assembly, officers of the communal administration, officers of important non-governmental organizations and institutions) in the same commune were classified under five categories: centre, less than 5 km, 5-10 km, over 10 km, outside the commune territory.

[1] The research was designed and carried out in the Administrative Research Division of the Institute of Social Research of the University of Zagreb. The research team included, beside the author, B. Aviani, M. Branica, E. Derosi-Bjelajac, I. Dujmović, S. Dvoržak, I. Golušić, L. Horvat, S. Ivanišević, Z. Pavić, I. Perko-Separović, S. Petković, M. Ramljak, and B. Sorokin.

TABLE 2

	Rotated factors						
	I	II	III	IV	V	VI	VII
Budget:: revenue per inhabitant	0.697[1]	0.107	−0.079	−0.035	−0.023	−0.068	−0.233
Expenditure on schools per inhabitant	0.522	0.019	−0.117	−0.163	−0.307	−0.144	−0.004
Number of inhabitants per employee in local administration	−0.040	−0.351	0.251	0.122	0.243	−0.309	0.024
Number of items received per 1,000 inhabitants	0.041	0.332	−0.388	−0.130	−0.079	0.167	−0.159
Number of items transacted per employee	0.025	0.023	−0.023	0.007	0.083	−0.064	−0.055
Education of employees in local administration (percentages)							
University	0.325	0.256	0.041	0.071	0.022	−0.256	0.016
College	0.106	−0.112	0.338	−0.030	0.022	−0.023	0.148
Secondary school	0.046	−0.076	−0.146	0.071	−0.134	0.012	0.831
Elementary school	−0.275	−0.016	−0.089	−0.123	0.068	0.121	−0.738
Local budget (percentages)							
Personnel expenditure	0.067	0.104	−0.256	−0.462	0.038	−0.082	0.288
Material expenditure	−0.217	0.126	−0.066	−0.545	0.174	0.059	−0.101

[1] The communality of the seven factors is 56.54 per cent. All correlations above 0.50 are italicized.

In ten communes grouped under three heads (urban, suburban, rural) 211 officials were interviewed on what they considered the most important task of the commune. At the same time 329 items from the minutes of communal decision-making bodies in the same communes during the last quarter of 1965 were content-analysed in order to discover the frequency of the various tasks.

The results of the statistical analysis indicated that the process of industrialization and urbanization is the principal factor concerning which communes in Yugoslavia differ (Table 2). There is a significant correlation between this factor and several indicators of the financial capacity of the commune, whereas none could be discovered between this—or practically any other—factor and the indicators of administrative quality.

Indicators of size (in square kilometres and number of inhabitants) however, show a much less clear relationship both to financial and administrative capacity (Table 3).

TABLE 3

Financial indicators	Area of commune (km^2)		No. of inhabitants	
	All communes	Non-urban communes	All communes	Non-urban communes
Budget: revenue in absolute terms	0.217	*0.562*	*0.852*	*0.854*
Budget: revenue *per capita*	—0.190	—0.193	0.020	*—0.671*
Total income of commune in absolute terms	0.179	*0.522*	*0.907*	*0.929*
Total income of commune *per capita*	—0.291	—0.382	—0.348	*—0.510*

The data relate to the 111 communes of Croatia. Correlations larger than 0.50 are italicized. "Total income" includes, beside the budget, separate funds for special purposes (such as roads, education, child welfare, public utilities and urban infrastructure, etc.) which are not included in the budget but are subject to the decisions of and control by the communal assembly, the representative body of local government.

Size is positively related to the total absolute amount of financial resources available to the commune. The correlation is, understandably, higher when non-urban communes only are compared. It reaches its maximum when size is measured not by territory but by number of inhabitants. But size is, on the whole, negatively correlated with *per capita* public income, and significantly so for non-urban communes where size is defined by population.

There is no significant relationship between territory and indicators of local administration and, more surprisingly, between financial capacity and administration as Table 4 shows.

TABLE 4

	Area (km²)	Budget: revenue per inhabitant
Number of inhabitants per employee in local administration	0.160	—0.076
Number of items transacted per 1,000 inhabitants	—0.048	0.080
Number of items transacted per employee	—0.187	0.025
Education of employees in local administration (percentages)		
University	—0.101	0.257
College	0.121	—0.037
Middle school	—0.190	—0.063
Elementary	—0.129	—0.077
Local budget (percentages)		
Personnel expenditure	—0.146	0.053
Material expenditure	0.008	—0.077

The data cover the 111 communes of Croatia. Not a single coefficient of correlation reaches even the threshold of significance, the absolute value of 0.32.

The results of the survey of local orientations and the influence of distance on the image of the local authority are known here only in relation to the interest exhibited by the respondents for various roles in the commune and, within its service-role, for the typical groups of services.

Three main roles of the commune were abstracted from the responses and defined as "power", "service", and "coordination". "Power" includes all activities of local administration where the local body acts as part of the general machinery of government in the exercise of its coercive authority, primarily concerning activities falling within the categories of "law and order" and "finance".

"Service" means all activities performed directly on behalf of the citizens, in order to satisfy a specific need of the population. Finally, "coordination" covers all processes at work within local decision-making bodies (the communal assembly, the various communal councils) where individual and local group interests confront each other and solutions are reached through consultation and bargaining without resort to manifestations of power.

The questions were designed to elicit which of the commune's roles interested the respondent most.

In Table 5 N indicates the number of times a role was mentioned in response to a question. As certain respondents mentioned several of the commune's roles as being important in their view, the number of responses is larger than the number of respondents.

The differences between the three zones are of little statistical significance. Where the figures are larger (e.g. 15.4 per cent of "don't know" answers in Zone I), they run counter to the expectation of greater interest to be found nearer to the centre. The control group shows, by comparison, an even more clearly pronounced interest in the service-role of the commune, a better understanding of its coordinating role than the experimental groups, and a quasi-total absence of interest in its power-role.

TABLE 5

Role of commune	Zone I[1]		Zone II[1]		Zone III[1]		Control group	
	N	%	N	%	N	%	N	%
Service	282	72.5	385	79.4	308	78.1	165	93.8
Power	41	10.5	47	9.7	41	10.4	2	1.1
Coordination	6	1.5	2	0.4	5	1.3	9	5.1
Don't know	60	15.4	51	10.5	40	10.2	—	—
Total	389	99.9	485	100	394	100	176	100

($\chi^2 = 10.55$; $0.01 < P < 0.05$ (only for experimental groups))

[1] Distances from the centre of the commune: Zone I, 6 km; Zone II, 11 km; Zone III, 20 km.

Within the service-role of the commune Table 6 shows how interest in the various services is unevenly distributed among the respondents in the three zones.

The interest in public utilities decreases with increasing distance from the centre, while the interest in health services, on the contrary, increases in Zones II and III. The interest in economic services (the investment by the commune in small industries and shops, agricultural extension services, forestry etc.) is considerably higher in Zone I and III than in Zone II; education is interesting in Zone II, social welfare in Zone III. There is no pattern which could relate these differences to the factor of distance from the centre. In all zones the interest in public utilities dominates all other interests.

TABLE 6

Commune as service	Zone I[1]		Zone II[1]		Zone III[1]		Control group	
	N	%	N	%	N	%	N	%
Public utilities	214	75.9	264	68.6	162	52.6	127	73.0
Health services	13	4.6	64	16.6	38	12.3	1	4.6
Economic services	48	17.0	15	3.9	71	23.1	26	15.7
Educational services	4	1.4	33	8.6	10	3.2	10	6.1
Social welfare services	3	1.1	9	2.3	27	8.8	1	0.6
Don't know	—	—	—	—	—	—	—	—
Total	282	100	385	100	308	100	165	100

$(\chi^2 = 120.6; P < 0.001$ (only for experimental groups)

[1] Distances from the centre of the commune: Zone I, 6 km; Zone II, 11 km; Zone III, 20 km.

TABLE 7

Main influence	Zone I[1]		Zone II[1]		Zone III	
	N	%	N	%	N	%
The commune generally	38	10.6	39	7.6	43	14.8
Representative bodies	33	9.2	20	3.9	22	7.6
Individual member of representative body	49	13.6	76	14.9	25	8.6
Individual elected officer	19	5.3	86	16.8	26	8.9
Administration	27	7.5	15	2.9	51	17.4
Direct action by citizens, their groups and organizations	52	14.4	34	6.7	28	9.6
Nobody	6	1.7	9	1.7	15	5.2
Don't know	135	37.6	223	43.5	61	21.0
Total	359	99.9	502	98.0	271	93.1

$(\chi^2 = 172.55; P < 0.001$ (only for experimental groups)

[1] Distances from the centre of the commune: Zone I, 6 km; Zone II, 11 km; Zone III, 20 km.

The respondents were then asked (Table 7) how they envisage the influence, in relation to those of the commune's problems which are of the greatest interest to them, distributed among the various political elements within and around the commune.

Again there are a number of interesting differences among the zones. The proportion of "don't know" answers in Zone II is more than twice as large as in Zone III, though the assumption of greater interest correlated with shorter distance would lead one to expect something different. The belief in the effectiveness of direct action by citizens in Zone I is significantly more pronounced than it is in Zone II, with Zone III in between. The individual elected officer (in most cases the mayor of the commune) is seen as considerably more influential in Zone II, and the local administrative machinery in Zone III. Whatever the reason for these differences (at present only a matter for guesswork), they do not fall into a territorial pattern which would confirm the assumption that, with increasing distance, the image of the commune in the eyes of the inhabitants changes in a predictable way, and more particularly, that people farther away from the centre know less about the workings of the central communal machinery.

To the related question of how respondents would like to see the influence on local affairs which are of greatest interest to them distributed, the largest proportion of "don't know" answers— indicating lack of interest in the question—came from Zone I (38.9) compared with 34.1 from Zone II and 17.8 from Zone III.

It is interesting to compare these results with the answers to the question how respondents view the distribution of influence and power in the commune generally, without relating this influence to the problems which concern them as citizens (Table 8).

Here again the differences relating to distance from the centre of the commune run counter to expectations, the percentage of "don't know" answers being the smallest in Zone III. In comparison with Table 7, the image is much more "monarchial", vesting the main power in the person of the mayor. Also, there is less belief in the general influence of the individual member of the elected body ("our representative") than in his influence on the comparatively small matters of everyday concern to the population. Here again, Zone III shows a significantly greater belief in the power of professional administrators than any of the other groups.

The location of local officers in various organizations indeed shows a very strong bias in favour of the centre. Each addressee was

TABLE 8

Influential group	Zone I[1]		Zone II[1]		Zone III[1]		Control group	
	N	%	N	%	N	%	N	%
Commune generally ("they in the commune")	4	1.6	3	1.2	6	2.5	4	3.0
Representative bodies	11	4.3	14	5.6	5	2.1	22	16.5
Individual member of representative body	12	4.7	4	1.6	19	7.9	5	3.8
Individual elected officer	71	28.0	84	33.3	79	32.7	78	58.6
Administration	10	3.9	10	4.0	59	24.5	6	4.5
Direct action by citizens, their groups and organizations	9	3.6	4	1.6	3	1.2	5	3.8
Nobody	—		—		—		—	
Don't know	137	53.9	132	52.3	64	26.6	13	9.8

$(\chi^2 = 132.99; P < 0.001$ (only for experimental groups)

[1] Distances from the centre of the commune: Zone I, 6 km; Zone II, 11 km; Zone III, 20 km.

checked for change of address after the election to his present office and no significant changes were found (Table 9).

The members of the Communal Council—the general political chamber of the Communal Assembly—are elected by all citizens over 18. Some of them do not live in the territory in which they were elected, but there is a very strong tendency for influential persons in the social system of the commune to live in or near its centre.

The results for the pattern of communal tasks were divided into four main groups, three of them comparable to the types already mentioned: commune as "power", as "service", and as "coordination"; the fourth "internal administration" being introduced in order to account for staff-tasks not clearly related to any of the other types. Table 10 lists the responses (R) of the 211 officers and officials in ten communes alongside the results of the content-analysis of 329 items from the minutes (M) for three main groups of communes: urban, suburban, and rural.

The striking difference between image and reality concerns the roles of "power" and "service". While officials of the commune consider the "service" role more important, most of the business transacted by the communal decisionmaking bodies is related to the power role.

TABLE 9

Organization and office	Centre	Under 5 km	5-10 km	Over 10 km	Outside of commune	Total
Number of voters	5 035	8 334	6 667	3 981		24 017
Communal assembly						
Communal Council	13	17	17	7	5	54
Council of Working Organizations	31	6	2	1	5	49
Communal administration	94	30	10	6	10	150
Political organizations	90	22	10	17	2	141
Non-governmental organizations	79	16	7	2	5	109
Enterprises and institutions	44	14	3	2	12	75
Total absolute number of officers	351	105	49	35	34	574
Percentages	61.15	18.29	8.54	6.10	5.92	100.0

The above results suggest some answers to the initial questions. Current assumptions about the relationship between the size of territorial units and the administrative process within them have not been confirmed. It would be definitely too early to say that these assumptions have been falsified. However, a more critical attitude towards them seems to be indicated, and a deeper analysis of the complex relation between territory and administration necessary.
1.   There is a widespread belief, not only in Yugoslavia, that the expansion of local territorial units is a constantly present tendency springing from the need for more resources and the concomitant impulse towards higher standards of administration. (In Yugoslavia this expansion was simply quicker and more pronounced than elsewhere.)

The results of the present research do not bear out this belief. No significant correlation was found between size and resources for communes generally, and for non-urban communes a correlation over 0.50 is shown only in relation to the absolute amount of income, not to its proportion per inhabitant. The same is true when popula-

TABLE 10

	Urban (%)		Suburban (%)		Rural (%)		Average (%)	
	R	M	R	M	R	M	R	M
Power	11.8	50.7	5.0	39.4	9.2	44.8	9.0	45.5
Service	47.6	19.1	72.5	14.4	57.5	22.0	57.8	18.7
Coordination	18.8	16.9	5.8	33.7	22.0	21.2	16.2	23.2
Administration	21.7	13.3	16.7	12.5	11.2	12.0	16.9	12.7
Total	99.9	100.0	100.0	100.0	99.9	100.0	99.9	100.1

tion is substituted as a measure of size, though this is by no means equivalent (increase of population is due more to urbanization than to an increase in area). There is even a noticeable negative correlation between number of inhabitants in non-urban communes and the *per capita* income of the commune. This points to the tentative conclusion that, from the point of view of services to be performed for the population the large commune is less fortunately situated than the smaller unit. If we take the service-consuming inhabitant as the measure for the size of the task of the communal service network and its financial responsibility, then the larger commune must assume a greater financial burden with fewer resources per inhabitant to help carry it. If, in spite of this, we see local units constantly expanding in size, with the argument of more resources being constantly invoked, one possible explanation is that the resources referred to are not those needed for services to the population but for other communal purposes, primarily as an agent of governmental power. We shall return to this aspect in our conclusions.

This suspicion is strengthened when we see that the principal indicators of administrative quality are unrelated not only to size but also to the factor of industrialization and urbanization and even to actual budgeted revenue. This datum makes the units of local government appear as parts of a general system, staffed and financed according to centrally-determined standards, and not really dependent on the economic and financial capacities present in the area under their jurisdiction. The existing system of central grants to local governments which cannot meet central standards makes this explanation even more plausible. This, however, contradicts the image of the commune as the independent expression of the community of citizens in its area, primarily serving their needs and subject to their authority.

2. On the other hand, it is accepted doctrine that the tendency towards territorial expansion of local units must be checked in order that these may not reach the size at which the interest and participation of citizens at the periphery cease to be forthcoming.

The commune where this doctrine was spot-tested is the result of twenty years of expansion. It includes many former basic local units, its territory is mountainous, ordinary transport and communication facilities are below average, the population is mainly composed of small peasants. It is a case where, if anywhere, the theory that interest for communal affairs abates with distance from the centre should have been proved correct. However, it was not. The interest of the population for local affairs (what there is of it) is more or less evenly spread over all distances, and if there are differences they point rather the other way. People are mainly interested in the services the commune is expected to render. This is even truer of the urban workers than of the peasants in the three zones which acknowledge the presence of the commune-as-power. Their image of who-can-do-what in the commune also does not depend on distance from the centre, though it is interesting for other reasons. It features the mayor as the powerful figure in communal affairs generally; but in negotiating the needed services it is more ready to resort to methods closer to self-help (individual member elected in the local area; direct action by the citizens themselves).

3. Distance from the centre of the commune does, however, affect very much an inhabitant's opportunities to participate in the leadership of various organizations in the commune, including the communal government. The selection which operates may be due to perfectly natural causes (e.g., difficulties of speedy transportation); but the fact remains that a citizen living in the central locality of the commune seems to have ten times as many chances of being elected to communal office as one living only some 11 kilometres away.

4. It is not only the people who consider service more important than power. Responsible communal officials and elected officers see their role and the role of the commune as being essentially to provide needed services to the population and develop the area in question into a progressive community of happy people. This idea is so strong that it influences decisively their notions of what the commune is actually doing. When asked about this, they dwell on the service tasks, underestimating the activities of government-as-power by about five times. That this is not due to their contempt for ad-

ministrative routine is shown by the fact that they tend rather to over-estimate a little the internal staff work performed in the various agencies and institutions within the commune.

The implications of the above for the development of local government and administration could be far-reaching.

The commune is seen at present mainly as an instrument of government. To see it as an autonomous community embodying the free consensus of the citizens and subject to their collective will and decision is an elusive ideal. The danger of such an attitude lies in tending to obscure the facts of local political life. Not only is the commune still very much defined by its power role, but there is a tendency towards the formation of local élites, centralized within the communal area, looking towards the central government instead of towards the local population, judging communal affairs, resources and capacities, in the last resort, from the institutional point of of view of strengthening, enlarging and stabilizing the commune as a governmental and organizational system. The constructive function of the commune as a service-centre serves, often probably unconsciously, as a legitimizing ideology.

There is, however, a much more practical and acute aspect of this discrepancy between communal image and reality. The old territorial power system, of which the commune-as-government is an integral part, is no longer the ideal instrument for providing services which, with the onrush of industrialization and urbanization, are becoming necessities. To have the million inhabitants of a city come together in one meeting place and decide their concerns after wise deliberation to their common satisfaction might be Utopia. But to have roads, sewers, water-mains, electricity, gas, local transportation, sanitation, parks, schools, recreation facilities is certainly not utopian. And, if we read the indications contained in this research correctly, people are clearly aware of the importance of these practical aspects of local government. Beyond the governmental reality of the commune, beyond its communal ideology, both citizens and local officials—in rural as in urban areas—concentrate on the local services it renders.

This situation implies a reappraisal of the relationship between area and function. The various aspects of what was traditionally a multifunctional local unit exhibit an increasingly strong centrifugal tendency. The local area, as part of the larger system of government, is the conservative element in this combination. Circumscribed by fixed boundaries, its jurisdiction defined, based on its power to coerce and, incidentally, to collect taxes, local government acts as the central agency on which all activities in the area depend.

Local service institutions, however, fit less and less well into this framework. Based, as they are, on functional, institutional forms of organization, free of coercion in their technical activity, able to finance themselves by user charges and other forms of financing independent of general taxation, with a rather fluid area of action, different for each service, tending to associate into larger functional networks, they begin to look upon their dependence on local government more often as an inhibition than as a support.

There is, again, a territorial aspect to local services, not necessarily related to government but involving very decidedly the interests of the population. A number of services owe their existence simply to the fact that there is some form of settlement. These 'specifically local' services are indispensable if normal life is to go on and cannot, therefore, be left to the discretion of an individual. They have to be organized, to function, to charge acceptable rates even if enjoying a virtual monopoly. There must exist an organization for the protection of the local service-consumer. This is another function of local government (this time as the representative of the population) with other requirements as to organization and, possibly, to area than the ones arising out of both the arbitrarily fixed boundaries of government and the fluid gravitational lines of the service institutions themselves.

There is also the aspect of the interest-confrontation between different services, faced with scarce resources, and without a technical criterion of comparison between each other. Is it more important to repair the theatre or to build a new sewage-collector when resources are not sufficient to do both at once? There should be a platform where such questions can be decided. But the area over which this adjustment-mechanism can function optimally should, again, be not necessarily the same as the territorial definition of the other functions.

There is, also, the problem of technical contacts between different service networks. How to coordinate all the services interested in the ground beneath the surface of the roads? How to bring together the health service and the educational network in order to organize a school medical service? The contact points within the network can be organized at any level. Sometimes circumstances may require that this level be fairly close to the operations themselves and therefore "local". But there is nothing fixed, permanent or predetermined in this respect. Much greater elasticity in adjustment will probably be needed than that available under the rigid local government system of today.

Local government today is possibly facing a process of decomposition whereby its functions will gradually be absorbed by regional and higher levels and, in the first place, by institutions and service networks. But this will usher in the new, and probably much more complex question of providing novel, more versatile forms of integration adapted to the interdependent world society of our day.

APPENDIX

A REAPPRAISAL OF THE UNITED NATIONS SOCIAL
SERVICE PROGRAMME

*(U.N. Document No. E/CN.5/AC.12/L.3/Add.1 submitted to the
Ad Hoc Working Group on Social Welfare, 17th February 1965)*

The original UN Document also included a section on Policy Developments (Chapter
II) and Chapter IV "Problems of Organization and Coordination". These have been
omitted here in view of their irrelevance to the contents of this volume.

FOREWORD

This report has been prepared in accordance with resolution 903 D (XXXIV) adopted by the Economic and Social Council on 2 August 1962. It represents one part of a continuing effort by the United Nations to evaluate its activities, including the technical assistance programme, in the social field. A report[1] on the first five years (1947-1951) of the programme of advisory social welfare services established by General Assembly resolution 418 (V) was submitted to the Social Commission in 1952. A second evaluation[2] covering the period 1 January 1953 to 31 December 1959 was prepared for the thirteenth session of the Social Commission.

The Economic and Social Council in its resolution referred to above requested the Secretary-General of the United Nations to "...reappraise, particularly considering the needs of developing countries for family, child and youth welfare services, the United Nations social service programme, including the technical assistance programme and the increased activities with the United Nations Children's Fund and the regional economic commissions in this field, and to prepare recommendations for strengthening the United Nations social service programme for consideration at the fifteenth session of the Social Commission..."[3]

The objective and scope of the proposed reappraisal were elaborated in a memorandum prepared by the United Nations Secretariat for the guidance of the consultant appointed to make the present study. According to this memorandum, it was not intended that the reappraisal should be an evaluation in the sense of systematically measuring results, nor merely a comprehensive account of

---

[1] *Evaluation of the Programme of Advisory Social Welfare Services, 1947-1951,* United Nations publication, Sales No.: 52.IV.18.
[2] "Evaluation of Selected Aspects of United Nations Technical Assistance Activities in the Social Field". United Nations, E/CN.5/350 and Corr.1.
[3] *Official Records of the Economic and Social Council, Thirty-Fourth Session, Supplement No. 1* (E/3671), p. 15.

the achievements and limitations of the programme as an isolated or fragmented approach to specialized social needs and problems; rather, the study should undertake an examination of the United Nations social service programme in terms of its present and potential place and contribution to social development, taking into account particularly the needs of the developing countries within the comprehensive framework of the United Nations programme, and an exploration of the most effective ways of using available resources to assist countries interested in establishing, extending or upgrading their social service programmes, especially those for family, child and youth welfare.

The present reappraisal, which focuses mainly on policy and programme developments during the period 1959-63, is intended to open a perspective on future developments of the United Nations social welfare programme without specifying the content of the programme or the methods to be employed, except that they should promise definite results in accelerating and facilitating national development.

The underlying concepts and findings of this study are presented in four parts containing respectively:

I.   An elaboration of the underlying considerations against which the United Nations social welfare programme was examined, including concepts of national development and social change, the specific social situations characteristic of the different aspects of change and the social services designed to cope with them.

II.   A discussion of the development of United Nations policy in the social welfare field and of the impact of the various programmes, particularly within the period 1959-1963.

III.   A prospective view on the United Nations social welfare programme, given the particular possibilities and the distinctive limitations of United Nations action and the evolving needs of the developing countries.

IV.   Some implications of past experiences and a perspective on the future structure of the United Nations as it affects the implementation of the programme in the social welfare field.

The review of the United Nations social welfare programme presented in this report is based on the following sources: visits to Indonesia, Pakistan and Turkey, which provided opportunities for observation and consultations with government officials, resident representatives of UNTAB, United Nations technical assistance advisers on assignments in these countries and, in some cases, field personnel of UNICEF; consultations during visits to the United Nations regional offices in Addis Ababa, Bangkok, Beirut and Geneva; discussions of certain aspects of the Technical Assistance Programme and research activities with officials and social welfare personnel in Washington, D.C., and Ottawa at the invitation of the Governments of the United States and Canada; and a review of relevant documents and consultations with the staff of the Secretariat and of UNICEF at the United Nations Headquarters in New York. The report also makes use of material provided by field reviews in Bolivia, Guatemala and Paraguay, as well as consultations with the United Nations regional office in Santiago, Chile, undertaken jointly by a member of the Bureau of Social Affairs and a member of the Division of Social Affairs, Economic Commission for Latin America.

In making his reappraisal, the consultant has taken into account previous evaluative studies of United Nations Technical Assistance programmes in the social welfare field. There have been, in addition, a number of valuable reports contributed by expert groups and other bodies appointed by the United Nations, of which the following deserve special mention for the stimulation and guidance they have provided in the preparation of the present report:

— *Report on a Coordinated Policy Regarding Family Levels of Living*, United Nations publication, Sales No.: 57.IV.7.

— *The Development of National Social Service Programmes*, United Nations publication, Sales No.: 60.IV.1.

— *Five-Year Perspective, 1960-1964*, United Nations publication, Sales No. 60.IV.14.

— *Report on the Organization and Administration of Social Services*, United Nations publication, Sales No.: 62.IV.1.

— *The United Nations Development Decade*, United Nations publication, Sales No.: 62.II.B.2.

It would be difficult, moreover, to undertake a meaningful discussion of social development and social welfare on a world-wide scale without the benefit of the series of Reports on the World Social Situation prepared by the United Nations Secretariat in cooperation with the specialized agencies.

The study was carried out during the last three weeks of December 1962 and between June and September 1963; it is recognized that the resources and time available for the study impose a number of important limitations upon the scope and depth of treatment afforded the subject.

The consultant wishes to acknowledge the full and helpful co-operation received from the staff of the United Nations Secretariat and from the regional social affairs units and offices he visited, and to extend his thanks to all those who, by their knowledgeable and constructive remarks, have helped to redress some of the shortcomings of the present report.

NATIONAL DEVELOPMENT AND SOCIAL WELFARE SERVICES

A. DEVELOPMENT AND ITS ELEMENTS

One of the crucial facts of our times is the emerging will towards national development. Its basis is the advance in the technology of production, the technology of the social services and the technology of organization. The productivity of human labour, in agriculture as well as in industry, is in the process of reaching — as far as available technology is concerned and considered on a world scale — a level where the satisfaction of basic material human needs can encounter only social and man-made — but no longer "natural" — obstacles. Advances in medicine, education, welfare, etc., make it possible to cope with problems which were earlier considered an unavoidable concomitant of the human condition. The mastering of the techniques of large-scale organization makes it at least theoretically possible to introduce changes rationally and quickly even in environments at a low stage of development.

There is an increasing restlessness in the broad masses of the world's population developing into a consciousness of human possibilities and a dissatisfaction with old ways, and culminating in a will towards achieving a better life for all. This will more and more motivates the groups spearheading progress and, at the same time, becomes a criterion to be applied by the masses in judging social institutions and policies.

The idea and practice of national development rest on two important conditions: one is the acceptance of change, the insight that a dynamic process is constantly going on in every community at all times, a process which excludes the possibility of arresting development at any one stage. The other precondition of national development is the possibility of people to influence systematically and decisively their own social destiny. It involves people in massive numbers in every stage of the development process. Not only in principle, not only through constitutional guarantees and by representation, but concretely, in detail, in the technical procedures from fact-finding through decision-making and implementation, to control and evaluation.

The ultimate goal of this general development drive — a better life for all — is clearly a question of values. As values change with changing traditions, cultural settings, historical and political backgrounds, it would be logical to expect the definitions of a better life also to change until, ultimately, there would be as many "better lives" as there are communities on this planet. It is the very reasonableness of this expectation which makes it all the more remarkable that a nearly general consensus seems to exist on what is meant by a better life for all. And not only do the indicators find wide acceptance, but most of them can be expressed quantitatively and therefore give a measure of the achieved level of development. A list such as the following — suggested only by way of examples — would probably be accepted in widely divergent cultural settings:

— A steady and stable improvement of living standards as measured by real family incomes;

— Decrease and eventual eradication of preventable disease as well as a steady and constant improvement of health standards;

— Progressive reduction of infant mortality;

— Steady improvement in life expectation;

— Stable improvement in nutrition;

— Reduction of illiteracy and stable improvement of educational and cultural standards;

— Achievement of regular full employment;

— Reduction of overcrowding and steady improvement of housing conditions;

— Reduction and prevention of neglect and destitution among children;

— Achievement of general security in relation to the common risks of existence (losses through disease, accident, loss of bread-winner, old age, etc.);

— Steady and stable increase in the quality of services given in cases of social emergency (disaster, breakdown of families or individuals, individual handicaps, etc.);

— Progressive improvement in the conditions of work;

— Steady and constant reduction of accidents at work;

— Steady and stable reduction of criminality and delinquency;

— Increased opportunities for active participation of people in the affairs of the community;

— Steady improvement in equality of conditions and in the universal sharing by members of a community of its resources, risks and benefits;
— Stable improvements in the climate of international relations and the achievement of peace;
— Steady and stable improvement of the social climate propitious to the growth of mature and well-balanced individuals.

The value of these indicators and the significance of their generality are in no way impaired by the fact that most of them are not, in a philosophical sense, ultimate. The place of any one indicator on the means-ends scale is relative. There is even considerable consensus on some of the clearly instrumental goals of development including the following:

— Steady increase of *per capita* national income;
— Steady and stable increase of productivity measured in terms of the number of man-hours required to produce a given quantity of goods;
— Steady and stable increase in amount of capital goods per person employed;
— Constant improvement in the ratio of savings to national income;
— Steady improvement in real wages and salaries;
— Steady and stable increase in the quality of public services in the community (transportation, public utilities, etc.).

The United Nations General Assembly, in its resolution 1710 (XVI), measures development by the criterion of growth in aggregate national income and defines the objective of the United Nations Development Decade in the following way:

... accelerate progress towards self-sustaining growth of the economy of the individual nations and their social advancement so as to attain in each under-developed country a substantial increase in the rate of growth, with each country setting its own target, taking as the objective a minimum annual rate of growth of aggregate national income of 5 per cent at the end of the Decade.[1]

In its resolution 1916 (XVIII), the General Assembly points clearly to the ends behind the economic targets of the Development Decade:

[1] *Official Records of the General Assembly, Sixteenth Session, Supplement No. 17,* Vol. I (A/5100), p. 17.

Convinced that economic and social progress, especially in the developing countries, cannot be achieved without a substantial change in outlook and a clear view of the ends to be attained, and without such alteration of certain social structures as may be necessary,

1. *Recommends* that the Governments of developing countries should take all necessary steps... for economic development, as well as for progress and social justice;[1]

It is clear that within the general social interdependence of aims and activities in any human community, the particular objectives of development exist only in relation to each other. Their influence is mutual and sometimes a clear chain of cause and effect relationship can be observed. The following quotation from a United Nations publication makes this point very clearly:

There is a primary need in less developed areas to increase agricultural production in such a way as to eliminate the chronic malnutrition which now affects more than half the people of those areas, and strengthen agricultural income, which is both insufficient and insecure. To help achieve this purpose, industrialization is required as a means of supplying fertilizers and equipment, providing a demand and a market for the increased production, and creating incentives to greater production in the form of inexpensive consumer goods. Modernization of agriculture also requires better education, without which the individual farmer is not apt to change his habits readily and make use of existing knowledge, and an 'infrastructure' of modern institutions upon which agricultural progress can be built—a proper land tenure system, credit institutions, marketing arrangements, and so on. Land reform in many cases is an essential first step that has yet to be taken. Substantial agricultural improvement can often be achieved only with irrigation works, sometimes it requires a river valley development. Finally, the population needs much better health if production is to be raised to modern levels—disease and debility now take an inordinate cut out of agricultural production in some of the less developed areas[2].

There are fields where cause-effect relationships are relatively easy to follow as, for instance, in the effect of taxation measures on a market economy or of a probation service on the incidence of recidivism. There are other fields where it is more difficult to relate effects to given causes, such as in the determination of the results of supportive and rehabilitative action in casework, or even to define the mutual interdependence with any clarity as, for instance, between

[1] *Ibid., Eighteenth Session, Supplement No. 15* (A/5515), p. 39.
[2] *Five-Year Perspective, 1960-1964* (United Nations publication, Sales No.: 60.IV.14), p. 12, para. 40.

juvenile delinquency and general levels of living. There are, conceivably, other examples where one item of development is a necessary but not a sufficient condition of another one. A better quality of public services, for instance, or more opportunity for participation in public life, are difficult to imagine without an improvement in economic conditions. But such improvement cannot be expected to bring about, on its own and as a matter of course, the desired social objectives.

In all these relationships, however, it is becoming increasingly better understood that human society as a whole is a dynamic process in which individual phenomena share a mutual interdependence that is ramified and complex, and that no field can be studied in isolation from any other field if purposeful practical action is the objective.

National development is, therefore, seen increasingly as a process involving human communities in all aspects of their existence where the relationships of ends and means is functional and sometimes reciprocal, as a web of simultaneous and successive measures in various fields of human activity, as an interlocking system of planned action.

In the general stategy of national development judgements of social worthwhileness are interrelated with, and often inseparable from, considerations of technological possibility and feasibility. Questions of value shade over into problems of priorities as well as into purely technical considerations.

Values held by people in a community are the starting point of development planning, though the value element is not always consciously present in decision making. For instance, should people be literate before they can put their skill to socially profitable use in an economy where prevailing production techniques require literacy? There is not only a judgement of priorities involved, that is how far an economy can progress before low educational levels come to constitute a bottleneck, but another question has to be answered as well: If education has an intrinsic value in developing the personality and enriching human life, have people an intrinsic right to education no matter to what socially profitable use they can put the acquired learning?

Decisions about *priorities* in development have often both technical and value elements.[1] Should a steel mill come before a shoe

---

[1] *Report on a Coordinated Policy Regarding Family Levels of Living* (United Nations publication, Sales No.: 57.IV.7), paras. 75-128.

factory? Steel is the material which goes into the building of any factory, while shoes are not technologically essential for the construction of a mill. Accordingly, the mill comes first. But does it not take a longer time to build a steel mill? Can we afford to wait so long for a return on our investment? Are we going to have a market for all the steel that is going to be produced? Is the scarcity of consumer goods going to cause inflation? Should we build a rehabilitation centre which, at best, will accommodate only a fraction of potential patients? We have to start somewhere and the plight of severely handicapped people is so humanly moving that whatever can possibly be done should be done. But just one centre might raise expectations which we will be unable to fulfil, and so make suffering only worse. What if the handicap has its source in prevailing conditions of life which are producing patients quicker than we can think of their rehabilitation? What if it is culturally accepted as one of the possible conditions of life? To what alternative uses could the resources used for the centre be put?

Various measures planned in the course of development are sometimes interrelated in the sense that the feasibility of one is a condition for the success of another. A geological survey is useless if there is no possibility to put the results to any practical use. Without a certain level of administrative infrastructure a census would be inordinately difficult to organize as well as unreliable in its results.

Beyond that there are the innumerable questions of how to do things. How to make a geological survey, to set up a steel mill, to organize a census, to start a literacy campaign, to build a rehabilitation centre, to undertake community development? There are technical answers to these questions, more or less precise, more or less complete, but they all involve essentially the same contingent type of judgement.

In fact, the approach to the different individual problems, as well as to the total situation of development, is itself not fixed; it changes and develops in its turn. Values define the point of view and, therefore, determine the aspect under which reality is seen. The relationship of different development factors to each other constitutes the framework delineating the sector which is going to receive attention. The network of relationships becomes, of necessity, progressively smaller as the focus becomes sharper with each decision on priorities that is made. The eventual contact with reality, however, always takes the form of some sort of action programme which, in turn, requires certain institutional arrangements for its implementation.

It is also essential to bear in mind that points of view are likely to *differ in specific social and cultural settings.* Values do not get the same emphasis in different countries. The relationship between different fields of activities has a different significance. Priorities are not always ordered in the same way. Techniques and institutions, finally, are different and can give different results for different social environments.

The differences among countries and regions are differences of accents, of total patterns of development, and very often not simple differences associated with different chronological stages of development. The political, legal, economic and moral factors and aspects of development do not necessarily develop at an equal pace or in harmony with each other, so that if we were to try to rank countries according to a common scale of development one country might rate higher on the scale than another on one aspect, but lower on a different factor. The changes that are occurring in a country depend on the concrete form of the total pattern as on historical and cultural peculiarities.

Yet, if we look for the probable direction of development in the future, it seems safe to assume that the tendency towards uniformity in the material conditions of life will result also in a greater uniformity in ways of thinking. Accordingly, whatever the present situation may be, it seems reasonable to expect a growing concensus with regard to certain fundamental considerations in analysing, planning and implementing national development.

B.   SOCIAL CHANGE

National development is more than a sum of planned measures; it is a social process, i.e., a process transforming the most fundamental patterns of man's social environment and of his personality structure. It alters not only the basic data of planning but the planners as well.

Social change, therefore, is not simply a non-functional or dysfunctional side effect of development planning. Actually, change goes on in all human communities independently of any purposeful development. In development planning social change should be considered as an objective fact, an independent variable whose movements the planners have to try to foresee and to adjust to.

The main areas of socially relevant change, as we know it from past experience, can be summarized under the following heads:

1. Changes in the way people work

Incidental to development is an essential modernization of work techniques. A new physical-chemical technology implies new materials, new sources of power, and the processes of mechanization and automation. The new biological technology is particularly operative in the fields of agriculture and medicine. The new social technology has made possible large-scale organization, the one most important new social institution of historical times; it has achieved considerable results in the field of education and in enabling large numbers of people to live together.

There is also under way an essential reorganization of institutional arrangements for work. In agriculture, the peasant and his family as the unit both of production and consumption producing essentially for subsistence and not for the market is gradually being displaced by a system of agricultural production for the market which employs different work arrangements dictated primarily by considerations of market efficiency. The crafts, with their concentration of the whole process of production from raw material to final product in one skilled craftsman, are replaced by manufacturing to which the detailed specialization of work procedures gives really a completely new character. More generally, the individual is losing his autonomy in the work process and tends to be integrated within the organization.

A new occupational pattern is in the process of emerging. The proportion of the population engaged in primary production is falling, while the proportion of those engaged in secondary and, eventually, in tertiary activities is increasing. This process, which is usually called — pars pro toto — industrialization, results in an increasing density of economic activity and, therefore, in increased employment opportunities, especially in the beginning phases of development, and in greater possibilities of seasonal labour. It is accompanied by a number of changes with far-reaching social implications, such as improved standards of living and the emergence of the differentiation and multiplication of occupations, etc. Changes in the occupational pattern must also be related to the process of specialization which is going on constantly within a society in the course of development. New occupations arise, new special skills are taught, people and functions become less and less interchangeable.

2. *Ecological changes*

Different occupational patterns, different institutional arrangements and new technologies necessarily entail different location-patterns of economic and social activities. One of the most significant of these changes is the process of urbanization with its rapid growth of existing towns, its creation of new towns often for a specific occupational purpose, and its generally accelerated rhythm of change in status and in the function of settlements. Villages change their traditional agricultural economy and become industrial villages before growing into cities, or, on the other hand, they grow into agricultural towns. Some settlements explode into huge metropolises and conurbations, others decay and die, all at a much quicker pace than ever before in history.

General movements of people are more massive than they have ever been since the era of the Great Migration; they are certainly more systematic and more purposeful than ever before. People migrate within a country and from one country to another in search of work, in search of better possibilities of education and personal development, or in order to escape political and other pressures. People travel in great numbers under orderly arrangements, or cross the borders as refugees. People are resettled in the wake of natural catastrophes or as a consequence of large development schemes.

Increasing population pressures, with a more and more unfavourable relationship developing between people and the living space available to them, promise to become one of the major determinants of the social situation in thirty years from now. The statistical projection of an increase in the earth's population to a total of over 6 billion by the year 2000 is already foreshadowed in a number of countries today. Some countries are already confronted with a population problem, a problem which would exist even with the most equitable distribution of land and other resources within the country. In other countries, the pressure of population is restricted to certain parts only of the country or is related to the prevailing patterns of land-ownership and of income distribution. There are also, on the other hand, some countries which suffer from a different kind of population problem — their population is too small to provide the manpower to develop their potential natural resources.

3.   Changes in social institutions

One of the most important and profound changes occurring in a social institution — and, in its eventual consequences, not yet completely understood — is the transformation of the family in the process of national development. From the large patriarchal or matriarchal family of the peasant to the small two-generation nuclear family typical of urban societies lies a path which has not yet been properly explored. It is certain, however, that on its journey the family is losing a number of social functions to other specialized secondary institutions. The family is no longer a self-contained economic unit; the place of work is divorced from the home; and the functions of social security, health protection, primary education, recreation, which were formerly to a large extent the responsibility of the extended family unit, have gradually become transferred to specific organizations.

What is true of the family is true also of the original small community, the community of the village. The social forms of cooperation and control are most frequently based on the village, and this is true even of those communities which pass through stages of centralized organization and political control in the course of their development, or where the unit of social identification is primarily the blood relation group, the totem, the clan, or the tribe.[1]

The nature of these metamorphoses occurring in a society is conveyed in the expressions from "Gemeinschaft" to "Gesellschaft", from status to contract, from ascription to achievement, all of which point to the gradual rationalization of social relationships. The course taken by this process is even more tortuous, although perhaps better explored than the development of the family. Old institutions based on emotional solidarity have to be replaced by new ones founded on reasoned cooperation.

Particular importance attaches to the emergence of the State and to its growth in power and possibilities of action. There is a political reason for this increased potential of the State, in its being the more

---

[1]   Melville J. Herskovits, *The Human Factor in Changing Africa*, (New York: Knopf, 1962), pp. 89-90, 100, 107.

acceptable — or, rather, less unacceptable — alternative for the organization of an increasing number of activities with implications for the common good. There is also an economic reason inasmuch as a number of poorer countries are unable to concentrate the necessary resources for development in any other way except through State action. Accordingly, limitation of the State monopoly of power becomes an increasingly pressing and pervasive political task. The methods used to achieve this limitation are various and range from the institutionalization of existing differences of interest and opinion in a society for political purposes to organized methods of mass control and to efforts at systematic organizational pluralism.

4. *Changes in interest positions*

No one social situation will appear in the same light to members of different groups or different interest-classes in a country. Existing social structures will usually express existing interest positions. The pattern of land ownership, caste arrangements, race barriers and colonial domination are both the expression and the source of groupings of people with different and often conflicting material and social interests in the same community. The interest positions of people often determine to a large extent their thinking, their attitudes and behaviour patterns. Sometimes, the mechanism of vested interest is very simple. In other cases, the relationship of attitude to interest is more complicated and manifests itself in the general propensity of certain interest groups to be influenced by certain views and arguments more than others. In any case, the breaching of old interest positions in the process of social change is probably one of the major single sources of tension in the course of national development.

As old interest groups are threatened and eventually dispossessed, new minority interests are often appearing and organizing themselves. Power cliques derived, perhaps, from movements which were instrumental in destroying the old order, together with the owners of new economic enterprises, the bureaucracies of emerging large organizations, particularly of the State, privileged geographical positions and dominant regions often form the basis of new minority interests. The poorer the country undergoing change, the greater the likelihood of this happening. As long as there is little to share, there will be minorities who will try to appropriate more than their share.

With every increase in a society's capability to satisfy needs and to take differing interests into account as a result of improvements in technology, productivity and growing wealth, there will probably develop a movement towards the recognition and implementation of wider community interests, the "general interest" of all members, along with and as a framework for the realization of individual and particular group interests. This tendency will sometimes take the form of simply emphasizing the importance of an over-all territorial organization of local or central government seen as encompassing all lesser interest groups in society and arbitrating among them. In other instances, the same tendency will find expression in ideologies and views of life stressing collective responsibility for the welfare of all.

C. SOCIAL PROBLEMS OF DEVELOPMENT

It is apparent that national development and the process of social change which it implies will be productive of a great number and diversity of tensions and difficulties. It is also clear that the manifestations of these tensions and difficulties will differ according to the natural and social environment.

More specifically, the term "social problem" might be applied to human situations to which a community attaches a negative valuation and to which it tends to react by deliberate measures of some sort. In this sense social problems are the natural starting point of a number of community activities, of various organized social services and, more particularly, of social welfare services.[1]

The particular configuration of social problems prevailing in a society is the direct result of various aspects of change. The transformations accompanying development and change are themselves sources of social problems. (From the fact that change results in problems, the mistaken inference is sometimes drawn that change itself is socially negative. Change is unavoidable and social problems constitute its hazards and risks that can and should be minimized by rational, planned action. In a number of situations

---

[1] The term "social welfare services" is used to denote organized services in the field of social welfare as summarized tentatively later in this report, while the expression "social services" is given a wider meaning including all or some—depending on the country—of the following fields: health, nutrition, housing, education, social security, manpower policy, social welfare, social defence, community development.

change is really an essential precondition for the solving of particular social problems.)

The sources of specific social problems of developing countries can be traced to two characteristic processes of development.

1. The break-through

The development of the technical, economic and administrative capacities of a country for conscious, systematic, rational, professional and mass activity, has often to start from a state of rural apathy, which is socially and culturally approved, confirmed by the economic situation, and undisturbed by any technical knowledge.

The actual course of development will depend on how the break-through from apathy to action is achieved. There are many ways in which this can happen, ranging all the way from numerous, patient small-scale efforts to the growth of a strong, charismatic and messianic movement, or the massive shock of a traumatic social experience such as national liberation or social revolution. Whatever course is followed, each alternative will have its specific appeal and will generate its characteristic problems and difficulties. While small-scale efforts may sometimes not add up to anything socially significant, the social cost of messianic action will sometimes be very high and the provision for orderly change of leadership and necessary change of method subsequently difficult to introduce. In any case, the question of motivation for development will have to be faced and resolved. One broad alternative is to rely on people's wish to improve their own individual situation. It should, however, be kept in mind that this source of motivation may sometimes either fail because of a limited perception of needs or because of the availability of alternative, socially negative possibilities of personal advancement; or that it may create subsequent difficulties through fostering active minority interests. The other general possibility is to emphasize the improvement of the situation in the community as a whole and to rely on this as a motivational force. Here, too, there is the danger of creating active élites and the difficulty of getting rid of them once they have performed their social function. Sometimes, moreover, the effectiveness of a motivational system which depends predominantly on centralized arrangements may be reduced by the inefficiency of the administrative machinery connecting the centres of planning and coordination with actual operations in the field.

In any case, "leading images" indicative of the future will have to develop in the consciousness of many individuals and ideas will have to take hold of the masses before they will move. This is essential even though the discrepancy between the dream and the reality may have the effect of adding to the social stresses already experienced by people caught up in the processes of development.

2. Unequal development

Development, if uncontrolled, will tend to assume a very uneven pattern, with the benefits, at least at the beginning, unequally distributed and favouring certain social groups at the expense of others. The lower the level at which a country first embarks on development, the smaller will the privileged groups tend to be and the stronger, therefore, the social tensions generated. The stresses resulting from urbanization and industrialization, from the break-up of traditional social groups and customs and from migration, will tend to be felt more acutely in the presence of inequalities in levels of living and opportunities of individual improvement.

Countries and regions where more rapid growth has been achieved in the past tend to move forward more rapidly in the future. Investment is drawn to investment, whatever the system of ownership; existing infrastructures are necessary for a number of economic and other undertakings, while a naturally favourable location offers multiple advantages. Human talent and capabilities accumulate where they can be used and, in turn, engage the attention of potential users. This tendency finds its institutional expressions in the urban agglomeration. The town is a nucleus of achievement exercising a gravitational pull on further elements of development. The inverse of this process occurs in the case of areas which have none of these initial advantages and continue even afterwards to experience difficulties in catching up. The flow of human and material factors of production is definitely against them. By their economic structure they are at a disadvantage in the distribution of the national income. They are left with the old, the infirm, the un-enterprising, while their human driving force — the best brains and the most forceful personalities — are constantly drained off to more favoured regions.

Because of poverty, lack of education, privilege and prejudice, the level of participation of people in public affairs is by no means equal in different countries and regions. The tendency towards development leads to a resentment of this inequality.

Varying levels of development in the social differentiation of labour make for difficulties in the transfer of techniques from one region or country to another, especially in the field of organization. Development usually involves movement from a pattern of un-differentiated social activities, directed at all kinds of need and problem situations and at a low technical level, towards more highly specialized services whereby increasing knowledge and resources are concentrated on smaller and smaller sections of the total social action field. The unevenness in this process of differen-tiation leads to a number of difficulties and developmental anoma-lies, such as professions which are established outside the context of the total situation, and which may result in a sort of degeneration, a change of content and of direction of the professional activity, an increasing turnover of its members, and a drop in its professional and moral standards. Or there may be a lack of certain needed professions because of their inferior social prestige (e.g. the middle educational range of technicians and specialists).

The uneven pace of development in the different sectors leads to well-known difficulties such as insufficient markets, inflation, agricultural lag, the creation of slums and shanty towns, lack of appropriately trained manpower, etc.

The unevenness of development adds generally and significantly to its cost. The backward regions and backward groups hold back general progress and increase tensions within a community. They influence adversely general productivity and a society's capacity for action in all fields.

The unsettling effects of change, which necessarily has to be accelerated for the break-through, together with the unbalancing effects of unequal rates of development in different sectors, in-evitably create problems in all fields. Most of the specific social welfare problems will probably be related to the common denomi-nator of *insecurity*.

It should be clearly understood, however, that this is a reference only to the possible negative side-effects of development and does not imply that insecurity is generally the typical atmosphere of development. It is often only the reverse side — the dark side — of a general optimism and enthusiasm.

The break-up of social institutions in the course of change leads to social isolation of the individual in new surroundings. The demise of the traditional institutions which formerly provided security, such as the extended family and the small community, leaves the individual alone in the midst of the material risks of existence. This change in his actual social situation tends to produce also psychological stresses and strains. How long new institutions and forms of social solidarity will take to develop and for how long, consequently, the "social interregnum" will last, depends largely on the social structure of the new society and the extent to which people share both the hardships and the fruits of development.

Changes in the occupational pattern result in the loss of acquired technological knowledge and skills. The individual has, in a way, to start professionally from scratch. The security of employment based on his professional expertise is gone. On the other hand, the new technologies he has to learn expose him to immediate occupational dangers and risks which he is ill-prepared to meet (for example, the accident rate in industrializing countries can be as much as ten times higher than the rate in industrially developed countries). Changes in the conditions and status of ownership create strong feelings of insecurity, especially among classes of small individual producers who have always been accustomed to owning their instruments of production.

Changes in people's place of residence, through migration and urbanization, leave them without their traditional social roots and background. Such changes impose a heavy strain on family ties and diminish the sense of security, formerly found in the emotional attachment to the small community. The over-all result is a loss of autonomy, a feeling of being moved by forces outside one's own control.

An increased incidence of problems in family relationships, such as marital incompatibility, divorce and family break-up, unwanted motherhood and child neglect, often follows in the wake of migration and changes in the relative status and opportunities of the sexes.

Where development does not extend equally to all areas and groups in a country, the sense of insecurity can reach disturbing proportions especially for those groups of the population who live in the poorer regions and do not enjoy any of the benefits of development and, in fact, may actually be discriminated against by the development occurring elsewhere. This effect is intensified by a certain structural hardening in the social patterns tending to arrest mobility along racial or other lines, and adding a sense of hopelessness with regard to the future to the disenchantment already with the present.

The whole situation has to be seen in many countries against a background of primordial general poverty, low standards of nutrition and housing, ill-health, reduced life expectation, lack of education, a pervasive apathy, as well as increasing population pressures.

The break-up of traditional social institutions means at the same time a break-down of social controls. The anomic effect of this disappearance of old controls is increased by under-employment in the villages and under-employment and marginal employment in the new towns. At the same time, the tensions of inequality generate anomic and anti-social behaviour which in its turn results in the degeneration of communities, old and new, in the deterioration of neighbourhoods and the general spread of lawlessness.

The stresses of insecurity tend to fall more strongly on generally weaker or specially vulnerable groups, such as children and youth, the aged, the sick, the handicapped.

Moreover, in an atmosphere of insecurity, personal or community calamities are felt more acutely and shocks are less easily absorbed than before. Certain situations — such as divorce, widowhood, unmarried motherhood — may become more difficult to deal with without the support provided by the former stable institutional framework.

New organizations — e.g., the industrial enterprise, the army, the school — may impose additional unaccustomed stresses on a number of individuals.

The definition of social problems as situations negatively valued by a community implies that what is felt as a social problem will depend on the prevailing scale of values and will therefore vary to a certain extent from community to community. One example of this is the divergent attitudes towards such social phenomena as begging, vagrancy or prostitution. Levels of needs and aspirations and notions of what is "minimum" and what "normal" are certainly not the same everywhere. Even within the same community, what is seen as a problem will often depend on the interest position or on the otherwise determined attitude of the group which defines the problem. Nevertheless, there are indications that in developing countries a greater sense of urgency will prevail with regard to mass social problems involving large numbers of individuals than with problems of small special groups or with individual misfortunes.

D.   SOCIAL WELFARE SERVICES

Social welfare is the sum of measures developed by a society in order to cope with its social problems. No human civilization can avoid dealing somehow or other with its social problems, and none has a monopoly of the right answers.

Social welfare is an essentially dynamic field where concrete measures reflect attitudes, activities, institutions and skills evolving out of general social development. In this general sense, it is certainly true that social welfare is a part of man's total effort "...towards a mutual adjustment of individuals and their social environment."[1]

There is little probability, however, of doing anything for the disadvantaged members of a society before a certain level has been reached in providing for the basic physical survival of the society and its members. "Sentimentality" towards the weak can even constitute an additional risk for the security of the group, and natural inclinations in that direction may be actively discouraged by certain social prescriptions (e.g., abandonment of weaker children to die from exposure and the abandonment of old people).

The basic independent variable influencing the development of behaviour towards weaker members in society is the growth of human knowledge. The accumulated fund of knowledge determines what a society can afford and what it can achieve in the treatment of its problems. Attitudes are shaped by economic possibilities and services grow out of a more powerful, more versatile and more many-sided technology.

This development, however, is neither continuous nor uniform. It is not continuous because the growth of knowledge and of its technological and social applications seems to proceed by "explosions", by spurts interrupted by longer and quieter periods of consolidation. During the spurts or the break-throughs, people are, as it were, turned towards the future, bent on a collective effort towards innovation. At the same time, there is as the other side of a widespread attitude of optimistic expectation an unwillingness to be bothered and held back by incidental human difficulties and problems, a mood of indifference in relation to the weaker members of society, often supplemented by an ideology of automatic and general social betterment. During the periods of more gradual

---

[1] *The Development of National Social Service Programmes* (United Nations publication, Sales No.: 60:IV.1), para. 6, p. 6.

change and of building the detailed institutional structures on the foundations laid in times of upheaval, there is both more opportunity and inclination to attend to the marginal problems, to situations of stress, and to individuals in need. Welfare thinking turns to concrete measures and services, rendered possible by the newly increased economic capabilities of the community and the actual level reached in the application of knowledge. Thus, development of social welfare on the whole seems to have advanced by a patient, gradual process of building up institutions, services, skills and attitudes, by a spreading of welfare thinking and of social responsibility for the welfare of increasing numbers of other people. The process has been interrupted by historical moments of scientific, technical and social break-through which, although often unproductive as far as new additions to the network of social welfare services are concerned — and which may mark an actual regression in general attitudes regarding the welfare of the individual — nevertheless constitute the necessary condition for further developments both in welfare ideas and services at new and higher levels of social capability. This discontinuous development is not uniform throughout a given society at any one moment in time. Regional differences, discrepancies among groups making up a society and other differentials add to the complexity of the picture.

Speaking internationally and historically, no system of social welfare measures and social welfare services can claim universal validity. A definition, therefore, of what social welfare services *are* might be not only difficult to agree upon, it could be actually misleading. It seems more useful to review, in summary, the various attitudes, activities, institutions and professional skills involved in the existing systems of social welfare.

This qualification does not imply, however, that there are no other possibilities besides those already tried. There are indeed strong reasons for the contrary belief that serious advances in tackling the social problems of developing countries can be achieved only by inventing new ways and finding new approaches. The following inventory of existing attitudes, institutions and techniques is necessarily compressed and simplified and is offered as no more than a point of departure for that undertaking.

1. *A question of attitudes*

In some instances, the initial diffuse helping activity — an expression of spontaneous solidarity in the human group — developed early into a systematic helping profession. In other cases, government, evolving from an early paternalism, became the main agent of welfare for the individual and the community, and governmental administration became the principal means of attending to social problems. In different situations again, the accent was on change, on social transformation and economic growth, and measures of a general nature were seen as the best way to attack social problems at their source. The different approaches taken to these problems were both a reflection and source of the particular attitudes associated with them.

In some surroundings, the objective isolation and/or psychological loneliness of the individual were productive of individualistic attitudes stressing the values of self-dependency and individual autonomy. In others, the experience of enduring basic stability in an agrarian society was more conducive to collectivistic attitudes valuing solidarity and seeing the individual as naturally dependent on the group. Whatever the reasons for adopting, usually, one or another combination of these two extreme attitudes, the attitudes are inevitably reflected in the approach to social problems. Thus, problems tend either to be seen more as subjective experiences, as problems of maladjustment, whose possible resolution is to be expected primarily from psychological insight and techniques, or to to be regarded rather as objective situations to be tackled by methods derived from sociology, economics or political science.

In any case, attitudes are evolving from a view of social welfare activities as a favour to the people concerned, towards acknowledging them as benefits to which people are entitled by right, however various the particular legal form may be in which these rights are expressed.

2.   The nature of welfare activities

Activities in the field of welfare like those in other fields of human action depend on prevailing levels of the social division of labour. At a certain stage, many specialized activities — e.g., nursing, home economics, auxiliary education, physical rehabilitation, social security, employment exchanges or even teaching or medical practice — do not exist as separate functions but are still fused in a general helping activity. At an earlier stage of development, activities may be even less differentiated with the same person performing very general functions. The village headman, the medicine man, the priest, the head of the patriarchal family, members of the village councils, all are consulted for advice and they function in relation to widely divergent situations which, in a more developed society, become the particular responsibility of different individuals, professions and services.

In order to comprehend the practically unlimited variety of activities designed to cope with social problems, some sort of classification is necessary, even though complete mutual exclusiveness of the categories cannot be achieved nor can all the possibilities be exhausted by the total list. It should be especially noted that the more the categories tend to coalesce, the less differentiation of labour there generally is in a society; that all of the functions have a more or less wide margin where they shade over into activities usually not associated with social welfare; and that the whole field is rapidly expanding, particularly in response to new situations in developing countries.

Types of activities:

a.   Giving *information* about available services, about rights (including elementary legal aid), about social conditions (to interested organizations in order to guide action, and to political and other decision making bodies), about behaviour intended to produce certain results (e.g., family planning, marriage guidance, parent education, child guidance, family counselling, informal adult education).

Related fields: vocational orientation, medical and psychological counselling.

b.   Assigning *income*, in money in the form of public assistance, family allowances, non-contributory social security benefits, emergency relief, etc., or in kind, such as free or low cost meals, school feeding schemes, distribution of clothing, fuel, etc., providing free or low cost housing.

Related fields: social insurance, measures of tax exemption, price limitations, credit policies, etc.

c.   Providing *services*, in institutions for full-time or part-time care, such as crèches and day care centres, homes for children and adults ranging all the way from infants to chronically sick aged persons, hostels, vacation centres, holiday homes, etc.; or providing services outside of institutions, e.g., different forms of home help, playgrounds and recreation opportunities for children and youth, services for migrants and refugees. A special group comprises services for the care and rehabilitation of physically or mentally handicapped children and adults, including the provision of employment or opportunities for productive work. Services for the handicapped are sometimes defined broadly to include services for alcoholics, prostitutes, vagrants, beggars, juvenile delinquents for whom remedial education, measures of work-therapy and economic support are provided. As a rule, all services have not only remedial but also preventive and, wherever possible, rehabilitative aspects.

Related fields: crime prevention and the treatment of offenders, medical and public health services, agricultural extension, home economics, education, the organization of recreation and leisure-time activities, employment services.

d.   Fostering *psychological support* through individual and group relationship, such as casework, individual discussion, organization of clubs, holiday camps, work groups and other group activities, community work and general educational influence through constructive mass action. Most of the activities in this class have important preventive aspects.

Related fields: clinical psychology and psychiatry.

e.   Regulating *social relationships* such as relations among family members, adoption, guardianship and custody, protection of women and children at work, registering social problem cases and licensing activities which have potentially harmful social consequences, etc.

Related fields: general legislative measures for the protection of workers, regulation of wages and work conditions, etc.

The methods employed in the various social welfare activities depend on the stage of methodological development and on the prevailing methodological doctrine as well as on the institutional context in which they are performed. Some of the activities, which in a sense are auxiliary and supporting in relation to the social welfare focus of concern, have developed methodological systems in their own right:

a.   Initiating, facilitating and assisting collective action of self-help or assistance to others in groups, communities and organizations, in the form of community development, neighbourhood leadership, activism in unions and other organizations. There seems to be here a potential for future development, particularly in developing countries.

b.   Management of organizations providing social welfare services, including their supervision and control, social policy planning, drafting of social legislation, etc.

c.   Training of personnel for the social services, including members of various professions, e.g., social workers, lawyers, administrators, medical workers, educational specialists, planners, applied sociologists and psychologists, etc., and non-professional and voluntary workers.

d.   Administration and systematization of work, such as record keeping, reporting, financial administration, dictating and typing, etc.

e.   Research in social problems and in the social services.

3.   The institutional context

In the course of development the principal institutional agents of social welfare activity are:

a.   The *family*, particularly in the early stages of development when it is practically the only institution of social security where weaker and vulnerable individuals (children, the aged, the handicapped) find a comparatively sheltered existence. In view of its basic function in relation to children, the family retains an important welfare role even in later stages of development.

b.   The *local community*. In early stages of development, it is the village, the clan, the brotherhood, the family cooperative, the tribe, etc. Later on, other organizations take over such as the community centre, the neighbourhood council, the local citizens advice bureaux, the information service, the community chest, the consultation centre, various citizens committees, village committees, local voluntary arbitration courts, councils and voluntary bureaux of social service, cooperative organizations, etc.

c.   *Inter-local, non-governmental organizations*, such as social welfare organizations, religious associations and churches, workers unions, organizations of women and youth, professional organizations, parent-teacher associations, social service exchanges and clearing houses, organizations for social surveys and research, voluntary individual consultants and inspectors (lawyers, medical workers, accountants, etc.), organizations of interest groups (e.g., old age pensioners), inter-local voluntary service centres and organizations.

d.   The *State*, meaning central and local government departments of welfare, social security, public assistance, social protection, etc., as well as other departments involved partly or wholly in social welfare activities (labour, health, education, agriculture) together with the relevant coordinating and planning mechanisms.

e. Networks of *self-governing social institutions*, representing a relatively new development which is occurring either through decentralization of government control and its gradual replacement by a system of self-coordination of institutions managed individually by committees composed of staff members or a combination of staff and citizens; or through the integration of governmental and non-governmental social institutions and organizations into an autonomous system of general planning and policy-making by elected mixed bodies.

The various institutional bases of social welfare activities are not hermetically separated from each other nor are they mutually exclusive. They do not necessarily follow a particular time sequence (e.g., non-governmental institutions may develop after governmental ones and central institutions may precede local ones) and it is not suggested that one kind of institution is necessarily better than another. Where the emphasis will be placed at a given moment during development will depend mainly on:

a. The level of organizational development, especially as it relates to how much a society has to depend on face-to-face groups for the necessary cooperation among its members and how far it has mastered the technique of organization;

b. The level of economic development permitting extension of the coverage of benefits or services to specific groups of persons;

c. The prevailing forms and strength of ideologies of social solidarity, derived from tradition or recently developed.

As development advances, the different institutional centres of social welfare activity tend to divide the task among themselves. According to the authority necessary for their performance, the various activities are clustered at different points along the voluntary-compulsory continuum. Regulative activity with an intended general impact is, as a rule, left to the State. There are, however, other forms of social compulsion which can be equally if not more effective than the physical power of government. Direct action, as opposed to indirect regulation, tends more often to be left or transferred to non-governmental agencies. Social policy planning, as it first develops, is traditionally a responsibility of the State. Only at later stages have there recently begun to emerge methods of polycentric planning which possess the possible advantage over

State planning of greater elasticity and adaptability.

The choice of methods as between providing services or supplementing the income of potential beneficiaries depends in part on the pattern of attitudes towards social welfare prevailing generally in a country at a given time. Some rational criteria for this choice might be found in the relationship of available resources to the nature and extent of the problems to be treated,[1] and in the cultural norms relative to the use of income.

4. *The professional variable*

As the various social services differentiate and branch out from the original general helping activity, corresponding patterns of new professions emerge, e.g., educators, doctors, nurses, administrators, planners, judges, criminologists, agricultural extension workers, home economists, community organizers, social insurance specialists, social workers, physical rehabilitation specialists, applied psychologists, applied sociologists and others. What the concrete pattern will be in one country or another at any moment, as well as the time sequence of the emergence of different professions, depend on contingencies of development, doctrine and history. In one case, the accent will be on governmental activity and, in time, general administrators will specialize in social welfare administration, in social insurance organization and accounting, and in social welfare policy planning. In another situation the professions of education, medicine, law will be already entrenched and claim the neighbouring fields of social welfare, such as institutional care, family and child care, juvenile delinquency. Sometimes the profession of social worker will emerge comparatively early and establish a systematized body of knowledge and skill, stake out an extensive field of its own, and practice both in what are called primary settings — i.e., organizations where social work is the principal activity — and secondary settings, where social work is practised as auxiliary or complementary to the main activity (as in schools, hospitals, courts of law, prisons, etc.), only to have its own claims disputed in turn by

---

[1] "Services as such are far less costly to an economy in which manpower is the major asset in spite of the cost of training and supporting specialized personnel, than programmes in which direct economic benefits are extended on a social basis to a substantial group of people."
1963 Report on the World Social Situation (United Nations publication, Sales No.: 63.IV.4), p. 109.

new and more specialized professions based on psychological, psychiatric, sociological and other knowledge.

Over longer periods of time these differences tend to grow less wide and the pattern of activities to follow the pattern of social problems rather than any preconceived idea of what social welfare is and what it is not. Even so, there are in different parts of the world different "profiles" of cadres in the social welfare services. These distinctions are reflected in, and reflect, differences in the kinds of training and previous preparation from simple short courses for volunteers to systematic study of several years at the postgraduate level, and from secondary subjects attached to main courses in other fields to the teaching of specialized knowledge and skill in social welfare.

Differences in the systems of training may also be reflected in different modes of professional identification, in the relative importance attached to different aspects of professional ethics, and in the different emphasis given to particular aspects of social problems and methods of coping with them.

II

UNITED NATIONS ACTION IN THE FIELD OF SOCIAL WELFARE AND RELATED SERVICES

A. THE PROGRAMMES AND THEIR IMPACT

The actual impact of the various United Nations programmes on the countries where they are implemented does not depend only, or even mainly, on the intentions of United Nations policy; it is the result of the convergence of two objective elements: the concrete instruments of United Nations action and the situation in the country, its specific characteristics as well as the actual stage of its development, its social problems, and its receptivity to a given policy.

In relation to social welfare programmes and services, the attitudes and ideas of people in a country will change with changing economic and social conditions and these changes will be reflected in the type of measures and activities which are most likely to be accepted. When existing social problems, by their extent and growth, present a clear threat not only to development but to normal life in a community, the tendency will be to fight the symptoms by emergency measures and to leave the sources untouched for lack of means, skills and the necessary conditions for attacking them. This situation is also often associated with repressive attitudes and an inclination towards prohibition or some kind of regulation of activities considered socially harmful (vagrancy, begging, prostitution, gambling, usury, etc.).

In the initial and subsequent early stages of development, interest will usually be concentrated on economic growth and social measures will be discussed primarily from the point of view of their probable effect on the economy. Social welfare programmes will tend to stress material assistance, both in money and in kind, institutional care, physical rehabilitation and other "tangible" forms of aid. A lack of understanding of long-range social policy measures might still be prevalent.

In time policy makers come to realize the essentially composite and interrelated character of development and to evolve methods by which to approach problems of development in a more systematic and radical manner and in all their aspects. As social security systems begin to grow and broad measures of social policy are taken, a more mature understanding of the causes and mechanisms of individual difficulties and social breakdowns begins to supersede earlier more emotional approaches.[1]

Classifications can serve only to illustrate. The pattern of knowledge and ignorance is not the same in all countries; for a host of reasons, responsible people in a country can be unaware of a problem or of methods to cope with it; hundreds of elements combine in hundreds of patterns. For purposes of international collaboration and for any practical action, every situation must be considered really unique. Accordingly, there is a limit to the usefulness of the kinds of generalizations which have to be made in a general report.

The same reservation has to be made about the classification by programmes of United Nations activities. Any classification is to a certain degree artificial, since one programme shades over into another and substantive action overlaps with functional facilitating or auxiliary activities (e.g., family and child welfare programmes with training or administration). The programmes discussed below are all directly related to family and child welfare even if they are not classified under that heading.

1. Family and child welfare services

The needs in this sector of social welfare are obvious. One study calculated[2] that the proportion of the child population in social institutions ranges from 0.3 to about 8 per 1,000 in developing, and from 10 to 40 per 1,000 in developed countries. It is probably realistic to assume that the proportion of children in need of institutional care is everywhere at least 10 per 1,000 child population, it being understood that the estimate is related to the possibilities in developing countries for providing this care rather than to the actual

---

[1] See *Report on the World Social Situation, 1963* (United Nations Publication, Sales No.: 63.IV.4), pp. 106 ff., and its distinction of "the formative stage of social service development", and "the stage of limited programme development" and "moves towards social entitlement and inclusiveness".
[2] Alice Shaffer, *Possibilities of UNICEF Aid for Social Services for Children* (E/ICEF/377), p. 7

needs for such care. This means that at least 1 per cent, or eight million of the roughly 800 million children[1] in developing countries, are in situations where institutional care is necessary, while many times that number need some form of social assistance. With the social upheavals of development, with industrialization and urbanization, with rising population pressures, that number is probably increasing at an accelerating rate.

Family and child welfare programmes have a much smaller place in developing countries as well as in international collaboration than the extent of the need would warrant, and demands for these programmes are constantly increasing.[2] Apart from the needs situation, programmes for children have a great emotional appeal and at the same time they symbolize a national orientation towards the future. Concern for children naturally includes the family and points towards the necessity, in many countries, of adapting the position of women to the requirements of a modern society and to the importance of planning for young people, the provision of needed resources and the avoidance of potentially damaging situations incidental to development.

Among the new features of United Nations action in this field since 1959 has been the extension of the activities of UNICEF into family and child welfare services, and a movement towards more comprehensive and more flexible forms of assisting children and youth in developing countries. Meetings of the UNICEF Executive Board in March 1959, June 1961, and June 1962, paved the way for this broader approach, which in turn brought UNICEF into closer contact and continuous collaboration with the Bureau of Social Affairs and with several other United Nations specialized agencies. A number of arrangements and, in particular, an inter-agency meeting in Geneva, 1961, defined the conditions of collaboration; UNICEF was to provide primarily material assistance, while the technical agencies were made responsible for technical advice and support. In social welfare programmes for children and families UNICEF is working in close cooperation with the Bureau of Social Affairs.

[1] See *Compendium of Social Statistics: 1963* (United Nations publication, Sales No.: 63.XVII.3), table 2 "Percentage distribution of population per sex and age: two latest available censuses", pp. 31-47.
[2] See *1963 Report on the World Social Situation*, pp. 106 ff., and "Progress Made by the United Nations in the Social Field During the Period 1 January 1961 to 31 December 1962, and Proposals for the Programme of Work 1963-1965" (United Nations, E/CN.5/377), p. 21.

Implementing its new policy in social welfare, UNICEF has branched out into new areas of activity covering, incidentally, new categories of people; these include aid for supplementary feeding, equipment and supplies to institutions, services and centres, assistance in training of various categories of personnel, establishing and aiding specific projects (e.g., foster care, adoption, rehabilitation, hostels, clubs, playgrounds). Women and youth as well as other groups in the population have often been the direct or indirect beneficiaries of aid aimed at complex projects or institutions. UNICEF is consciously striving to find its place in the United Nations Development Decade within the task of "building the human resources of development".

UNICEF brings to this task its considerable financial capacity and administrative experience as well as a solid network of regional, area, country and liaison offices throughout the world. By its method of working with countries on the basis of agreements and plans of operations, as well as by its policy in favour of establishing advisory committees and other mixed consultative bodies relative to the needs of children within each country, it is in a good position to make a contribution to the development of planning and the fostering of coordination among the different social services within the administrative machinery of the recipient countries. Its willingness to enter into policy questions and participate in discussions about fundamental problems of policy within a country — limited, of course, to the neutral and generally acceptable field of helping children — as well as its generally pragmatic and flexible policies, give UNICEF considerable leverage towards making an effective contribution to family and child welfare services.

The various UNICEF programmes involve a number of technical agencies of the United Nations. Generally speaking, day-to-day collaboration seems to be best where the organizational structure of the partners is most similar. In the field of social welfare some difficulties are unavoidable in view of existing organizational differences. The Bureau of Social Affairs has to rely more on central machinery for the most efficient pooling of general experience and for the organization of a world-wide programme of exchange through experts, advisers, fellowships and training opportunities. UNICEF is oriented more towards a decentralized form of organization in order to be able to carry out on the spot and in the quickest and most efficient way complex operations of material aid in a large number of countries. Collaboration at the Headquarters level seems to have been most satisfactory. At the regional level, UNICEF representatives have sometimes found that the regional offices of the Bureau of Social Affairs lack authority to decide issues and that the necessary clearance procedures through the Bureau of Social Affairs are time-consuming. The Bureau of Social Affairs, it is true, does not have the necessary staff in its regional offices to transfer to them the responsible task of technical expertise in the many UNICEF-assisted projects. At the country level, collaboration between UNICEF officers and the experts sent under programmes sponsored by the Bureau of Social Affairs depends, generally speaking, on the elasticity and adaptability of the experts. There are instances of very good collaboration where experts have been eager to put the considerable resources of UNICEF to the best possible use within a broader definition of their assignment to the country. There are also examples of much less satisfactory relationships when experts feel that they should interpret their terms of reference more restrictively and consider themselves as simply technical personnel with a specialized job to do. On the other hand, it is certainly not easy for the Bureau of Social Affairs to encourage experts in its programmes to take too great liberties with their terms of reference, considering the nature of their responsibility and the possibility of complications within the country of assignment.

The Bureau of Social Affairs has adapted both its internal structure and its programmes to the possibilities opened up by cooperation with UNICEF.

Specialized personnel within the Social Services Section are assigned full-time to liaison with UNICEF. The number of experts, fellowships (with the exception of 1961) and seminars in the field of family and child welfare has been increasing since 1959, and the Bureau of Social Affairs is concentrating on getting a better grip on the problems involved in the planning of broad national programmes of social welfare services for children, youth and families.

Before the various questions of organizational structure and day-to-day operations can be tackled, it will probably be necessary to solve a deeper problem of orientation. UNICEF with its wide array of possible activities is constantly drawn into broad programmes for children in which the social welfare aspect is only one component. The Social Services Section of the Bureau of Social Affairs, on the other hand, is inclined, naturally, to emphasize social welfare services without being restricted to a specialized clientele such as children and youth. Experience seems to point to the conclusion that activities are more successful, on both sides, when each side is least mindful of specializations and restrictively defined responsibilities and is more concerned with meeting the always complex and many-sided problem situations encountered in the different countries. Approached in this way, it soon becomes evident that programmes of family and child welfare cannot be divorced from problems of general policy, planning and administration.

2. General social welfare policy

The factors which motivate a country to ask for United Nations advice in the field of general social welfare policy, planning and administration are usually related to the demonstration effect and to the realization that something useful might be learned by international collaboration with countries that have experienced similar social problems in an earlier period of development.

Problems in the planning and coordination of activities of the relevant ministries, agencies and departments, and of regulating the partnership with non-governmental agencies, seem to be especially baffling in the field of family and child welfare for administrators in young administrative systems. Some kind of administrative machinery, legal regulation, as well as methods to avoid duplication and guarantee the minimum of foresight necessary for policy, seem to be essential for the functioning of any kind of specialized programme.

Questions and alternatives with which general social welfare policy advisers are faced in different countries tend to conform to a common pattern:

a.   What should be the respective spheres of action of governmental and non-governmental bodies in the total social welfare effort at any given moment in development? Traditional non-governmental agencies (local organizations of mutual aid and self-help, religious organizations, voluntary associations with a social aim) often represent an important reserve for action in welfare which it would be wasteful not to use. On the other hand, these same forces sometimes embody attitudes which are opposed to the aims of development and of broader social policy measures. Where Governments have subsidized non-governmental organizations, examples of abuses have occurred with resulting demand for more control, standard setting and licensing of non-governmental organizations by the State. The problem is, however, that the State lacks — and usually precisely in these situations — the necessary machinery to perform this function.

b.   What should be the relative degree of uniformity or variety to be aimed at in the organization of social welfare services? To concentrate on one sector or to spread out into many though small-scale actions? In a given set of circumstances and having regard to the prevailing administrative tradition, which arrangement is better: a single ministry or department of social welfare or social welfare units in a number of different departments and coordinated by an inter-departmental committee or a broader national consultative body (including non-governmental representatives)?

c.   What should be the place of institutions (that is, relatively self-contained organizations with a degree of financial and operational autonomy within the administrative system) in the future network of social welfare services? Institutions are often a welcome way to avoid bureaucratic rigidities and other handicaps, but they pose problems in standard setting and control with which a country may be unable to cope. Furthermore, they require personnel and specialized organizational knowledge which may not be available.

d.   What should be the respective spheres of action of central and local agencies? Most activities in the field of welfare are local by nature on account of the close contact required with their clientele and the comparatively small concentration of resources needed for their performance. On the other hand, new services, whatever their nature, will have to be sponsored, developed and controlled by a more advanced centre before they can really take root locally.

In spite of the often excellent quality of the advisers, programmes of international collaboration in general social welfare policy and administration seem to have been less successful on the whole than other programmes. The following reasons have been advanced for these relatively negative results:

a.   In discussing general social welfare policy in a particular country it is sometimes not possible to avoid entering into delicate questions of national politics or touching upon problems which involve the emotions of the adviser's national counterparts to such an extent that the rational aspects of an issue become obscured.

b.   In a development situation, characterized by frequent and radical changes in political and general administrative orientation, the results of years of patient negotiation by advisers and of persevering efforts by the country's social welfare administrators may be swept away in one major general reform.

c.   Transplants with widely ramifying roots — as is the case with systems of administrative organization and of law — may very well find the ground or the climate of another culture unpropitious. Examples abound of theoretically excellent structures that are unable to function because the personnel manning them do not even approach the level which was tacitly assumed; or of meticulously drafted laws which never come to life because of the absence of the necessary machinery for their implementation or the indispensable attitudes of respect on the part of citizens.

d.   Besides the requirements of broad experience in different sub-fields of social welfare and a high level of synthetizing intelligence and considerable talents in negotiation, the task of an adviser in general social welfare policy usually calls at a certain stage for specialized knowledge and skill in the field of public administration. The scarcity of appropriate personnel necessarily limits this type of international collaboration to exceptional cases.

e.   It is particularly difficult to evaluate adequately the contribution of advisers in this field, where the significance of ease of contact and frequency of suggestions may be easily overestimated and where the end-result is usually claimed by a host of agencies and individuals. In the case of choices between alternatives, the evident drawbacks of the alternative selected will usually be compared with the presumed advantages of the one rejected.

It is probable, nevertheless, that international collaboration will have to be extended occasionally to questions of general social welfare policy and administration, at least in order to assist and supplement the effectiveness of other programmes. One general experience seems to point, again, to the advisability of combining, undogmatically, what is separated at more advanced stages, and of concentrating and simplifying to the utmost limit of what is necessary to perform a function.

3. *Training for social welfare services*

It has been discovered with impressive regularity in different countries, at various stages of development, that the main element in upgrading welfare services for children and families, as well as the principal factor in establishing social welfare administration, is trained personnel.

International collaboration as such, in its most important aspect, stands for training either directly or indirectly. The best results have been achieved by advisers and experts who were able to transfer their knowledge, skill, expertise and experience to the greatest number of people in a country. It is only natural, therefore, that international programmes have been inclined to formalize training procedures, to start with them and to stress their particular importance.

Formal training for various functions in social welfare contains a large element of teaching in the social and behavioural sciences, based on internationally valid findings, which are often thought to be largely independent of local peculiarities and therefore easier to provide within the framework of international action.

The result is that in most countries where there are United Nations programmes in social welfare, training has an important and some-times dominating place, most recently with UNICEF participation and aid. Yet in spite of the favourable convergence of need and opportunity, there are increasingly serious doubts about the useful-ness of the current training schemes considered in relation to the priority requirements of the countries where they are introduced.

The misgivings are caused by the fact that frequently the initial decision to introduce training for personnel of the social welfare services means begging the most important question: what kind of training? The programmes and methods of training, as well as the student "profile", are largely determined by the schools and training centres where the training experts and advisers themselves received their education, or which served, in one way or another, as inspi-ration for the new training projects. It so happens that specialized training for social work was first developed and with particular intensity, in countries with a pronounced individualistic outlook on social problems and a corresponding understanding of social welfare services as a means of helping in the process of individual change and adjustment. Even though most of these countries have them-selves progressed far beyond this stage of thinking towards an awareness of other components of social problems and towards the development of systems of broad measures of social policy, past attitudes have been preserved, sometimes perhaps unconsciously, in the training programmes. They are transmitted even more readily to developing countries whose level of economic capacity seems to exclude, for the time being, costly systems of social security or complex mechanisms for the redistribution of income.

In spite of the most sincere efforts to increase "flexibility", to adapt programmes to "different levels" and to take into account "specific situations", the influence of the ruling doctrine is usually too strong for these efforts to achieve anything better than a watered-down version of the original, in which case "adaptation" may mean nothing more than to settle for less than first-class standards. The whole problem of training has, evidently, to be examined critically in the light of the most recent experiences in international collaboration:

a.   A programme without adequate staff cannot function as planned; the resulting difficulties and disappointments are likely to discredit not only the programmes concerned but the very idea of international collaboration in social welfare. The importance of trained staff, therefore, should really not be underestimated.

b.   To organize systematic training is the quickest way to disseminate knowledge, to create a radiating influence which, possibly, will start a number of other developments.

c.   A country's social policy can ultimately be developed only by a country's people. Training institutions help to create a group of people with the necessary knowledge who, in their own interest, will want to put forward and to develop the social welfare point of view and will follow it up through all the vicissitudes of a country's development. Beyond its immediately useful effects, a training institution, if it is a good one, will develop a philosophy and become a social force.

d.   The arguments listed in favour of training are independent of the question: what kind of training would be most useful in a given country at a given stage of development? There are other arguments which, again without prejudging the sort of programme and teaching methods which would be most appropriate in a given situation, speak for systematic schooling at academic levels — what is usually referred to as professional training:

— higher levels of training, by and large, give a right to expect greater proficiency in practice;
— higher levels of training, by definition, recruit students of greater maturity and a better educational background;
— it is important that the personnel of the social welfare services should be of equal professional status with other professions (medicine, teaching, etc.), particularly in view of the fact that the possession of academic degrees in the changing social

structure of developing countries tends to assume a dispropor-
tionate importance.

These arguments with regard to the more particular problem of
the level of training to be aimed at are usually opposed by the
following counter-arguments:

a.   Students with academic training, especially in developing
countries, usually have higher ambitions than to stay in the social
welfare field;

b.   They are particularly unwilling, and often unable, to work at
the level of the villages and the depressed fringe areas where the
most important social problems are;

c.   Consequently, the drift of graduate students out of the social
welfare profession is alarmingly high, making this form of training
exceedingly costly (e.g., in one country it was noted that over 30
per cent of graduate students have left the profession two years
after their graduation; in another it was indicated that the majority
of graduate students work in administrative jobs — for which they
were not particularly prepared — instead of direct social welfare
work, for which they were);

d.   Higher professional education is sometimes said to produce
clannishness and professional narrow-mindedness in graduate
students and to constitute a handicap in their practical work.

There are other arguments as well which are directed not against
the necessity of training in principle — this necessity seems to be
acknowledged generally — but rather against a one-sided and too
simplified approach to the problem:

a.   The prevailing approach to training, it is pointed out, does not
start where it should, namely with the question: What will people
working in the social welfare services actually have to do? The
answer to this question would show, it is assumed, that most of the
social welfare service operations most necessary in the mass-problem
situations of developing countries are essentially simple, and that
even if they call for some training and preparation this should
certainly not be a costly formalized education;

b.   Large-scale social problems do not mean that the need for
trained social welfare personnel is unlimited, especially as other
professions emerge and assume responsibility for some of the problems. The establishment of schools and other permanent training
institutions is usually not based on a realistic assessment of personnel requirements but starts from the unstated assumption, the more
the better;

c.   Opportunities for systematic education are scarce in developing countries and when investing in the creation of such opportunities the total situation of personnel needs should be considered, i.e., the need for trained personnel in the social welfare services should be measured against the competing claims of other special fields.

d.   Within the different possibilities of training for social welfare services a more rational process of selection should operate. Are highly trained professional workers oriented mainly towards individual social welfare services more needed than, for example, personnel with the appropriate training for serving in social institutions? Would some kind of elementary orientation for volunteers have sometimes a higher priority, being both less costly and more effective? Would an addition to the standard training of other professions (e.g., teachers, nurses, doctors, administrators) be sufficient to cope — for the time being at least — with the needs of the social welfare services? Would it, on the other hand, prove to have been more forward-looking to push specialization in a different direction and to prepare — with a longer time perspective in mind — applied sociologists and applied psychologists for services in the field of welfare? The question at issue is not whether any of these solutions is useful in itself but if, under given conditions, it is more useful and more economical from a social point of view than any of the available alternatives?

e.   Furthermore, a given form of training should not be considered only on the strength of its theoretical possibilities or of its achievements in another country. There is considerable danger that the high investment involved in creating a permanent training institution might not pay off because of practical difficulties. Component parts considered essential for a training programme may be exceedingly difficult to organize, as shown by the experience with field work training or with research training in developing countries. The teaching staff has often to be improvised and may not be up to the task of teaching complex subjects. The educational background of the students may be lower than the standard indicated by their formal qualifications and the students therefore unable to follow the teaching (as witnessed by the frequent complaints about the teaching being too "theoretical"). There is sometimes a significant difference between what is thought to be taught and what is really taught;

f.   Social reformers and social policy makers cannot be created in schools, though some of the students might be more likely to develop in that direction if given a different approach to social problems than the one they get in the schools of social work of the prevailing type.

The two lines of argument are really not contradictory. One points to the necessity for some kind of preparation and training for the personnel of the social welfare services; the other draws attention to the dangers and shortcomings of the present somewhat one-sided approach to social welfare by the United Nations agencies, as well as to the hazards and difficulties involved in the transfer of training institutions generally. It is certain that if training is to realize its potential advantages in helping developing societies to cope with their specific pattern of social problems within the limitations of existing possibilities, the whole question of training has to be radically re-thought, a greater variety of variables and possibilities taken into account and new forms of training developed corresponding to new welfare services in social situations which really have no precedent.

4. *Community development*

One factor is attracting increasing attention among the elements of any plan for international collaboration in developing countries, namely, the limited scope for division of labour. There is less specialization of functions than at later stages of development, fields which are going to separate later on are still integrated and differences among professions and skills are less detailed. Accordingly, the classification of social welfare services current in more developed countries is less meaningful, while even the line between social welfare and neighbouring fields may not always be clear-cut. This situation has implications for programmes of international collaboration, especially in a comparatively narrow field such as family and child welfare. It has brought social welfare programmes increasingly into contact with programmes of community development.

An extensive though rather eclectic body of theory of community development has grown over the years while at the same time considerable experience has been accumulated in its practice. In these developments United Nations action holds a very important place.

Community development is being evolved as an answer to some of the baffling aspects in the task of national development generally: the limited scope for division of labour; the disintegration of tra-

ditional institutional structures; the restricted level of organizational capacities and possibilities; the absence of a reliable network of
local services and local government; the prevailing apathy of
poverty; the paternalism and antiprogressive traditionalism
restraining efforts towards change and development; the mass
character of the existing problems; the existence of a wide margin of
under-employment in the villages and in the urban fringes. Community development as a common denominator to a variety of efforts
represents the quest for forms of mass action which are felt to be
necessary. It stresses widely acceptable democratic values, and as a
movement it has a stronger emotional colouring than other programmes — which might be a distinct advantage in situations
where emotions rather than rational calculation are likely to move
people. It is by definition widely adaptable and versatile and in a
country it can more readily get the attention of high level policy
circles than more specialized activities.

Evaluation of the extent to which community development is
able to realize its far-reaching goals is an extremely dificult task.
Community development means different things in different settings
and it is too complex in its network of organizations and activities
(governmental — non-governmental, central-local, economic-
social, etc.) for a given effect to be ascribed to an identifiable cause;
moreover, the time factor is too dynamic for any conclusion to have
a serious chance of claiming more than ephemeral validity. It is
therefore, not surprising that there is actually little reliable material
on the results of community development.[1]

The criticisms, therefore, which are levelled against community
development — like the listings of its advantages — are more decla-
rations of principle than well-documented results of experience.
Sometimes it is simply asserted that community development as a
concrete programme is falling short of achieving the desirable goals
it has set for itself. It is pointed out that community development,
working in a given community setting, does not take sufficient
account of the existing social stratification and the conflicting
interest positions in the community, and examples are cited of
community development working for the advantage of privileged
groups or of programmes otherwise misused for politically non-
progressive aims. The achievements of community development

---

[1] *Community Development and National Development* (United Nations publication,
Sales No.: 64.IV.2), para. 7, p. 4.

show too small an increment over what would happen in the communities anyway as a result of existing communal feelings and traditional institutions of local solidarity. In general, there are indications of a slight disillusionment with community development, mainly caused by the disproportion between what it wants to achieve and what it is actually able to show.

Social welfare is one of the programmes associated with community development. Within community development schemes, however, the theoretically postulated balance among the different special programmes associated with it is not always maintained. There is usually one of the components — economic improvement, local public works, health measures, communal services, or social welfare — which takes precedence over the others and gives the whole programme its main characteristic.

The actual experiences are at present inconclusive. There are examples of social welfare activities being carried by community development into rural regions, especially where the community development movement coincided with mutual aid traditions or ideologies existing in the country. There are also impressive instances of the coordination of community development with institutional welfare services in some urban projects. This kind of combination of resources would appear to offer some of the most promising possibilities for new welfare services in the developing countries.

A number of questions remain open:

a. What should be the relative emphasis, in various situations, on governmental and non-governmental action within community development?

b. What should the contribution of professionals consist in and what should be the role of volunteers?

c. Does community development require already organized communities or can it be considered as a starting point for their growth?

d. Does it precede or can it only follow the development of specialized technical services?

e. To what extent is there an inverse proportion between the need for funds, equipment and technicians, and the element of mass participation in community development?

The question has been raised — particularly as it concerns the relationship of community development to social welfare services —

as to the extent to which social work training can be considered a professional preparation for community development, and whether social welfare personnel should be given the role of coordinating other special programmes within community development activities.

At the present time, community development appears to be sufficiently fluid in its theory and versatile in practice, to offer a promising starting point for attempting a solution of some of the central problems of international collaboration for development. But the very amplitude of the promise is productive sometimes of exaggerated expectations and overstated claims. Present doubts may be merely a reaction to these claims. As in training, however, the "kernel of truth" in community development seems to require much more elaboration — nationally as well as internationally — before its contribution can reach its full value, and before even its relationship to the different special services — social welfare among them — can be fully clarified.

5. *Other social welfare services*

Other United Nations programmes in social welfare may be mentioned as illustrative of certain problem situations and attitudes as they relate to children and families. They concern either services for special groups, such as rehabilitation, or services in special settings, such as medical social work. In both cases, family and child welfare might be largely, though not exclusively, involved.

These services are characterized by their relatively small scope and, consequently, by their comparative expensiveness. In developing countries they often give the impression of being somewhat apart from the main problems of development.

Some of them (for example, rehabilitation) illustrate the fact that a cost-benefit analysis is not the only criterion in deciding what kind of social welfare services to organize. Comparatively large resources have been invested by the United Nations in programmes for rehabilitation and, as it seems by the results, on the whole rightly so. The relationship between investment and visible direct contribution to development from rehabilitation of severely physically handicapped persons appears to be unfavourable. But the human appeal of grave distress is so strong that people are prepared to divert resources to its alleviation independent of any reasoned calculation. In assisting these efforts much more is probably won in goodwill, in general awareness of social welfare problems, and in mass education towards humanism than can be shown or demonstrated in a tangible way. This is even more true when the rehabilitation efforts are directed towards victims of wars, assistance to whom is felt as a national obligation.

Other services, e.g., medical social work, should perhaps be considered rather as experiments, as a demonstration of what can be done with modern specialized methods even though, for the moment, only on a small scale. Such "token of the future" programmes should not be judged summarily. Each of them should be considered on its merits. In particular situations — for example, when it is necessary to increase general awareness of the importance of seeking early medical intervention — these merits can be considerable. Nevertheless, as a rule, such programmes should not cost too much, and should not overlook the possibility that the future may take a different course from the one implicitly assumed in the programme.

6. Relation of social welfare to other United Nations programmes

The general fact of a more limited scope for the division of labour in developing countries brings about a constant blending of problems and makes contact between different programmes and the overstepping of boundaries practically unavoidable. The awareness of this fact was reflected in an increasing number of cooperative projects in exploration and study, particularly through seminars in the various regions, of subjects of overlapping and common interest to two more United Nations agencies, such as the relation between research, planning and social policy, the convergence of social security and social services, the social aspects of housing and urbanization, the administrative aspects of community development, the economic side of the social services generally, the relationship among various types of trained personnel in different social service settings, etc.

The day-to-day working contacts of social welfare with other programmes are mainly through community development and through UNICEF — which adds value to both. Community development brings social welfare into contact with mainly rural programmes, such as land reform, home economics, cooperatives, and with local government. Urban community development projects relate social welfare to housing and urban planning programmes. UNICEF provides the base from which social welfare works together, to an extent, with health, education, vocational training and some FAO programmes.

There seems to be a rare consensus about the insufficient impact and use of the United Nations information and publication service. The material often does not reach the reader and when it does it is too stereotyped, not fully relevant nor completely understood. Except for some outstanding efforts of individuals in the Information Service, the dominant mood is critical with the feeling that there is room for a lot of improvement.

Examples seem to indicate that full-scale formal cooperation in the field across United Nations organizational lines puts too great a stress on the United Nations framework. In the few instances when such collaboration was brought about it quickly went beyond the United Nations altogether. At the same time, it should be stressed that the occasional working contacts in the field which arise in the normal course of events do not usually present any problem. There is a natural solidarity among people working on contiguous tasks in a country other than their own and they manage to get together and to get along. The problem is at the level of programme planning where more coordination would have a very high chance to improve results and to reduce costs. In view of the long lines of communication between Headquarters and the field, the strategic place to join operations would be at some intermediate point in space and in time, most conveniently in the existing regional organizations during the preliminary discussion of draft programmes. We are not unaware of the fact that every conceivable solution presents quite formidable problems of organization, some of which will be discussed later.

B. EVALUATION OF UNITED NATIONS PROGRAMMES IN SOCIAL WELFARE

The first evaluation of the advisory social welfare programme of the United Nations, covering the five years from 1947 to 1951, resulted in a report submitted to the Social Commission in 1952.[1] The report of the second evaluation, covering the time from 1953 to 1959, was

---

[1] *Evaluation of the Programme of Advisory Social Welfare Services, 1947-1951*, United Nations publication, Sales No.: 52.IV.18.

before the Social Commission in 1961.[1] The third and present reappraisal is mainly concerned with developments since 1959 up to the end of 1963. Evaluation tends to become more frequent, more continuous and, in a way, a constituent part of the programmes themselves. In order to assess the place of evaluation it is, therefore, essential to see clearly the most important difficulties of the evaluative process and its inherent limitations.

The first of the recurring difficulties in evaluating United Nations action is related to the question of how to measure the action itself and its results. There is first of all the problem as to what constitutes the object of measurement: is it United Nations action, corresponding governmental action, total governmental action in the field, the total amount of social welfare effort in the country, changes in the general social situation, especially as they relate to an increase or decrease of particular social problems, or even the total development of a country? It has been observed that, given the principle of multi-causation in respect to social phenomena, the greater the level of generality the less it is possible to ascribe a given effect to one given cause. While it is comparatively easy to demonstrate the connexion between a single measure in a country and a given United Nations programme, it is very difficult to achieve this demonstration when it comes to more general effects such as the over-all social welfare programme or even the country's social development. Furthermore, United Nations programmes are essentially programmes of cooperation. These programmes do in some way influence the situation in a country but, on the other hand, a country's own development influences the direction the cooperative effort is taking. A better response in the country, for instance, is likely to call forth a greater effort on the part of the United Nations.

All evaluation depends mainly on subjective sources of information (opinions of experts, fellows, officials, citizens, etc.). One of the aims in the development of a methodology of evaluation should be the use of a greater proportion of objective criteria (statistics, economic and financial indices, case-studies, etc.). The difficulty in objectifying and quantifying social and organizational phenomena has been felt especially in the quest for a unit of measurement, a criterion by which one would be able to say in advance what is to be considered as successful action. It is too infrequently realized, how-

[1] *"Evaluation of Selected Aspects of United Nations Technical Assistance Activities in the Social Field"* (United Nations, E/CN.5/350).

ever, that there is a considerable and constantly expanding number of activities where such units are obvious.

Often the most valuable results of United Nations action take a considerable time to become apparent and this poses a difficulty in correctly evaluating successes and failures.

The information which is subjected to analysis in the evaluation of United Nations activity is, as a rule, second hand and the possibilities of distortion, therefore, especially great. Apart from the usual handicaps of bias and preconceptions in the evaluator, there is a danger of simplification, of trying to find regularities which obtain in all countries and are valid for all the programmes. Also, the readiness of informants to help any evaluation to the best of their ability should not be taken for granted. The implications for bureaucratic aggrandizement or diminishment within the governmental system of a country, or even within the United Nations organizations, are too great.

It is often felt that United Nations evaluative action should be more positive in its recommendations. It should not be forgotten, however, that the larger the geographic or functional area covered by an evaluation, the vaguer the general conclusions arrived at must necessarily be; and moreover, that in the United Nations it is an accepted form of behaviour to say nothing openly negative of any Member country or about any programme which a Member country sponsors.

The difficulties enumerated suggest even more clearly that evaluation should be made a constant and integral part of all United Nations programmes for only then can it become a factor in continuous self-improvement and growth of the services. The necessary conditions for successful evaluation include clear and measurable goals capable of being defined in advance, reliable measuring techniques, and objective machinery for evaluation. All of these ideals are to be constantly striven for, even though they can never be completely attained.

C. SOME GENERAL CONCLUSIONS FROM THE PAST

1.   Social welfare services in United Nations international action have moved away from an early emphasis on methods, on technical questions, and on a simple transfer of techniques — derived mainly from one kind of social welfare tradition — without questioning the

attitudes and values underlying the techniques. The movement has been towards a broader concept of welfare services as multi-purpose community services, organized in local centres and development projects. At the same time, while training for welfare services was still thought to be one of the most promising approaches to international collaboration or assistance in the field, there was also a subtle change going on in the understanding of the content and meaning of training. There was less dogmatism with regard to the curricula prescribed or the methods of teaching employed while greater store was set by the versatility and essential flexibility of the training provided. The generally increased attention given by United Nations policy-making bodies to national development found expression in the social welfare field in a greater interest in questions of over-all social welfare systems, their organization, administration and planning.

But at the same time, the possibility of exploiting these favourable developments in understanding and policy was limited by difficulties in recruiting suitably qualified advisers. These developments called for advisers who would be not merely technicians but would have sufficient knowledge of the country they were advising, and a breadth of viewpoint and enough creative imagination to enable them to underplay the knowledge acquired in their own countries and yet be able to help people of a foreign country who have themselves given a certain amount of thought to the problems in question. Limited resources, both material and human, technical as well as professional, are among the essential limitations of assistance action generally, and are limitations inherent in the medium.

2. The second movement in policy development in the social welfare field is towards the realization that some of the basic concepts need to be rethought more systematically, that they are simply not yet ripe for direct technical implementation. This is especially true of the concept of balanced development itself, of the interrelationship of different factors — functional and dysfunctional — in the process of social change incidental to a community's progress; of the concept of social planning, of planning for social objectives and for rational action to obtain certain predetermined results in the complex and very dynamic situation of changing societies; of the concept of community development, its real meaning, its different institutional realizations, especially its methodological possibilities and the variations depending on the milieu where it is applied; and, finally, of the concept of training in relation to the other problems

and needs of developing countries.

All that has emerged so far is uneasiness about the place of social welfare services in national development, about the very meaning of the discipline under different conditions, especially in the context of a narrower range of social differentiation of labour in a community.

It is still an open question how to adapt the range of specialization obtaining in the United Nations to the different stages of development, and how to consolidate what may be widely separate programmes at Headquarters in one action-unit in the field.

At the same time, it must be acknowledged that the existing forces of the United Nations in the social welfare field have been fully engaged in current programme operations which leave no margin of freedom in which to turn to the new and pressing tasks of re-thinking and programme-division, tasks which are time consuming and require a different tempo than operational activities. These have been some of the basic limitations of the programme.

3.   The third movement is towards the realization of the necessary interdependence of policies and programmes. Where development is taking place, it is impossible for all practical purposes to separate the planning and programming of welfare services from community development, from problems of land tenure and agrarian reform, from deviant behaviour and the methods to cope with it, from housing, planning and building, from population pressures, from levels of living, from the trends towards industrialization and urbanization, from the prevailing patterns of government and the possibilities of public administration. Appreciation of this fact was responsible, to a certain extent, for the joint exploration with other United Nations agencies of subjects of overlapping interest, such as the social aspects of housing, the relationship between welfare services and social insurance, the social problem implications of demographic trends, the training of leadership personnel in social welfare organizations, problems of urbanization, of planning, etc. The regional seminars have been especially useful in promoting these inter-disciplinary interests and activities.

But the organizational compartmentalization within the United Nations, besides procedural and other barriers, sets natural obstacles and limits to the possibilities in that direction. These have been the limitations inherent in the structure of the organization.

4.   The fourth trend has been towards an understanding of international action in the social welfare field as partnership and cooperation rather than as simple assistance. Attempts at mere trans-

plantation have shown a tendency to degenerate or to wither on the vine. The undeniable success of the European Social Welfare Programme, based as it is on the principles of exchange and partnership is clear evidence of the inappropriateness of assuming that the possibilities of fruitful international cooperation in the social welfare field are restricted to countries at particular stages of development. All countries are developing, all countries are in a position to make socially costly mistakes and they can only profit from international cooperation in avoiding them. It has been clearly recognized by the countries from which experts are most often recruited and which act most frequently as hosts to fellows from other parts of the world that they have profited considerably from being exposed to the necessity of adaptation, of fresh thinking and of re-examining their own programmes.

At the same time there is an unavoidable limitation inherent in the specific tradition of each country and in the knowledge and skills developed there: this kind of limitation may be described as belonging to a particular point of view or attitude of mind.

There seems to be an individual optimum for each country with regard to the amount of outside assistance it can usefully absorb in dealing with its own problems. This optimum is not identical with the maximum. Too much outside interference, however well meant it may be, can have the effect of immobilizing the country's own forces, of creating the sometimes unconscious impression that a certain problem field can be safely left to outside assistance. This is not to say that a formal system of matching, such as is sometimes employed in United Nations programmes, would invariably produce fortunate results. But it should always be kept in mind that a balance between what people in the country are doing themselves and what other people can do in cooperation with them has certainly to be preserved.

The question of the optimum length of a programme of collaboration is related to the one just discussed. Economic considerations as well as psychological factors, such as the necessity for a period of preparation in order to overcome resistance in the recipient country, have been advanced as arguments for the extension of established programmes. On the other hand, the danger of bureaucratization, of the loss of adaptive capacity to changing conditions and the possible over-all deterioration of a programme have all been cited as reasons for setting a limit upon the duration of an assistance programme.

Programmes may be too large for United Nations resources adequately to maintain them and too complex for evaluative appraisal to relate particular effects to particular causes; on the other hand, they may be too small to influence development to any appreciable extent or even to leave their imprint on the consciousness of people. It is essentially a problem of scale.

It is sometimes surprising how blandly advisers will suggest to another country the adoption of measures and programmes which even in their own country have not yet been introduced or which have had to wait not only for a given level of economic productivity and administrative capability, but also for an often dramatic and long-drawn political struggle to overcome opposing vested interests. This does not mean that such measures should not be suggested or advocated. It does mean, however, that they should not be presented simply as exercises in planning and rational implementation. They should be analysed for their social and political implications and perceived as problems of social action in a situation of conflict.

Programmes of international collaboration and assistance cannot — and should not — avoid policy questions. While the making of political decisions is always the responsibility of a country's policy-making authorities, assistance within the framework of international cooperation should and will contribute to the identification and delineation of the different policy alternatives and their consequences, and will draw attention to the values involved; it will add to the skill available in the country for distinguishing among different courses of action and their implications, and will broaden the horizons within which significant relationships are perceived.

It is especially important that experiences and services offered as part of a programme of international cooperation should not be presented statically. The impression should be avoided that there is a recipe to be invoked or even an idea to be striven for. Care should be taken to maintain an historical perspective on development and not to lose sight of the importance of social creativity.

The United Nations should at all costs avoid not only the practice but also the appearance of paternalism in relation to Member countries. The United Nations should start from the principle of helping countries to help themselves, and should facilitate the exchange of experiences, refraining scrupulously from imposing any one form of solution or pattern of services under the guise of "United Nations doctrine". It is also the clear responsibility of the professional staff of the United Nations agencies to know and to make known the different existing systems and approaches, and no difficulties in communications should be considered serious enough to exonerate the competent units of the United Nations machinery from this responsibility.

The only rule is movement. There is really no general prescription for behaviour in dilemmas such as that posed by the tendency to concentrate on one main task or a few programmes as opposed to the wish for a greater variety of activities, or the choice between general and special programmes, between strict rules of priority and allowing for "imponderables" such as readiness of the country, emotional involvement of the people, etc., between regional and country projects and many other similar choices to be made, decisions to be taken anew in every action.

This element of never-ending development and change is probably at the same time the most deeply satisfying and stimulating aspect of international collaboration. As we quoted in a United Nations document,[1] here actually "what is past is prologue". What is past looks at best as a promising beginning. The main task remains always for the future.

---

[1] *Five-Year Perspective, 1960-1964* (United Nations publication, Sales No.: 60.IV.14), p. 120.

III

THE POTENTIAL PLACE AND CONTRIBUTION OF THE UNITED NATIONS SOCIAL WELFARE PROGRAMME

It is an extraordinary fact that at a time when affluence is beginning to be the condition, or at least the potential condition, of whole countries and regions rather than of a few favoured individuals, and when scientific feats are becoming possible which beggar mankind's wildest dreams of the past, more people in the world are suffering from hunger and want than ever before. Such a situation is so intolerable and so contrary to the best interests of all nations that it should arouse determination, on the part of advanced and developing countries alike, to bring it to an end[1].

In trying to live up to that determination United Nations future policy in the field of social welfare should be guided by the following considerations:

a.   The progress made in fundamental and applied social science and in the analysis of development, particularly with regard to the dynamics of the evolution of social problems;

b.   The changing consciousness of and attitudes toward social problems and the possibilities of corresponding social welfare services in the country concerned;

c.   The potentialities of United Nations action.

A.   VARIABLES IN DEVELOPMENT AND IN THE PERCEPTION OF SOCIAL PROBLEMS

The social sciences have recently been applied in a more complex and less onesided way to the study of the phenomenon of development. Economic growth is seen more and more as one aspect of

---

[1]   U Thant, Foreword to *The United Nations Development Decade—Proposals for Action* (United Nations publication, Sales No.: 62.II.B.2.), p.v.

general social change, just as economic behaviour is increasingly recognized as human behaviour in one type of social relationship. The periodicity of the will to achieve has become a subject for study,[1] and the hypothesis has been formulated that groups with a special predisposition to development are to be found in each society.[2] Even if the current basic hypotheses appear to be merely reaffirmations or transpositions of earlier theses, there is evidence of some progression in the fact that speculation tends to be more and more supplemented by investigation.

Certainly, practical action and international collaboration for national development ought to proceed from the insights of theory, just as theory would have everything to gain from a more systematic and more significant link with practice.

The main result of current theoretical efforts seems to be an understanding of development as the interplay of a number of constantly changing variables and sub-variables which produce by their interaction the apparently static "stages of development" and their corresponding configuration of problems.

Among the significant variables which have been identified are the following: economic growth with its technological and professional infrastructure, its speed, its particular direction and content, and its institutional framework; political development viewed as the process of defining and redefining different interest positions in a society; the cooperation of different interest groups and the conflicts among them, the frequency, extent and intensity of conflicts, as well as the methods of domination, reorientation or compromise employed to channel, solve or suppress existing situations of social conflict; organizational differentials related to the size, the incidence and the type of organizations and the range of differentiation among them; ecological change along the rural-urban and other continua; evolving types of family and family life, ideological and religious movements and shifting social loyalties; modifications in the prevailing motivational patterns in a community. These and other variables, their never-ending metamorphosis and their manifold mutual interaction are the background for any analysis of development and, therefore, for any effort towards induced and planned change.

[1] See, for example, David C. McClelland, *The Achieving Society* (London: Van Nostrand, 1961).
[2] See, for example, Everett E. Hagen, *On the Theory of Social Change* (Homewood, Illinois: The Dorsey Press, 1962).

The concept of social problem as basic to the planning of social welfare services implies the introduction of value judgements into the complicated interaction patterns of development. To declare that a situation presents a social problem is to say that it is not satisfactory according to whatever standards are applied.

In the case of developing countries, more than one set of standards is usually invoked. At the lower end of the scale are standards intrinsic to the culture of a country and related to its actual capacity for acting on them. At the other end are standards based on the most exacting requirements existing anywhere in the world and which assume an optimal capacity in the country of their realization. The values actually held by the different groups engaged in development will tend to scatter or cluster somewhere along this scale. It is pointless to plan a system of social welfare services without taking into account the values of those who define particular situations as social problems, the standards which are actually applied, and how this pattern of values is likely to change in the future.

Assuming, for illustrative purposes, a situation in which two sets of standards are applied to the definition of social problems in a given developing country — viz. the traditional standards of the country itself and the standards assumed by an agency of international collaboration — the result is likely to be two "layers" of social problems:

a. Situations of groups and individuals which are considered exceptional and unacceptable according to standards traditional in the country; and

b. Situations of groups and individuals which, even if they are not exceptional in the country concerned, are considered unacceptable according to standards professed by international agencies or those held by groups in the country as a result of external influence.

Usually there are more than two value-positions which are maintained by various groups. But they tend towards the two points indicated. And the two positions, even if they are not distinct and clearly distinguishable from each other — even if they change during development and shade over into each other — result nevertheless in important analytical and policy differences:

a. The number of cases falling into the social problem category is likely to be much smaller according to the first viewpoint than the second. Judged by traditional standards indigenous to the country concerned, the various problem situations will appear as "marginal" compared with a picture of "mass" problems which emerges from the application of more exacting standards derived from outside the country.

b. The marginal problem situations call more for individualized treatment, while the mass problems suggest large-scale general measures. While mass problems appear much more important from the point of view of general development than marginal problem situations, they are also more likely to be affected visibly and, to an extent, "automatically" by economic betterment. In contrast, the problems conceived of as marginal not only often remain untouched by rising economic levels but are followed, as a rule, by new social problems which develop in the wake of economic modernization and concomitant industrialization and urbanization. It is difficult to conceive of mass problems as a fit subject for treatment by a particular profession trained to cope with them on the basis of a well-defined, professional full-time activity. They would appear to be more amenable to general measures of social policy and of political action.

This results sometimes in the paradoxical situation that the marginal problems which the policy-making group in the country recognizes as social welfare problems do not seem to them to require any special or elaborate attention; for the time being, while the country is attending to more important questions, these problems can be left to the traditional ways of coping with them that were good enough for so many centuries. On the other hand, the mass social problems, which do seem important to everybody, are unlikely to yield to the social welfare methods usually advocated and are not associated therefore, in the minds of the country's policy makers, with social welfare activity. This is the reason why social welfare programmes in developing countries, themselves the product of the mutual influence of the two value-positions on each other, frequently give the impression of posing an assortment of issues pertaining to quite different points in time.

In planning welfare services, standards prevailing in the country will have to be taken into account as a starting point, together with the services considered appropriate to whatever is defined as a social problem in the country. International collaboration is a process of mutual education. In time, international agencies will learn that standards are meaningful only if they can be honoured within a given time-period; and social policy circles in a country will begin to see as social problems what they had hitherto accepted as normal

— though perhaps unedifying — conditions of life. What this compromise position on the scale of possible standards is going to be, and how quickly it is going to evolve towards higher levels, depends mainly on the possibilities for effective action, of doing something about problem situations recognized as such. Within the limits set by resources, the capacity for action depends on the available instruments.

The actual welfare measures and services evolved cannot possibly conform to any one pattern. In principle, they should reflect the unique combination of a country's particular pattern and rate of development, its economic, technical and social possibilities, its particular configuration of problems and the knowledge available internationally. To help countries achieve an optimum combination of these factors, rather than to "adapt" any one existing solution from another country — this is the essential task of international technical collaboration in the field of social welfare.

B. SOCIAL WELFARE SERVICES—SOME DIRECTIONS OF DEVELOPMENT

As to the actual conclusion to be drawn from the analysis of problems of development and the different understandings of social welfare services, no more can be attempted than to outline the general direction which concrete discussion about any one programme would have to take. The reasons for this are not only the obvious limitations of time and space. It would clearly be a mistake to try to develop any kind of general programme: too few of the relevant factors can be taken into account in a blueprint which tries to fit every situation. What follows, therefore, is only a tentative list of questions which should be posed when considering the social welfare programme of a country.

1. Social action research

That any rational programming has to be based on a picture of the pertinent facts is self-evident. That it is so rarely done, or even considered necessary to do, is probably the consequence of three groups of factors:

a.   Research is costly and requires manpower which is either non-existent or in very scarce supply in the developing countries;

b.   Research is often oriented to the past; the time it takes to accomplish a research project makes the picture already a little out of date on the day the report is published, especially in quickly-moving situations of accelerated social change;

c.   Groups which are in key positions for influencing progress in a developing country are usually strongly motivated by an ideal, though somewhat simplified, representation of the future course of events, and/or by specific interest positions, and they tend to be impatient with facts that do not fit their ideal, over-simplified plans or their interests.

To overcome these handicaps, social action research should be oriented, as much as possible, to quickly usable results, even at the cost of a loss in theoretical significance by not considering every aspect of a composite problem situation. Research should be oriented to practically available and applicable methods. The fact, for instance, that no reliable census data can be produced, or that the use of questionnaires would meet insuperable technical diffi-culties does not mean that research is impossible; it only orients it into practicable methodological channels. It will probably be necessary to develop methods whereby the research results can be used to throw a beam of light on the future instead of the past, a kind of forward-pointing motion-picture of social change. Further-more, research activities should from the beginning be placed at the centre or near the centre of political decision-making. Research institutions should identify themselves fully with the general development aims of the country, and at the same time occupy a position "...whose scientific independence would be assured..."[1]

Moreover, it must not be forgotten that the degree of research specificity increases when the subject of investigation is one country or even a region in a country within a given time-period, compared with research into development generally with the whole world as subject. Again, therefore, there is not much that can be said usefully about social welfare research in the abstract.

2.   Social programmes

The statement in the *1963 World Social Situation Report* to the effect that "If social services are to play an essential role in the social

---

[1] *Report on European Seminar on the Relation between Research, Planning and Social Policy*, The Hague, 27 October-3 November 1957, Report (United Nations, Geneva, 1958) (UN/TAA/SEM/1957/Rep.3), p. 92

structure rather than serve as a kind of philanthropic frosting on its surface, they must inevitably change their form and scope as the society itself changes",[1] may be considered as generally accepted. The main efforts, nationally and internationally, should be directed at the goal to find out more specifically how, where and when this change should take place and what the new forms should be.

In accordance with what has been said earlier, the accent should be on programmes oriented towards the future. Therefore, social welfare programmes for children and youth should have high priority; youth programmes especially should get much more attention than they have in the past. The possibilities inherent in such bodies as voluntary youth work brigades or "Peace Corps" organizations for mass activities by the youth of a country and their joint activity among a number of countries should be systematically explored and developed. The idleness of youth in its formative years is one of the great problems in the new towns of the developing countries and elsewhere as well.

Unemployed and underemployed youth, on the other hand, are an important reserve of labour, of drive and energy for development, which no country can afford to waste. It is important to remember that a man, and especially a young man, "does not live by bread alone", and that the emotional appeal of a programme to the generous instincts of youth is sometimes more important than its rational side. The education of youth to maturity is a many-sided process, and practical action is an important part of it. There is a functional relationship between the activities the youth of a country engage in and the atmosphere in which they live. The quality and content of mass recreation and entertainment programmes (e.g., films) for youth have a fundamental importance for this atmosphere, an observation which has somehow, unaccountably, escaped systematic attention.

The accent should be on programmes directed towards building security in both a social and a psychological sense. Community-creating programmes of the most diverse forms, ranging from clubs and recreation centres to religious revival and political movements, can play an important role in this respect, but it should not be forgotten that the basis of security, especially in poor countries, is material security. Programmes of social security ranging from cooperative and small-scale community action to large social

---

[1] *1963 Report on the World Social Situation* (United Nations publication, Sales No.: 63.IV.4), p. 105.

insurance systems and, finally, to social security for all should be in the forefront of thinking, undeterred by any argument about the time not being yet ripe for such "costly and complicated" programmes. The truth seems to be that material security programmes can be started in very simple forms, that they can be selective as to the groups covered, favouring more vulnerable or, in the process of development, more involved categories of the population, and also that the opposition to them often reflects simply the interest of groups who think they do not need them and would have to defray a part of the costs.

Programmes of constructive social action which build solidarity and social consciousness are most likely to counteract the anomic effects of the break-up of traditional social institutions.

Programmes to improve the condition of women in many countries have a direct social welfare relevance through their influence on the role of women in child rearing and family planning, as well as through the potential contribution of women to all activities in a community. The experience of countries where women moved more quickly towards a status of equality points clearly to the possibilities in that direction.

The community development movement is certainly an important beginning towards devising the concrete forms of these new activities. It is a possible form of mass action. It is a plausible answer to the lack of functional differentiation, and more limited range in the social division of labour in developing countries.[1] It can be at least a temporary substitute for services as well as an introduction to them. It is a conceivable method to stimulate the will to achievement and to motivate people towards the goals of development.

There is as yet, perhaps fortunately, nothing definitive in community development. The programme content and direction will have to depend on independent programme planning. The practice of community development will also reflect the prevailing social and political realities in a community. It will probably have better

---

[1] "The potential scope of social service activity in such countries is affected by the complete or relative absence of other specialized services. Fine distinctions of functional specialization have little meaning in places where there are few if any services of any kind. It is for this reason that, so often, workers sent into relatively untouched villages—whatever their original designation and sponsorship—in fact quickly become 'multi-purpose workers' teaching the first principles of hygiene and child care, administering simple remedies, advising on farming and housekeeping practices, conducting literary classes, stimulating cooperative activity and undertaking a variety of tasks performed by more specialized workers in a more highly developed community setting". *1963 Report on the World Social Situation*, p. 106.

chances to grow wherever it succeeds in becoming the instrument of the underprivileged masses towards a better life and towards social justice. Here again, the orientation towards the interests of the masses and the resulting emotional atmosphere, together with the appeal to deep-seated feelings in people, might count for more in the end than the tidy coordination of specialized technicians.

It is, however, neither possible nor advisable to design social welfare programmes along purely logical lines. The question of priority of a given social welfare service within the total picture of national development should not be pressed too hard. Welfare services sometimes have to meet urgent and dramatic claims which, in theory and considered in relation to the over-all needs of development, may have no priority at all (for example, services for the rehabilitation of war invalids). The order of priorities will obviously differ from one country to another.

If the objective is to achieve the maximum benefits of a multiplier effect in the social welfare services, the best results will probably be achieved by concentrating on seminal programmes such as training, well-publicized discussions especially in policy-making circles, successful and popular periodical publications, etc. All these programmes have the capacity for stimulating change in ever-widening circles. If, on the other hand, the main consideration is economy of programme, first attention should be given to activities which are in a way complementary to already existing institutions or services. For instance, a school lunch programme which would help to raise the school attendance level, or a reception and orientation home which would help make an established programme of foster-home placement really successful, would all be activities promising the greatest return on investment. Occasionally, too, small-scale services merit consideration in the setting of priorities, especially when they can serve demonstration purposes.

3. Training

The preconditions for the necessary development of a new outlook on training are, first, the recognition that some kind of training for the performance of different functions in social welfare is necessary and, second, that none of the existing patterns of training necessarily has general validity and universal applicability.

On the whole, it seems that training for a number of possible functions should start at a younger age than the present requirements of maturity would allow, that it should stress values and develop attitudes to a greater extent than, on average, it does at present, that its forms should be more versatile and the educational results more adaptable to various later careers and specializations. It should both encompass a greater range of existing possibilities and provide scope for a greater diversity of future orientations than the present system of educational specialization generally permits. Furthermore, training should be as economical as possible from the point of view of society as a whole. It has been calculated[1] that more than 6 per cent of the national income and a period of thirty years are needed to introduce elementary education in a country. The training of social welfare personnel can be made more selective in relation to the strategic importance of particular functions they are expected to perform as well as to the content of training and the methods employed.

The following possibilities are suggested only as examples of the directions which thinking about training might take and are not to be taken as an exhaustive list of the various forms of training for the many different categories of personnel staffing the social welfare services:

a. It is conceivable, for example, that youth leaders could be trained at a comparatively early age, somewhat along the lines of certain Scandinavian programmes, and, perhaps, employed on practical work in youth camps, recreation projects, work brigades, schools, etc. After several years of such practice, candidates might be selected from the ranks of youth leaders for further training in community organization, community development, or as union activists, adult education organizers, home economics advisers, auxiliary social workers, public health educators, etc. On completion of training, they would return to practice and, after a further lapse of time, certain ones among them might be trained in advanced theoretical and practical understanding of social processes. This method would have the double advantage of engaging larger numbers of younger people in activities of social prevention at comparatively low training-cost, and at the same time it would set in motion a natural selection and placement process permitting a much more documented and balanced judgement about the potentialities and motivation of the candidates.

[1] A. Sauvy, "Demographic Considerations in Planning for Children: The Case of Education" (Report for the Round Table Conference on Planning for the Needs of Children in Developing Countries, UNICEF, CC/WP-4, 1964), pp. 3, 9.

b.   The preparation of senior personnel in the social welfare services could make much more effective and efficient use of international collaboration than it does today. Fellowships and observation tours could be planned to be more flexible and adaptable — leaving more room for special inclinations and professional interests of the fellows — as well as more intensive so as to include periods of formal concentrated study, intensive discussions with theoreticians and practitioners in their particular field, writing and the experimental direction of a project. These comparatively expensive forms of training should be prepared and conducted with the full participation of the trainees' superiors, and might very well include some kind of regional and inter-regional comparison of the results achieved. Selection of candidates should be more rigorous and individuals not meeting the required standards should be given instead scholarships for formal training. The accent of the effort in developing observation tours and fellowships as a form of training should be on devising ways to include the fellows in responsible, independent action and leadership in their particular field of interest while they are engaged in the study programme.

c.   Mass training for volunteers should be given much more attention than it has received hitherto. There are world-wide voluntary organizations, such as the Red Cross, which have accumulated through the years very valuable experience in mass training (e.g., courses of basic education in health, public hygiene, first aid, etc.). The League of Red Cross Societies is planning to extend the activities of Red Cross societies in the field of social welfare. This could be taken as a starting point for the development of new, inexpensive and effective forms of mass training for volunteers in social welfare services. Including the volunteers at the same time in a voluntary mass organization would increase their effectivenesss and improve the return on the training investment.

d.   Mass training programmes for some form of social action are going on all the time in many countries, such as the training of activists in political and other mass-action movements, of members of religious organizations, etc. It would be worthwhile to explore the possibility of increasing the content related to social welfare in these forms of training. Even slight modifications of training in that direction could increase the value of these cadres for certain forms of social welfare action, in view of the fact that they are professionally very often faced with social problem situations.

e.   The training of a group of individuals of academic status and oriented towards giving leadership in social welfare administration and in social policy can yield satisfactory results only if the training plan includes from the beginning the development of other types of personnel with appropriate forms of training in addition to the creation of a nucleus of leadership personnel. The initial "elite" group would be responsible for starting the whole process, for giving social welfare the necessary place and status among comparable activities, to win for it the attention of policy-making groups, and to provide the first generation of coordinators and leaders in the field, with the understanding that new leadership would be selected later on from the ranks of the field workers and would not remain a monopoly tied to an educational prerogative. The initial high-level courses in social welfare policy could develop later into, or revert to, social science teaching with a possibility of postgraduate specialization for different fields of practical action derived from the social sciences.

4. Planning and administration of social welfare services

Since organized large-scale services are bound to emerge, sooner or later, in any type of development, there should be from the very beginning an awareness of, and an effort towards learning to cope with, complex organizational structures and procedures in the social welfare field. The experience common to developing countries of having new forms of governmental administration superimposed on older traditional structures is likely to create problems so complex as to baffle even more seasoned administrators than are, as a rule, to be found in the country experiencing these events.

The preparation of a concrete plan or action programme, on the other hand, is necessary even in the most rudimentary stages of a social welfare service. Methods of planning and structures for the implementation of plans and the coordination of action will, in many cases, have to be developed at the same time. Whether social welfare is the responsibility of one governmental sector or whether it is divided among several sectors, the simplest and therefore most successful method of planning will probably be the method of gradual approximations. In developing countries the advantages of this method of planning, compared with other more sophisticated methods, are greater ease in recruiting and coordinating planning personnel and the repeated contact with reality which it enforces on the planners.

As a guiding principle, the plans should be prepared where the action will take place. Central action should be planned centrally and local action locally. The better quality of available technicians at the national level will be counterbalanced by the greater contact with life and the more favourable conditions for comprehensive planning for social welfare in small communities. Moreover, if we grant that planning means the mobilization of people on behalf of certain courses of action, it is at the local levels where the participation of wider circles of the population can best be organized.

The body responsible for planning should combine technical competence with political responsibility. The best combination will probably be a small collective body on which political representatives and senior technicians have equal standing. Whether this is going to be a purely governmental social welfare planning board, an inter-departmental committee, a mixed body of governmental and non-governmental representatives, a departmental commission combining with members of the relevant committee for social policy or social welfare of the legislative body and representatives of interested citizen groups and voluntary organizations, will depend on the position of social welfare in the administrative machinery and the general organizational structure of public activity in the country.

As a rule social welfare will have several centres of gravity in government and outside of it, and the main problem of planning and administration will consist in assuring the maximum of coordination and the minimum of friction among them.

5. The cost of social welfare services

The problem of the cost of welfare services is receiving increasing attention from economists, specialists in public administration and social welfare practitioners alike and for a number of reasons interest in the subject is likely to continue. For example, people in developing countries are naturally cost-conscious in a situation where the problem of scarce resources is especially acute. Social welfare is easily labelled as "unproductive" with the mistaken inference that it can be left to take care of itself without entailing any serious consequences for development one way or another. As social planning becomes increasingly integrated with economic planning there is need for a common language, preferably one employing quantitative terms. "Insufficient effort has thus far been devoted to locating and preparing relevant data in the quantitative terms most useful to planners", asserts a meeting devoted to the question of planning for children and youth.[1] Efforts to arrive at quantitative data by short-cuts often lead to rather unfortunate results, to mistakes both in the assessment of the costs involved as well as in the evaluation of the benefits to be expected from social welfare services.

Careful study of the question is needed in each country as well as internationally. It is particularly important to understand, and to express in objective terms, the notion of total social cost and benefit, which is not at all identical with the visible input and the assumed output in money terms. Social welfare services, for instance, do not invariably represent a new social charge, though they may figure in the budget as a new outlay. The cost of a welfare service can often be considered as a substitute for, or reduction in, some corresponding individual expenditure; e.g., the organization of crèches permitting mothers to go to work, are probably a net benefit socially as well as economically. Old people taken care of through a system of pensions would otherwise, at least in part, burden the family budgets. The social benefit consists sometimes simply in a transposition of the accent, a change in the conditions governing the selection of beneficiaries. A community health service will tend to benefit the patients who are most in need of treatment rather than those who can most easily afford to pay for it. A system of scholarships will tend to favour the brightest children and not necessarily those of the richest or most influential parents.

The techniques of assessing social costs and social benefits and of comparing them reliably are still in an embryonic stage. But in the less complex situations of developing countries these beginning efforts will probably be easier, and the techniques more likely to grow naturally with the increasing complexity of the planning tasks.

C. POTENTIALITIES OF INTERNATIONAL COLLABORATION

Increased international collaboration in all fields is indicated for the future as a result of the increasing productivity of the economically developed countries and the growing awareness everywhere that

---

[1] *Children and Youth in Development Planning—Conclusions of a Round Table Conference held at Bellagio, Italy, 1-7 April 1964* (UNICEF), p. 5, para. 7.

the development of the earth's resources, material and human, is the common responsibility of the earth's inhabitants.

Even if much of this collaboration occurs on a country-to-country basis, the United Nations is really the only fitting organization for undertaking it. The idea of a universal organization of men has an increasing rational and moral appeal to people all over the world. Among all the possible forms of international organizations, only the United Nations has political authority by virtue of being an association of governments. The United Nations is also one of the few politically catholic organizations where the coexistence of different systems and ideologies is not based on misunderstandings and glossing over of differences, but on a frank — if sometimes uneasy — exchange. The United Nations is an organization that can assure a continuity of policies on a world-wide basis. It has enough of a "general staff" to be able to undertake basic tasks of research, fact-finding and even some modest implementation. And its growth and further development is really the only alternative worth considering when discussing constructive world-wide technical action in any field.

On the other hand, the United Nations in its present form and for its foreseeable future, has certain limitations which have to be taken into account if the proposed action programme is to be realistic. There are not only basic political and ideological orientations unfavourable on principle, to United Nations action, but also prejudices and susceptibilities on minor points. The action of the United Nations agencies is further limited by the framework of international law and regulations governing its different activities as well as by the existence of various national legal systems. The world-wide scale of United Nations organs and operations imposes a technical limit to what can be done. The United Nations cannot, as a rule, assume leadership in relation to an individual country except for very restricted programmes and a very restricted time-period. Its experts, officials and representatives are always in the position of outsiders in relation to a country's policies and essential decisions. For the time being also, the most obvious limit to United Nations action is the amount of money available to finance its activities, as well as the number and quality of people undertaking its assignments.

It is clear that the necessarily limited scope for action of the United Nations must be exploited by applying its resources at particular points where they can produce results more than proportionate to their size. It has been, for instance, the consistent experience that the same action undertaken at different points in time can have very different results. If several favourable circumstances coincide one action can trigger an ever-increasing number of related activities and, directly or indirectly, achieve results far beyond those that were originally intended or even dreamed of.

United Nations policy in the social welfare field, generally speaking, should aim at a synthesis of all the various styles characteristic of international collaboration over the years. In each of them — international legal regulation, direct material aid and assistance with services, and technical assistance to develop the country's own resources in the field — there is a kernel of truth, each of them corresponding to a still existing need.

A fourth "style of action" should perhaps be added: direct efforts to develop, internationally, new insights into problems and new methods of action. The United Nations is in a particularly favourable position to draw on the world's best resources in thinking and to maintain, at the same time, immediate contact with a world-wide variety of practical problems and situations.

Between the extremes of grand panoramas of social change and purely pragmatic every-day action, the most promising solution still seems to be a "middle-range theory" approach. There is reason to believe that the material already collected by the various United Nations agencies is potentially capable of contributing to such a body of theory. It would be worthwhile to try to assemble these elements, to relate them to each other systematically, to integrate them, and to plan further investigation and critical scrutiny of the facts.[1]

The creation of the regional planning and development institutes, as well as the United Nations Institute for Social Development Research in Geneva, are steps in the right direction designed to provide the United Nations with the instruments for systematic scientific thinking. One of their first tasks should be to continue what has been going on already for some time in an *ad hoc* manner:

---

[1] Essentially the same point was made in a previous evaluation report, stating that "further steps towards a more effective exploitation of the accumulated body of practical knowledge and experience derived from technical assistance operations would be in order. It seems, however, that in using available resources for research work a balance should be maintained between work related to immediate operational needs and longer-term research aimed at the development of sound social policies and international programmes of assistance". (*Evaluation of Selected Aspects of United Nations Technical Assistance Activities in the Social Field*, E/CN.5/350, para. 86.)

that is, to analyse the different stages of development, to refine the indicators and take more differences into account, and then to evaluate systematically the success of various forms of social welfare services tried out in different stages, with the aim of establishing correlations between stages of development and forms of service which have given optimal results in a given stage.

The varieties of training and methods of community development could be perfected much more quickly and brought to bear on the problems of developing countries with much greater relevance if the wealth of practical experience and the scattered theorizing could be subjected to continuous, systematic analysis, the hypotheses brought into relation with each other, restated, and subjected to a process of continuing confrontation with the facts.

There should be a more elastic transfer of experiences generally among United Nations agencies and among regions (e.g., the results of the European Social Welfare Programme should be utilized more in other regions).

The question of volunteers in international projects should be given more careful consideration.

The lessons which seem to emerge from an examination of past trends of development in United Nations social welfare policy and their implications for the future seem to be, first of all, the necessity to develop new programmes in the welfare field that are especially relevant to the needs of countries with mass problems of levels of living and a limited range of occupational specialization, including programmes for youth, for community building, for the development of security, primarily in the economic and social sense, and of appropriate forms of research and training, especially the training of higher level policy personnel, and of legislation and administration. There should be systematic help in perfecting survey techniques, in the organization of such work and in conducting large-scale programmes as well as in the long-range assessment of manpower needs. Provision for systematic follow-up and evaluation should be built into all programmes from the beginning.

It seems to be repeating the obvious to insist once more on the necessity of coordination and cooperation both within the United Nations family and outside its member agencies in relation to social welfare problems and programmes. Possibly greater attention to coordination of programmes within a country or region would give more satisfying results than the same effort at United Nations Headquarters level.

It is clear and accepted that policy thinking with regard to the social welfare services, as for any other field, has to be done in the interested country itself. The consequences to be drawn from this principle are, first, a greater attention to policy-making circles in a country. These circles will profit most from a systematic international exchange on an equal footing. They cannot be reached by technical advice alone.

This does not mean, however, that techniques might not be useful and their exchange necessary. The particular nature of the techniques and who might most profitably develop them and pass them on are questions deserving more thorough examination. There will be countries whose circumstances and background naturally equip them to develop and adapt their own experiences in, say, techniques of social welfare administration and research to the requirements of international programmes, while others may be more expert in techniques of legislation, and still others in the skills required in rehabilitation programmes, etc.

In conclusion, it seems essential to strengthen the flow of communication generally between the United Nations and Member countries. It has been noted very often that the diffusion of United Nations material is very limited, that it does not reach the circles with a primary interest in it and who might profit most from it, and that the material is sometimes not written in a form conducive to easy communication. On the other hand, communication from individual countries to the United Nations should flow through more than diplomatic channels. Knowledge about social situations and social forces, the possibilities and interests in a country's development, would appear to be essential for any rational planning in the United Nations.

The basic problem in the present situation is to find ways in which the express desire of the advanced countries to help the developing countries can be translated into effective action. New methods of technical cooperation, added to those already well tried, will have to be found to take full advantage of the new economic and technological possibilities which have emerged in recent years[1].

---

[1]   U Thant, Foreword, *op. cit.*, p. vi.